The
Life and Death
of
Trade Unionism
in the
USSR, 1917-1928

The
Life and Death
of
Trade Unionism
in the
USSR, 1917-1928

Jay B. Sorenson

ALDINETRANSACTION
A Division of Transaction Publishers
New Brunswick (U.S.A.) and London (U.K.)

for my Mother and Father,
who know the meaning of toil

First paperback printing 2010
Copyright @1969 by Transaction Publishers, New Brunswick, New Jersey.

This book is printed on acid-free paper that meets the American National Standard for Permanence of Paper for Printed Library Materials.

Library of Congress Catalog Number: 2009041273
ISBN: 978-0-202-36350-9
Printed in the United States of America

Library of Congress Cataloging-in-Publication Data

Sorenson, Jay B., 1929-
   The life and death of trade unionism in the USSR, 1917-1928 /
   Jay B. Sorenson.
       p. cm.
   Originally published: New York : Atherton Press, 1969.
   Includes bibliographical references and index.
   ISBN 978-0-202-36350-9
       1. Labor unions--Soviet Union. I. Title.

HD6732.S67 2009
331.880947'09042--dc22

                                                      2009041273

THE AUTHOR

JAY B. SORENSON is Associate Professor of Government at Smith College and an Associate of the Harvard University Russian Research Center. In 1956, he was awarded a Russian Institute Certificate, and in 1962 was granted his Ph.D. by Columbia University. He has taught Soviet government and politics at Princeton and at Columbia and has published numerous scholarly articles and book reviews. In 1968, he received a Ford Foundation and Fulbright-Hays Research Fellowship for research on Sino-Soviet conflict.

Acknowledgments

Barrington Moore once said that a book is written by many authors. I could not concur more. There are many whose works I have read and benefited from. To these scholars, several of whom I know only from their writings, I owe much. The work of E. H. Carr and Isaac Deutscher has been invaluable. Deutscher's death is a great loss to all of us. I hope that his biography of Lenin will be published; judging from a conversation with him in 1967, I believe that it is rich in unusual insights into Lenin's personal life. Margaret Dewar's short but penetrating monograph on Soviet labor has also been particularly helpful. Leonard Schapiro's *The Origin of the Communist Autocracy* is one of the principal models I have utilized. I am in hearty agreement with Professor Schapiro's observations about Lenin and the Bolsheviks, and have benefited from conversations with him at Columbia and Amherst. I owe an inestimable vote of thanks to Daniel Bell. Not only did a conversation of many years ago help to start me on this topic, but his provocative essay, *Work and Its Discontents*, has spurred my interest in it over the years since the inception of this book.

I am indebted even more to those who generously undertook the difficult, time-consuming task of helping with this book—particularly Bertram D. Wolfe, who read the entire manuscript and offered valuable suggestions and criticisms. I have been aided immensely by his keen grasp and vast knowledge of the period. He always helped me most when he was at his critical best. Professor Aaron Warner of Columbia University taught me much and made valuable recommendations regarding my work on labor relations. To Professors John N. Hazard, whose encomiums urged me on over the years, and Zbigniew Brzezinski, whose original suggestions for revisions were so eminently sound, I am also grateful. Charles D. Lieber, my publisher, has provided many insights, recommendations, and urgings. He has helped to make me a better writer and this a better book.

I would like to thank the publishers who gave me permission to quote excerpts from two firsthand accounts of events in Russia during this period, *I Write As I Please*, New York, Simon & Schuster, Inc., Copyright 1935 by Water Duranty; and John Reed's *Ten Days That Shook the World*, New York, International Publishers, Co., Inc., Copyright 1967.

The Harvard Russian Research Center made facilities available for the completion of this book. I am particularly indebted to Professor Abraham Bergson, Director, as well as the other officers and staff, for their generosity and courtesy. Bruce Davis has proven to be a wise and judicious editor. I have not only benefited from excellent recommendations but have gained a friend as well. I should also like to thank all the Smith students, especially Miss Audrey Gartenberg, for their selfless and diligent help in preparing this manuscript for the typist and editors. Mrs. Sandra Olson contributed careful editorial work. At all stages my wife's help was so varied, fundamental, and invaluable. To others who have been generous with time and ideas, my thanks are unending. Though I hope that those who have helped me with this book may subscribe to its views, I alone am responsible for its shortcomings.

Contents

Whoever wants to arrive at socialism by a different road, other than that of political democracy, will inevitably arrive at absurd and reactionary conclusions, both in the economic and political sense.

LENIN, "Two Tactics"

1 ✊ On the Threshold

The Russian Revolution excited men. It captured their imaginations. The overthrow of the despotic Nicholas II did not appear to be an isolated event confined to Russia; rather, it appeared to be in keeping with the democratic revolutions that had been sweeping Europe from the time of the French Revolution, with its affirmation of the Rights of Man, to World War I. The Tsar had been overthrown; it appeared that a democratic republic was about to be raised in the least modern and almost last of the great European powers. Democracy, it seemed, was on the threshold of realization throughout the West. This indeed was heady news.

In addition, the Russian Revolution seemed to herald the fulfillment of the nineteenth-century socialist movement. The socialists believed that with the proper use of technocracy they could scourge poverty and hunger from the earth. They believed that with a social system based on equality and social justice they could overcome the traditional division of each society into rich and poor; that they could overcome a social problem which, seething and bubbling beneath the surface, threatened to be as destructive as wars fought between great powers.

These were the ideals and objectives of both 1917 revolutions. They were exciting and contagious. The Russians were seen by many as being on the threshold of a new and great experiment, one which would lead the world to peace, democracy, and security—the dream of ages. Support grew quickly. A world-wide movement committed to the extension of the ideological and moral principles of the Revolution and to the defense of the Soviet Union grew and became a significant factor in world politics, one result of which is that today Russia and America stand starkly opposed to one another. It would appear that ideological issues, beginning with opposing programs on a new world order, rather than conflicting national interests, lie at the core of this antagonistic stance.

If these democratic and socialist goals were the cherished objectives—and if U.S.-Soviet antagonism is one of the key impacts—of the Russian Revolution, the hopes and dreams for which it was fought are still to be attained. The Russians have traveled a long, hard road. Why? In retrospect, the explanation is to be seen primarily in the acts of men following March 1917 and less in the legacy of the pre-1917 period. The story of Russia is less a tragedy of the unavoidable than a tragedy of what might have been.

Much of the story of this tragedy is to be found in the labor fight—the split between the Communist Party, the trade unions, and the workers. The labor movement, which had been pushing for a democratic alternative, turned against the Bolsheviks soon after 1917, and labor opposition left the Bolsheviks at the crossroads of history. The Bolsheviks had to choose between dictatorship or democracy. Under Lenin's guidance they opted for minority dictatorship, the outcome of which was tyranny over the very people in whose name they fought.

A SOCIETY COLLAPSING

To gain insight into the question of what happened after 1917 we must glance quickly at the pre-1917 scene. Late nineteenth-century Russia was a nation falling apart. The old answers of the Tsarist Empire were not effectively solving the problems of backwardness, peasant unrest, industrialization, and moral malaise. At the same time, new values, a social revolution, and a power shift accompanying the industrial revolution had not taken complete hold. The net result during this period of transition was profound division, with the old and the new pushing and pulling the society in different directions. Russia was tottering, but she held on; society was more characterized by dissension on goals, disintegration, high levels of antisocial behavior, and polarized politics than by cohesion and growth.

It would be a mistake not to see centripetal forces at work producing cohesion and growth. The industrial revolution and a rapidly growing GNP resulted in a real rise in the standard of living and some upward mobility. Indeed, the prevailing condition for most workers remained actual or hovering poverty. But exploitation and human misery had been the mother of the Russian labor movement, so while poverty and sweatshop factory conditions were widespread, these did not represent a deterioration in the living standards of the working class as a whole. There were setbacks, particularly during depressions, for workers in "sick" industries and for peasants just off the farms, but the working-class standard of living did go up with over-all economic growth, and the skilled and second-generation workers enjoyed a climb in status and wealth substantial enough to create a rift between them and the unskilled. On a national political level, however, an improvement in standard of living and upward mobility served as a unifying force creating greater opportunities for social cohesion. "Trade unionist" and evolutionary socialist demands evident up to 1913 were indicative of this temporizing trend. Health, education, and welfare reforms also served to stabilize Russian political action.

Yet the society was crumbling. One negative effect of the industrial revolution was the loss of traditional cognitive orientations which had made life stable, predictable, and meaningful. In the rapidly growing urban centers the municipal authorities seldom had the inclination or presence of mind to cope with the great influx of men, women, and children from the villages. The workers were the new migrant group. They were a marginal class and had to fight hard to establish a place for themselves. For most of them, family ties were torn, old village customs were rendered absurd, city mores were either unknown or inapplicable, and intermediate associations were lost. For those remaining in the villages—many of whom were on the verge of being forced out—life was not very different. Individuals and groups were atomized, lost and anxious. Insecurity became a way of life, even for those who found themselves climbing the social ladder and for those who were downward bound. In many cases, men, rendered psychologically marginal by change, became either social deviants, criminals, or innovators of the new society.

There was another problem which exacerbated tensions. The rising standard of living did not produce an increase of working-class consumption on a level comparable with that of the bourgeoisie. It was less the need for forced savings than the bias of a self-centered middle class—which was dreaming about a bourgeois life, not social equity—that lies at the heart of the wide and growing gulf in living standards. More improvements could have been made. But the middle class, comfortably ensconced in a bourgeois world, was not prepared to share it with men who, in their eyes, were inferior socially and intellectually. The glaring inequality was at the source of profound workman discontent, particularly since their value system and that of the middle class were not congruent. Indeed, as the economic situation improved, the mood of anger and dissatisfaction heated as well. The sharp outburst of widescale political strikes in 1913 and 1914, a period of economic progress, sprang not only from anger over wages but also from criticism of the political posture and values of the bourgeoisie. Two "nations" existed in Russia, and for one—regardless of all improvements—life was a living nightmare.

A social revolution also divided the nation. Autonomously triggered by the industrial revolution, it produced a redistribution of status, wealth, and power, and had deep unsettling effects. The Tsar and the nobility fought and lost on every level. The industrial middle class emerged as the major beneficiary, though never powerful enough to carry through the revolution for which it stood. The urban working class did not acquire any tangible increases in status and wealth, but it did grow in power. Although small in numbers compared with the peasants, the urban working class played a role far in excess of its size in shaping Russian politics. The shift in status, wealth, and power was not planned or intended. It was a by-product of the industrial revolution, and it occurred willy-nilly. Like a great crescive wave, it rolled over the shoals of autocratic Russia, washing away the political dikes protecting the old order. So unsettling was it that the Tsar and the middle class, independently of one another, pursued policies designed to maintain social stratification. Neither wanted to create an equalitarian society or one in which the working class emerged politically dominant. Indeed, after the 1905 Revolution both lived in fear of a social revolution carried to its conclusion. Their policies were very effective. This was a period of comparatively high mobility, yet the son of a worker remained, with few exceptions, a worker. Thus a war was waged against a social revolution at the very time one was independently transforming Russia. The result was tragic. If a comparison may be ventured, the Russian worker was in a position akin to that of Negroes in the present-day urban ghettos of the United States. He was a newcomer to the cities, with some improvement in earnings, standard of living, and opportunity; yet he suffered from strong class discrimination, limited economic opportunities, and social exclusion. As life improved he felt more angry and frustrated about the impenetrability of the middle and upper classes and about his own artificially depressed position.

As the political structure weakened, the prospect of revolution grew. The Tsar contributed substantially to his own decline. As a result of his political reaction and the breakdown in societal goals and values, the Tsar was incapable of introducing change and unable to restore order. He suffered a serious loss of support and power. Increasingly he held the system together by armed force. A precarious situation it was for a nation undergoing rapid change and torn apart by intense internal conflict. By 1913 no consensus existed in Russia. Then, caught up in World War I and suffering one defeat after another, it became only a question of time before naked force, increasingly less effective, failed.

In the context of social malaise and a breakdown of political power, a movement for democracy took hold, and it was this force that opened the possibility of new alternatives for Russia. It originated in intellectual and moral anger, and was manifested in mass strikes, demonstrations, and pressure for real constitutional rule and a redress of injustice. Political parties were formed which were committed to a representative system, a meaningful national Duma, and local self-government. One impressive fact is that in 1913 there were few men or parties among the Left or the middle class that did not believe the Tsar would have to go. Within the ranks of the middle class the great debate was whether this would take place by evolutionary or revolutionary means. Indeed, the constitutional reform movement, along with strong economic growth and socially congealing tendencies, have led many scholars, including Bertram D. Wolfe and Alexander Gershenkron, to believe that if World War I had not interfered with the over-all economic growth rates and cohesive trends, Russia would have missed the entire Bolshevik experience and even followed the West to a form of constitutional rule.

THE RUSSIAN WORKER

Much has been written about the Duma and the movement for democratic reform, but since the primary interest here is in the roles of labor and the Communist party, we should focus directly on them. The Russian worker, for the most part like his brother peasant, rated high on an authoritarian scale. This judgment applies less to the second- than to the first-generation worker who was just off the farm, poor, unskilled, and of low cultural-educational attainment. The Russian worker was, for the most part, the product of a paternalistic family structure and a messianic apocalyptic church. He was traditionally pro-Tsar, usually prejudiced with regard to religion, race, and class, and open to extremist right-wing appeals, like those of the Black Hundreds, or to left-wing extremism, such as Bolshevism.

There is, as Durkheim and Wallace have argued, no necessary one-to-one correlation between a social system and personality; indeed, the personalities of men in a social system will vary over a wide range, but not one without limits. That range is determined by the environment, values, and tensions atomizing a system; yet, taking all these factors into consideration, the Russian worker was still a political authoritarian. A corollary may be added to the Durkheim and Wallace observation. There is no one-to-one correlation between psychological authoritarianism and political commitment and impact. It may be likely that an authoritarian personality plays an authoritarian role, but it is also possible he may not. Indeed, the Russian worker, an authoritarian, played a democratic role and had a democratic impact on Russian politics. It was this worker who constantly demanded social equality and political liberty, and opted for socialism and democracy. Of course many remained torn, apathetic, and paralyzed by conflicting loyalties or a low level of expectation; some remained conservative or reactionary; but a large majority, it would appear, came out on the side of socialism and democracy at all the critical moments: 1905, 1914, and 1917.

The paradox of an authoritarian worker coming out on the side of democracy and having a democratic impact is to be understood in the context of political despotism and a highly fragmented system where radical ideologies and politics flourished. It was the existing political order that structured the alternatives open to him. As a member of an oppressed social class, the workers' choice was either: (1) to accept the old order, which was incongruent with a newly developing industrial value system, and remain a member of a class subjugated and discriminated against, or (2) to seek changes that would relieve the tension and enable him to realize his objectives of material comfort, social equality, and human dignity. To do the latter, however, was to be a political deviant or a radical and to attack the established order itself. Even the intention of achieving such marginal gains as trade unions, the right to strike, political representation, freedom of press and assembly—to say nothing of social equality or a redistribution of wealth—was to demand a new and different Russia. It was the Tsarist system, dictating the role the worker had to play to win a better life, that made his role and impact a democratic one.

Yet, taking a note from Max Weber, the fact that a democratic and socialist ideology was adopted cannot be explained solely as a response to a political environment. Why were democracy and socialism chosen over other values?

It was a small group of dissatisfied intellectuals and worker elites who, committed to socialism as the most desirable way to eliminate social inequity, managed to capture the mind and spirit of the Russian working class. These revolutionaries worked day and night. Social democracy was advanced by them as a competitive ideology to the traditional value system of autocracy and as an alternate to capitalism. Social democracy served as a main reference point for analyzing the existing system, for moralizing and mobilizing for action. It enabled them to establish a link between personal feeling and social action. Their socialist system contributed to a sense of hope; it reflected a sense of what a just society should look like. Interestingly, there was high congruence between their socialist analysis and the existing system, yet when they spoke of that "unjust society" they were rather utopian in their outlook. When all is said and done, it was the socialists, acting as a moral fountainhead, who captured the imagination of the majority of the Russian workers.

The entire experience with Police Socialism and Father Gapon on the eve of the 1905 Revolution is a *prima facie* case of how successful the socialists were. To insulate the workers from the socialist preachers, the Tsarist police officers, even against Count Witte's admonition, decided it was essential that unions be organized. Once set up, these unions backfired. They had merely incorporated all the demands that the socialist intellectuals and worker "aristocrats" had been preaching. Gapon negotiated with the Leftists as he drafted his manifesto, and at least four different drafts were written. Significantly, the one that was decided upon called not only for a redress of grievances but also for freedom of speech, inviolability of person, freedom of assembly, and all the other liberties one associates with a democratic society. Gapon's manifesto, if not the police unions themselves, indicated the Left had won. The Left had captured the minds of the workers. The police and Gapon were acting in response to it. If the socialist intellectuals and second-generation worker elites were weak organizationally, they had won the battle of values.

I want to emphasize two points. First, the importance of the bridge between the social democratic intelligentsia and the worker elites, and the workers themselves, cannot be minimized. It highlights the difference between the workers and the peasants. All efforts by the radical intelligentsia to establish ties with the peasantry failed; but not so with the workers. The reason for success in one case and failure in the other was not merely one of personalities and tactics. Clearly, a different milieu existed for the worker—perhaps he felt improvements could not be won without altering the existing order—but it was one that made him distinctly more susceptible to socialist arguments than was the peasant. Second, I contend that the worker was politically oriented and committed to social democracy, and was not just seeking bread-and-butter wage gains.

By the sheer weight of numbers, the relative importance of their class position, and the role they played, the workers gave substance to a major thrust in the direction of democracy. They helped make it a political force of substantial credibility. They helped open a new alternative for a Russia steeped in autocratic tradition. This was so in spite of a strong tradition of historical and class authoritarianism, in spite of a political situation of profound disequilibrium and extreme political polarization.

THE BOLSHEVIKS

What of the Bolsheviks? By no means were they an aberration. They reflected the deep currents of Russian life. They sprang from the profound turmoil of the social revolution. They were a radical party in an age of transition, in an age when shifts from rural life to industrialization, from monarchy to republicanism, left few men moderate in their position. The main questions, however, are: How important and effective were they in the pre-1917 period? What following did they have in working-class circles? How predictable was it that they would emerge as the ruling party or that a dictatorship would be the logical consequence of pre-1917 politics?

The traditional observation of Western and Soviet scholars has been that, after 1903—except for short spurts—the Bolsheviks were a secondary force, though Lenin indeed enjoyed great prestige. Today some scholars see the Bolsheviks as a primary force. Leopold Haimson, a foremost Western scholar, has offered impressive evidence indicating that the Bolsheviks were making a remarkable recovery in 1913 and were a genuine party of the workers in 1914. Contemporary Soviet historians, on the basis of similar evidence, go even further and argue that Russia was on the threshold of a revolution in 1914, one, they suggest, that the Bolsheviks could have won.

Without detailing the information, Haimson is correct. The Bolsheviks made a comeback in 1913-1914. But the crucial question is: What effect did it have? The answer appears to be: not very great. Haimson States that their victories do not suggest "that by the outbreak" of war the Bolshevik party had succeeded in developing a secure following among the masses of the working class." Rather, he says, "The first year of the war showed only too clearly how fragile [the Bolsheviks'] bonds to the supposedly conscious Russian proletariat still were. Indeed, it bears repeating that the political threat of Bolshevism . . . stemmed . . . not from its [organizational success or ideological indoctrination], but from the workers' own elemental mood of revolt." * The coincidence of worker mood and Bolshevik appeal is the key point. This does not mean the Bolsheviks had a great effect; in fact, they were weak. They did not direct the labor movement, set its goals, or mold its views. Their temporary comeback was no indication that they did. The situation was wide open. Although Martov lamented the Bolshevik success in 1913, the Mensheviks had far greater effect than did the Bolsheviks in reaching the workers and shaping their attitudes, though their success was also limited. The early days of March 1917 testify to this.

The telling point is that Bolshevik support quickly evaporated after 1914. By March 1917 they were little more than a small isolated sect. Outside of a handful of unions—though indeed some important ones, such as the metal workers'—and a handful of worker-Bolsheviks like Shalyapnikov and Tomsky, Lenin was hard pressed to find worker support for his party. By 1917, he had lost the support of key unions, including the Printers' Union. Also he had lost most of the executive committees of unions, for many formed in 1917 quickly became Menshevik-dominated. Add the fact that most workers did not really know who Lenin was or what the Bolsheviks stood for, and the Bolshevik defeat at the Third Trade Union Conference, and the relative position of the Bolsheviks in the pre-1917 period become academic. At the Third Trade Union Conference in July, which was called for the purpose of creating a national trade union movement and had representatives from many major unions and regional councils throughout the nation, the Bolsheviks suffered a stunning setback. At this Conference, the Menshevik and socialist moderates had a comfortable majority, with the Bolsheviks holding only 36 per cent of the votes. Menshevik policies on peace, the Provisional Government, and the Revolution were adopted. The labor movement, under Menshevik auspices, officially and firmly committed itself to the support of the Provisional Government. The Bolsheviks could not have suffered a more humiliating defeat.

It was also in the initial period, when the Bolsheviks were weak

---

* Leopold Haimson, "The Problem of Social Stability in Urban Russia, 1905–1917" (Part One), *Slavic Review*, XXIII; 4 (December 1964), 639.

in the unions, that they supported the "workers' control" movement against the trade unions and actively worked to split the labor movement and discredit the moderates. The syndicalist idea of workers' control, resting ultimately upon the demand for the complete and direct management of the plants by the workers themselves, gained popularity immediately. The "factory committees," in organizing collective management in the plants and attempting to run them, put the idea of workers' control into practice in a crude but effective way. Workers' control became the official ideology of the factory committees and was competitive with the ideas of socialism and nationalization (state control) at the time. So strong was the identification that "workers' control" became synonymous with "factory committees."

The idea of workers' control gave rise to much acrimony. Prominent labor figures like Lozovsky and some Bolsheviks like Ryazanov saw it as isolated and anarchistic shop-level action that would sap (rather than reinforce) the political power of the Left. The principal opponents of workers' control, for political and ideological reasons, were Mensheviks and trade unionists. They were strong in the trade unions and were looking forward to a unified labor movement led by the Menshevik-oriented national trade unions. The factory committees, heavily syndicalist in orientation, looked instead to a system of autonomous factory committees introducing a maximum program of workers' control.

Lenin, in disagreement with some of his fellow Bolsheviks, directly supported the committees and workers' control. He favored workers' control in the pre-November period less because of ideological convictions than because of his weakness in the unions. He needed a foothold, and indeed he won one. After he came to power he shifted his position—but this is a story to be told later.

The disagreement between the factory committees and the unions, however, continued unabated until the First Trade Union Congress in January 1918, at which the proponents of workers' control were defeated in a bitter floor fight. Conciliatory efforts were made, but little quarter was actually granted in the heated debates and political maneuvering that took place. The tragedy of the battle lies in its self-destructive character. The unity of the labor movement was dissipated at the moment of its emergence as an independent force, but it worked to the benefit of the Bolsheviks at a time when they were very weak. Indeed it was Bolshevik weakness and not strength that triggered the ensuing civil war in the labor movement.

To sum up: The Bolsheviks were not very effective in the pre-

1917 period in spite of their comeback in 1914. Only at rare moments did they come close to a mass following. They did not set the goals or direct the labor movement; they helped shape but did not make events. Their permanent effect was negligible. It was more a question of their mood and that of the workers coinciding in 1914.

Regarding the Soviet view of imminent revolution and Bolshevik victory in 1914, it is doubtful that a revolution would have been successful at that time. In any test of strength the workers could not have succeeded without the support of the army, or at least its neutralization; the disaffection of the army played a role crucial to success in 1917. There appears to be no evidence to indicate that army support of the autocracy was crumbling in 1914. It took World War I and military defeats to "eat up" its will to fight for Nicholas II. It thus appears that the prospects for a successful worker revolution in 1914 were not very good. The critical role of the war in contributing to the army's neutralization seems to support those who contend that it was World War I to which one must look for an explanation of the Bolshevik success.

There is the additional point that if a revolution had broken out in 1914 and had been crushed, it probably would have taken years, even decades, to build and organize for another revolution. Who knows what would have happened in the interim, particularly if the economy continued to grow and living standards kept on rising. Gradual reforms and strikes for limited gains undoubtedly would have continued, and surely they would have continued to produce some short-run beneficial results. Lenin, in exile a few short months prior to the March Revolution and despairing over the slim hope of ever seeing a revolution in his lifetime, gives us a clue about his assessment of the level of cohesion that had set in. Well-informed he was, but he was not properly evaluating Russia's war failures or internal weaknesses. The judgment of Western scholars such as Alexander Gershenkron, Bertram D. Wolfe, and Arthur Mendell that the war, not the strikes of 1913–1914, was of decisive importance to Bolshevik victory appears to be the sounder of the two.

To turn to the Bolshevik victory and the ensuing political dictatorship, it is difficult to see either as unavoidable outcomes of pre-1917 chaos and polarization.

To treat political dictatorship first, the question is the weight to assign to the democratic movement against a situation of extreme polarization and a tradition of autocracy. The over-all context was hardly conducive to democracy, but the autocratic past and extreme division of the country were hardly barriers to the creation of a new system. Most certainly they did not totally dictate the future; other options existed. The incipient democratic movement born in the earlier period shaped Russian politics and, on a spectrum of possibilities, democracy became very much a marginal but real alternative. The March Revolution was more than a revolution to end the war. It was not an accident that the autocracy was smashed, political freedom introduced, rank and privilege abolished, and a redistribution of power and property rights effected. The people made their democratic demands in the streets and in the creation of the Soviets and the Provisional Government.

With the overthrow of Nicholas II in March 1917 and the introduction of free speech, press, and assembly, the main thrust of the earlier democratic movement carried Russia to the threshold of democracy. The situation was very fluid; Russia was at the crossroads of history. Some were afraid, some opposed, and some dared to hope, while yet others were foolishly or dangerously optimistic; but a new option had been created, a revolution in expectations had occurred, and a strong desire and commitment for democracy existed. A tough road lay ahead for Russia if a democratic system were to be established, but the first step had been taken. In spite of a strong tradition of autocracy, Russia could have gone democratic.

There would have been serious problems, but not insurmountable ones. The peasants posed a big question; they constituted the vast majority of the people. Would they have gone democratic? Did they know the meaning of democracy? Would they have sustained it? Conclusions are hard to draw, but projecting from the evidence available, I do not think the peasants would have posed an impossible problem. First there is negative evidence. The peasants, for the most part, stayed out of politics and were not that decisive a political force in the Revolution. For the most part they just seized the land; they had little to do with the overthrow of the monarch or with the November seizure of power. In other words, it was not the peasants who were the initiators of the Revolution, who determined its outcome, or were the authors of the ensuing political dictatorship. They definitely were not as important as the workers and soldiers, who in turn were not as decisive as a small band of radicals. Against this there is the positive fact that an overwhelming majority of the peasants had voted for Chernov and for democracy and socialism in the elections to the Constituent Assembly. Chernov's program had its appeal, and the peasants seemed willing to follow him. The big issue in their minds was land. Since land was being seized and since it would have been most unlikely for Chernov not to underwrite peasant land seizure as land reform, the major question that might have led to peasant unrest and an abandonment of a democratic commitment would have been by-passed.

The prospects for building a democratic society were better with than without peasant support. Indeed their ignorance and lack of any strong self-governing tradition lowered the prospects, but it would appear that the peasants were not the decisive obstacle to a democratic system. It is also worth noting that the right-wing counterrevolution did not begin until after the Brest-Litovsk negotiations, and it is hard to say it was not more directed against the Bolsheviks than the entire democratic revolution. One wonders what the war would have been like had the attack been directed against a Chernov-led Constituent Assembly supported in the villages throughout Russia by the peasantry. For the monarchists the war would have been considerably more difficult to wage.

Peasant commitment was one problem; social revolution and political polarization were others. The country was so badly split and lines were drawn so sharply, that at first glance the conditions necessary for stable democracy do not appear to have existed. The social revolution was a very real problem dividing the middle class from the workers and peasants in 1917, but centripetal forces were also at work in 1917, producing the conditions necessary for cooperation and stability.

The ouster of the Tsar alone was not enough to unite the people and no decisive action was taken to end the war or to provide bread and land. In part the failure was a symptom of the profound social split, but it was also partially a product of Kerensky's personal failures. Like an Othello character, he was excessively jealous of his power and possessions and was incapable of either yielding or solving problems for fear he would be excluded from any new government. He not only hesitated on peace, bread, and land, but he equivocated on calling elections to the Constituent Assembly until it was too late. By refusing to grant rights and power to the Democratic and pre-Parliament conferences, he destroyed the assemblies which he himself convened to deal with Russia's internal difficulties. He left a wake of chaos and destruction in his path. He failed either to ameliorate conditions or to pull the nation together when possible. He was a tragic figure, paralyzed by indecision and pride; without his presence, Lenin undoubtedly would never have ruled Russia.

Independent of Kerensky, a possibility for political stabilization and social cohesion began to emerge. It is difficult to place it exactly by date, but by the fall of 1917 it was evident that the middle class had decided to accept a major transfer of power, wealth, and status to the workers and peasants as a fact of life. Their acceptance of the Constituent Assembly election results, if not the numerous other statements and acts of men like Miliukov before November 1917, testify to their willingness to yield. This did not mean they would not continue to resist or try to preserve what status and wealth they had left. They were willing, however, to abide by a democratic election to work within the framework of a government created by the Constituent Assembly, and to help create a new Russia—a Russia ruled by a multiparty system and committed to rectification of the old abuses. Grounds for stabilization and cohesion evolved. The Russians were on the threshold of solving their problems within the context of the March Revolution, contrary to contentions of those like I. Deutscher, who feel the November Revolution was essential for a resolution of Russia's social and political problems. It is hard to say that dictatorship was an inevitable consequence of 1917.

On the basis of pre-1917 events, it does not seem at all predictable that the Bolsheviks would emerge as the ruling party. The Bolsheviks were a product of the social revolution, a symptom of it. They contributed to the social revolution but they were not its initiators, nor its only or most effective spokesman; nor were they responsible for the overthrow of Nicholas II. If any party was brought to power by the Revolution, it was the Socialist Revolutionaries, who had won the Constituent Assembly election by an overwhelming majority. The Bolshevik. victory is to be explained in terms of a seizure of power, from above. It was a *coup d'etat* which occurred within the context of a political vacuum created by Kerensky's inept handling of the situation. The Bolsheviks came to power without a formal majority or the support of the great majority of the people in the nation. And they have waged a fifty-year war with the people. They did not unite the country and they espoused a way of life unacceptable to most. Indeed, if an effective, united, and resolute leadership had existed, the Bolsheviks might never have come to power at all. Unlike the March Revolution, November was not an unavoidable consequence of the social revolution and political polarization. But this shall be traced further in the next chapter.

To conclude, the pre-1917 period set the context for the later period and allows a closer examination of key questions. The chaos of the time did not close the door to any system but dictatorship. The pre-1917 period does not explain the success of the Bolsheviks

—or what happened after 1917. A democratic movement was slowly emerging and slowly shaping Russian politics. The workers provided a mass base in this process, playing a role that made the drive for democracy a real political force. Russia could have moved in a number of different directions in 1917. To explain why the democratic trend which was building and could have carried Russia in a different direction was aborted, one must look to the Bolsheviks. One must look to factors like an autocratic tradition and economic chaos, but most of all one must look to the Bolsheviks.

2 ❧ The Dilemma of Power

"Never mind," he said finally. "You know me. My name is Trotsky."

"You haven't got a pass," answered the soldier stubbornly. "You cannot go in. Names don't mean anything to me."

"But I am the President of the Petrograd Soviet."

"Well," replied the soldier, "if you are as important a fellow as that you must at least have one little paper."

Trotsky was very patient. "Let me see the Commandant," he said. The soldier hesitated, grumbling something about not wanting to disturb the Commandant for every devil that came along. He finally beckoned to the soldier in command of the guard. Trotsky explained matters to him. "My name is Trotsky," he repeated.

"Trotsky?" the other soldier scratched his head. "I've heard the name somewhere," he said at length. "I guess it's all right. You can go in, comrade." [1]

A rising of the masses of the people [Trotsky rapped out], needs no justification. What has happened is an insurrection, and not a conspiracy. We hardened the revolutionary energy of the Petersburg workers and soldiers. We openly forged the will of the masses for an insurrection, and not a conspiracy. The masses of the people followed our banner and our insurrection was victorious. And now we are told: renounce your victory, make concessions, compromise. With whom? I ask: With whom ought we to compromise? With those wretched groups who have left us or who are making this proposal? But after all we've had a full view of them. No one in Russia is with them any longer. A compromise is supposed to be made, as between two equal sides, by the millions of workers and peasants represented in this Congress, whom they are ready, not for the first time or the last, to barter away as the bourgeoisie sees fit. No, here no compromise is possible. To those who have left and to those who tell us to do this we must say: you are miserable bankrupts, your role is played out; go where you ought to be: into the dustbin of history! [2]

November 7, 1917, marked a great victory for the Bolsheviks. With major discontent working in his favor, Lenin had successfully guided the Bolsheviks, a handful of men, to power. Then he had convinced the Second Congress of Soviets, composed primarily of soldiers and workers, to legitimatize this act by proclaiming the Soviets to be the new government.

It was these two separate forces, the Bolsheviks and the mass of workers and soldiers, each going its own way, that crossed paths briefly to sweep Lenin into power. Trotsky was both right and wrong: It was more than a mere conspiracy to the extent that the workers and soldiers overthrew Kerensky, but it was not an insurrection. The Bolsheviks, as a party with its own well-defined ideology and intentions, came to power independently of the workers, soldiers, and peasants. The vast majority of the masses of workers and soldiers, particularly outside of Petrograd, do not seem to have been sure of who Lenin and the Bolsheviks were, or to have known that the Soviets had split or that some of the moderate socialists were organizing to bring down the Bolshevik government.

A telephone conversation of Lenin's with Sheinman, the chairman of the Helsingfors Soviet, and Mikhailov, the chairman of Tsentrobalt (the Baltic fleet), in Finland, illustrates the confusion as well as Lenin's apprehensions and tactics.

> *Lenin: On behalf of the government of the Republic,* I urgently request you to begin sending these forces immediately [to defend Petrograd against Kerensky]. Please inform me also whether you are aware that a new government has been formed, and what is the attitude of your Soviets to it?
>
> *Mikhailov:* All we know about the government comes from the newspapers. The transfer of power to the Soviets has been welcomed here [Helsingfors] with enthusiasm. . . .
>
> *Lenin* [Earlier in the same conversation, to the chairman of the Helsingfors Soviet]: The news is that Kerensky's forces are approaching and have taken Gatchina, and as some of the Petrograd troops are exhausted we are in urgent need of strong reinforcements.
>
> *Sheinman:* What else is new?
>
> *Lenin:* Instead of your question "What else is new?" *I expected you to say you were ready to come and fight.*[3] [my italics—J.B.S.]

The conversation took place on November 9. Lenin placed the call by direct wire and made no effort to conceal the threat facing the new Soviet Government. But Robert Payne states that he was "deliberately disingenuous" [4] in his conversation with the two men, for he did not introduce himself by name or party. He simply called himself the spokesman for the new Soviet Republic. Furthermore, when asked for additional news by Mikhailov and Sheinman, who really did not know what was going on, he "ducked" the issue of the opposition of the moderate socialists and left the distinct impression that the Soviets were united. While Lenin attempted to create an image of unity, his questions also reveal that he was not at all sure how the Bolshevik seizure of power would be received or whether his new regime would be supported by the Helsingfors Soviet or the Baltic fleet. Clearly Lenin was fishing for the strongest support on the vaguest information.

Lenin had been correct in the analysis he presented to the Central Committee in his two secret letters of September advising a seizure of power. He had argued that the time was ripe even if the Bolsheviks did not have a popular majority in the country, that no one was strong enough to stop them, that they should not wait for the Constituent Assembly, that revolution never waits for anyone, and that history would never forgive them if they did not seize their opportunities.[5] As George Lichtheim states: "To do him justice, Lenin himself did not pretend that the November Revolution was 'necessary' in the sense of being inevitable; on the contrary, he insisted through the critical months that if the chance were missed, it might never return." [6]

The achievement of victory in this context testifies to Lenin's greatness as a leader and strategist, but the ambiguity of his relationship with the soldiers and workers determined the very weakness of his victory and created the context for the ensuing problems.

LABOR SUPPORT

In March 1917 the Bolsheviks had only scattered support among the workers. For all practical purposes they were isolated. As late as August they were described by John Reed as a "small sect." During the period from March to November, the Bolsheviks emerged with a large following among the industrial workers and with control of a newly-created national union machinery and several unions.

The Bolsheviks made some initial gains in May, but it was not until the fall of 1917 that they really grew in numbers and strength. They profited from Lenin's extremely able leadership, but their support grew in correspondence to the workers' general dissatisfaction with the Provisional Government and the division and paralysis of the moderate socialist Soviet and trade union leadership. The Bolsheviks rode the rising wave of discontent, letting it carry them willy-nilly as it engulfed Kerensky.

But this was not merely chance. The Bolsheviks worked hard at destroying the Provisional Government by wedging their way into the labor movement. In May and June they won majorities in the workers' section of the Petrograd Soviet and at the Petrograd Conference of Factory Committees. As the fight between the factory committees and the trade unions opened the door for the Bolsheviks, they established their foothold in the labor movement and challenged the Mensheviks.

In the fall they made their breakthrough. The September municipal elections in the large cities revealed that the Mensheviks and Socialist Revolutionaries had suffered a sharp drop, against an abrupt increase for the Bolsheviks. In the Moscow central and ward dumas the SRs dropped from 58 members in June 1917 to 14 in September, while the Mensheviks decreased from 12 to 4. Bolshevik membership, on the other hand, rose from 11 in June to 47 in September.[7] By November 400,000 workers were members of the Red Guards and the Bolsheviks could report that their membership was 60 per cent worker in composition.[8] By January 1918 membership had increased to 115,000 from an alleged 23,000–24,000 in January 1917. Also in January the Bolsheviks won a majority of workers' and soldiers' votes in Moscow, Petrograd, and other large industrial centers in the Constituent Assembly elections. They had not won the election, but they had won one-fourth of the votes. There is no question that the Bolsheviks had a mass base, and that they had outflanked the Mensheviks.

To what did they owe their success? Reed puts it neatly: "They took the crude simple desires of the workers, soldiers, and peasants, and from them built their immediate program."[9]

The Bolsheviks had become the Phoenix symbol of the March Revolution. Out of the failures of "do-nothing Kerensky" and the "hesitant" Mensheviks and Socialist Revolutionaries, the Bolsheviks, the party of action, appeared as the party most willing and able to resist the right wing and to complete the March Revolution. "All power to the Soviets" and "bread, peace, and land"—these were great slogans of the Revolution; and if the Bolsheviks were willing to fight for them, many workers were willing to support the Bolsheviks.

There were also other factors: One was anger at a time of revolution. The workers and soldiers were full of hatred, and Bolshevik entreaties encouraged them to give full vent to their demands for retribution. Political ignorance and confusion were also factors; the workers lacked knowledge of and familiarity with the intricacies and subtleties of party politics. Aware as they were of many things, they were confused by the interparty bickering and struggling of the various socialist parties. They frequently did not know whom to believe or what to do, and at times this confusion worked to the advantage of the Bolsheviks.

The quotations at the beginning of this chapter point up this confusion. It is sufficient to cite one additional case. At about 3 A.M., during one of the sessions of coalition negotiations between the moderate socialist parties following the Bolshevik Coup, a delegation of some 15 young and old workers from the Putilov munitions works, having threatened to barge in by force if necessary, were allowed into the room where the negotiations were taking place. A member of the group stepped forward and castigated all sides for a civil war between socialists: "Already for a week the two revolutionary camps have been shedding each other's blood in this criminal war. We demand this be brought to an end! We have had enough of it! You have been here for two days trying to come to an understanding, and it seems as if you were in no hurry. We will not allow this civil war to go on. To hell with Lenin and Chernov! Hang them both! . . . We are telling you to put an end to this situation, otherwise we will make you pay."

Ryazanov, a Bolshevik representative, as deeply impressed as everyone else, jumped up shouting: "You are perfectly right! We Bolsheviks have been ready to come to an agreement from the first. We are making all kinds of concessions." Then he flatly asserted that it was the Socialist Revolutionaries, the Mensheviks, and the representatives of the city duma who were resisting agreement and were the cause of continued fighting. "Go to them," he said, "and demand the civil war be brought to an end." Accepting Ryazanov's statement at face value, the worker, still quite agitated, cried, "Very well, we will go there and drag them here." S. An-sky, an anti-Bolshevik infuriated by Ryazanov's speech, took the floor and pointed out that the representatives of these parties were present and that Ryazanov had distorted the facts. He then attempted to explain the differences in points of view. Finally the worker exclaimed: "The devil alone knows who among you is right or wrong. You insult the earth by walking on it. If we could hang all of you on one tree the country would enjoy peace. . . . Let's go, men. We have nothing to gain from talking to this bunch." [10]

Such were the sources of Bolshevik support. It was an unlikely combination of chance and confusion that worked for the benefit of the Bolsheviks, who themselves were badly divided and confused over the seizure of power. Lenin definitely had lady luck on his side.

John Reed, at the time of the November *coup d'état,* caught the element of chance in a graphic account of the debate that decided the issue for the *bronoviki,* the armored car troops.

> A little officer in a leather coat came running down the steps. "The garrison is turning!" he muttered in my ear. "It's the beginning of the end of the Bolsheviki. Do you want to see the turn of the tide? Come on!" He started a half-trot up the Mikhailovsky, and we followed.
> "What regiment is it?"
> "The *bronoviki.*"

Comments Reed, "Here was indeed serious trouble." The armored car troops were "the key to the situation." The question was whether they would listen to the Committee to Save the Revolution and remain neutral, or side with the Bolsheviks.

Rushing to the Mikhailovsky Riding School, where the armored car troops were garrisoned, and brushing aside the two sentinels at the door, Reed found about 2,000 *bronoviki.* They stood in a vast hall under a single eerie arc light, listening to the political speakers who climbed to the turret of an armored car to address "the dun-colored soldiers." Kanjunov, a former officer who had been president of the summer's All-Russian Congress of *Bronoviki,* pleaded eloquently for "neutrality." He said, "It is an awful thing for Russians to kill their Russian brothers. There must not be civil war. . . ." When he had finished another climbed up, said he was from the Rumanian front, and urged "peace at once." A Duma delegate also pleaded for "neutrality." One after another they spoke, pleading their cases. Reed wrote:

> Never have I seen men trying so hard to understand, to decide. They never moved, stood staring with a sort of terrible intentness at the speaker, their brows wrinkled, . . . sweat standing out on their foreheads; great giants of men with the innocent clear eyes of children and the faces of epic warriors.

Fortunately for the Bolsheviks, N. V. Krylenko rushed to the school. "In a voice husky with fatigue" he won the day by seeking the deepest desires of these soldiers and stating that the Bolsheviks were giving them peace and a Russia which "belongs to you." It was a stirring appeal few could resist. But, as Reed states:

> Imagine this struggle being repeated in every barracks of the city, the district, the whole front, all Russia. . . . And imagine the same in all the locals of every labor union, in the factories, the villages. . . . Think of the hundreds of thousands of Russian men staring up at speakers all over the vast country . . . trying so hard to understand and to choose, thinking so intensely. . . . So was the Russian Revolution.[11]

The incident reflects the tension, the agony, and the doubt of the moment—and the thin thread on which the Bolshevik victory hung.

THE PROBLEM

If the Bolsheviks did have an immediate, majority of the workers and soldiers, the relationship was a vague one, filled from the beginning with profound ambiguity and doubt. In the heat of the moment during those fast-moving, unpredictable days from September to December, the Party did not know what was going on, how much support it had, or how far the support would go. Lenin was counseling revolution, but he and all the other members were acting in the dark and were as dependent as not upon luck and what the others, including the workers, did or did not do.

But then the workers were also confused. They were not sure of what they wanted, of who the Bolsheviks were, as Trotsky learned—or what the Military Revolutionary Committee was, as John Reed found out the hard way. He tells:

> . . . and [they] led me to a wall, against which they placed me. It flashed upon me suddenly; they were going to shoot me!
> . . . Desperately I ran after the [soldiers as they walked out into the road]. "But comrades! See! Here is the *seal of the Military Revolutionary Committee!*"
> They stared stupidly at my pass, then at each other. "It is different from the others," said one, sullenly. "We cannot read, *brother* [sic]."
> I took him by the arm. "Come!" I said. "Let's go to that house. Some one there can surely read." They hesitated. "No," said one. The other looked me over. "Why not?" he muttered. "After all, it is a serious crime to kill an innocent man."
> We walked up to the front door of the house and knocked. A

short, stout woman opened it, and shrank back in alarm, babbling, "I don't know anything about them! I don't know anything about them!" One of my guards held out the pass. She screamed. "Just to read it, *comrade* [sic]." Hesitatingly she took the paper and read aloud, swiftly: "The bearer of this pass, John Reed, is a representative of the American Social-Democracy, an internationalist. . . ."

Out on the road again the two soldiers held another consultation. "We must take you to the Regimental Committee," they said. In the fast-deepening twilight we trudged along the muddy road. Occasionally we met squads of soldiers, who stopped and surrounded me with looks of menace, *handing my pass around and arguing violently* as to whether or not I should be killed." [12]

The workers did not know what the Bolsheviks wanted or where they were going. They did, however, look forward to a social revolution, with Russia belonging to the people.

The objectives of the two had coincided over bread, peace, and land. The workers and soldiers underwrote the Bolshevik *coup d'état;* but their support was quite mercurial, based on negative anti-Tsarist and rightist fears on the one hand, and on positive hopes for workers' control and upward mobility on the other—rather than on a positive commitment to the Bolsheviks. Most of the workers were not ideological Leninists. Lenin was aware of this; in part, it is the reason that he did not inform them of his real motives in refusing to form a coalition government with the moderate socialists, or of his goal of securing a Bolshevik dictatorship—which he had practically decided upon by the time of the dismissal of the Constituent Assembly, if not by the time of the coalition talks. The Bolsheviks could neither count on the workers nor trust them.

Lenin's problem was, in part, that his own seizure of power changed the very nature of the Revolution. With the seizure of power in November, the Bolsheviks had started another revolution, the values and purposes of which were not entirely congruent with those of the March Revolution. The Bolshevik Revolution was elitist, taking place within the framework of the larger social revolution of March. It had some mass support, but only formally. In reality, it was an act committed by a handful of men, by a small political party. Their objective was to steal power and shape the larger revolution, which had been left unfulfilled by Kerensky. Lenin wanted to attain a maximum socialist revolution within the March Revolution. In this regard the Bolsheviks were definitely conspirators and occupied a minority position.

Once Lenin decided in favor of a Party dictatorship he was asking the workers to follow him and his Party, and this was the "horse of a different color." It quickly became clear to Lenin that most workers did not want the suppression of strikes, the destruction of independent unions, or the arrest of Menshevik, anarchist, and SR leaders. The situation soon changed. Much of what the Bolsheviks did upon seizing power contributed to a substantial loss of worker support as early as the winter of 1917-1918. Perhaps the decisive act for many was the creation of the Cheka, which was instituted as a weapon of suppression against the workers and the Left, against strikers and political opponents. The army existed to combat the Right.

Working for the Bolsheviks was first the threat of counterrevolution, and then the civil war, which forced a closing of ranks between workers and Bolsheviks even while great friction existed between them. In tact; throughout the entire period when the Bolsheviks could claim worker support, when the party grew in numbers and recruited heavily from the ranks of the workers, the relationship that existed was a combination of agreement and disagreement. The bulk of the workers remained permanently outside the Party, even though some felt that social doors had been opened which placed the power of Russia within their hands. Even in November the Bolsheviks could not be sure of unequivocal worker support. Thus, the Bolsheviks, vulnerable because of the amorphous nature of worker support, had to look to organizational strength, and this they did at the First and Second Trade Union Congresses.

CONTROL THROUGH THE COMMAND POSTS: THE FIRST TRADE UNION CONGRESS

The First Trade Union Congress convened in Petrograd in January 1918. It was just at this time that the Bolsheviks were suffering over-all defeat in the Constituent Assembly elections, but were winning in Petrograd, Moscow, and most industrial centers. The Congress followed on the heels of three unsuccessful efforts by the moderate socialists to challenge the Bolshevik seizure of power: a strike threat by the Railway Workers' Union to paralyze Petrograd and destroy the Bolsheviks unless a coalition government was formed, a strike by the civil servants, and an attempt by the Committee to Save the Revolution to force the Bolsheviks to yield power. The Congress opened just after the Bolsheviks had promised to transfer power peacefully to the Constituent Assembly. It was a decisive moment and all knew it.

January was little different from July and November. Few could tell what the outcome of events would be, and many were predicting that the Bolsheviks would not last very long. The delegates, in other words, were as much thrown together by circumstance as they were drawn together by common leftist aspirations. Ambivalence about the Bolshevik seizure of power pervaded the atmosphere, but belief in a Russia ruled by the people pulled the delegates together; so did the fact that everyone favored the creation of a national labor movement, and that all were proud of this first assembly of labor delegates in Russian history. All previous assemblages had been appointive. In spite of the divisions, they felt that they were about to fulfill a dream nourished by blood and hope for more than two decades. It was with optimism, but also in anger and confusion, that the delegates gathered in the corridors and discussed the dominant issue before the Congress: the Bolshevik seizure of power.

Of 428 delegates representing two and one-half to three million registered union members at the Congress, 281 were Bolsheviks,[13] a clear majority of 66 per cent. But the Bolshevik majority was challenged. How it was "won" has bearing on the significance of their victory.

The mandate commission report reveals that on the All-Russian Union level Menshevik representatives outnumbered the Bolsheviks 12 to 9; on the oblast level it was exactly the reverse. On the local council level the Bolsheviks outnumbered the Mensheviks 28 to 12; on the local union level the Bolsheviks had an overwhelming lead of 232 to the Mensheviks' 34.[14]

A further analysis of the First Congress, undertaken for the International Labor Organization, indicates that Bolshevik support came from the local organizations while that of the Mensheviks came from the trade union apparatus (the Central Federation of Trade Unions); the recorded strength of each group did not necessarily correspond to its actual strength; no fixed or uniform method was used for electing delegates; some important industrial centers (and Menshevik strongholds), including Odessa, sent no delegates, while some towns were more than adequately represented; it was difficult to tell whether local unions had as many members as claimed and whether all paid dues; and not all of the delegates were elected legally. Thus, the Mensheviks lost control of the Congress by not paying more attention to the pre-Congress election procedures.[15]

Lozovsky's report [16] to the delegates on trade union progress revealed that, of a total of 28 All-Russian Unions, only 18 were represented at the Congress; of the 28, 8 were not yet affiliated with the national movement, and some of these were very important anti-Bolshevik unions, such as the railway and post and telegraph unions. He noted that a number of other unions with large memberships had not yet formed an All-Russian organization and were neither present nor affiliated with the All-Russian Central Council of Trade Unions, the chief administrative organ of the trade union movement, which possessed decisive institutional power and was controlled by the Bolsheviks. (See Chapter 10 for a full description of the A.R.C.C.T.U.) Negotiations, he stated, were under way with these unions, and some, like the railwaymen's union, appeared interested in joining. All the pro-Bolshevik unions, led by the large metal workers' and textile workers', were present, but their opponents were not. Once again the Bolsheviks had outmaneuvered their opponents. The Congress was theirs beyond question.

CONFUSION OVER DEMOCRACY AND DICTATORSHIP

As important as the question of a technical majority was, this was not the decisive factor that led to the defeat of the Bolsheviks' opponents. Enough dissension existed within party ranks for lines to be crossed. Men shifted positions frequently during the course of the debates. Any victory won on the floor was a result of hard work and effective arguments. Beyond doubt, having a majority to begin with helped the Bolsheviks enormously, but the opposition was defeated because it never organized an effective alternative. The opposition lacked the self-assurance and daring of the Bolsheviks. It was never the band of zealots, the millenarians, that the Bolsheviks were.

Of decisive importance in undermining the Bolsheviks' opposition was an ambivalent stand on the issue of democracy and dictatorship. Enigmatically, most of the delegates—Bolsheviks and non-Bolsheviks—were committed to dictatorship and democracy simultaneously, yet they held reservations about both, particularly dictatorship. While they were repelled by the antidemocratic posture of the autocracy, with few exceptions believed that dictatorship—albeit one of a majority over a minority—was the prerequisite for the realization of democracy and social reform. Yet few, if any, appear to have been committed to the idea of a permanent dictatorship. All were committed to democracy and thought of dictatorship as little more than a means to an end. All appear to have believed that under a dictatorship the majority of people would be free, that equality and justice would prevail, that oppression as a means for resolving conflict and maintaining harmony would be consistent with justice, and that dictatorship would ultimately give way to democracy. Yet most, if not all, revealed serious doubts about the effectiveness of the democratic process in resolving problems of revolution and internal war as long as private property and social conflict existed, as long as counterrevolution was a possibility, and as long as a heterogeneous political environment prevailed.

Martov's position typifies the confusion. He opposed Lenin's seizure of power because of the undesirable implications of a minority dictatorship, yet he did not reject the idea of a class dictatorship by a majority over a minority under the right conditions. In the summer of 1919 the Mensheviks presented their program in a manifesto, "What Is To Be Done?" It is noteworthy because, although the Mensheviks demanded civil liberties, free speech, secret elections, the abolition of terror, and so forth, they demanded these only for the workers and had no intention of extending them to opponents of the Revolution. They said: "The new labor democracy is the democracy of those who take part in public productive labor. The complete or partial forfeiture of civil rights to social groups outside this labor democracy does not violate the democratic principle of class dictatorship." [17] On this issue it is difficult to find much difference between the Menshevik and Bolshevik positions.

What is of particular interest about Martov's stand against the Bolsheviks is his apprehension about a minority dictatorship. There is little doubt he sensed the danger and feared it, but he did not base his arguments on this point. Instead, he opposed the Bolsheviks on the issues of socialism and industrial underdevelopment, arguing that Russia was still too backward, too agrarian in social composition, and too feudal in mien for the revolution to be socialist in substance. Only by stating that the "economic policy" of the government could not "consistently and clearly [express] the interests of the working class" did he implicitly warn against a minority dictatorship.[18] Tragically, Martov never directly raised this issue, which was crucial to the realization of the March Revolution.

This was Martov's dilemma, but in essence it was also the dilemma of a majority of the Bolsheviks' critics. It was the Hamlet-like equivocation, the confusion on the issue of democracy and dictatorship in that turbulent revolutionary jungle of 1917, that contributed to their paralysis and impotence in the struggle against the Bolsheviks. This point cannot be minimized. Later, in 1920-21, the Mensheviks and others did state their case, making a principled argument for democracy—but by then it was too late.

THE PROCEEDINGS

On the fourth day of the Congress, immediately after the reports of great union progress during the nine months since March, the issue was joined; the struggle for labor support began. Two extremes reduced the issue to the question of strong independent unions as against the absorption of the unions into the state system. The Bolsheviks maintained that in a workers' state unions were "public" organizations, socialist in substance, "and that their mission is to play a role in the organization of the state"[19] in fighting for socialism. G. Y. Zinoviev argued that unions should not confine themselves to advancing labor's cause within the framework of a capitalist system, but should begin to branch out and perform the duties of the class dictatorship. The Bolsheviks denied the meaningfulness of independent and neutral unions motivated by the parochial objective of defending the interests of their members and prone to calling strikes and causing economic stoppages. Unions had a new role in a workers' state. They should think in "class terms" rather than along the lines of particular benefits for specific groups. Conflicts should be judged in light of their effect upon over-all policy. If not, they implied, one hand will tear down what the other builds.

Arguing for the other side was a strange alliance composed of Mensheviks, a group of Lozovsky-led independents, and maverick Bolsheviks like Ryazanov, who refused to abide by Party discipline on union questions. Among these men there was little or no agreement on the nature of the Revolution or what course to pursue. Their coalition was negative, based on a protest against minority dictatorship and the difficulty of building socialism in an economically backward country. Unfortunately, although they saw the implications of the Bolshevik position, they had neither the power nor the will to unite and bring the Bolsheviks down.

Within this alliance, those most opposed to the Bolsheviks were the Mensheviks. Grinevich, a prominent Menshevik, warned that, with state absorption of unions carried, the unions would be swallowed by the teeming masses of peasants and would be incapable of defending the needs of the proletariat.[20] Maisky, one of the most anti-Bolshevik of the Menshevik leaders, forcefully addressed the delegates. Although acknowledging that the Menshevik stand was an unpopular as well as a minority one, Maisky said, "our revolution remains . . . a bourgeois revolution and the trade unions therefore have to perform their customary job."

Their position was formally outlined in a resolution presented on the fourth day of the proceedings. In addition to the arguments just mentioned, they stated that the Menshevik Party would be the primary organization to oppose capitalism.[21]

Lozovsky, Provisional Secretary of the A.R.C.C.T.U., assumed a leadership role. He argued in support of the plea for independent unions, but developed his stand along different lines. Enjoying large support and working from the Trotsky and Parvus position on permanent revolution, he made it quite clear that he believed in the necessity of a world socialist revolution as a prerequisite for the creation of a workers' state in Russia. He said: "In the present abnormal situation [to ensure the success of the revolution in Russia], it seems to us that trade union independence from Soviet organs of authority must be maintained."[22] Developing this latter point in a separate speech, he prophetically warned: "The unions would suffer immense loss, [that] if they become state organizations . . . decisions would be enforced by coercion and armed force." He further warned that "no account would be taken of the collective opinion of the workers employed in the various branches of industry." In essence, he said, "we would replace the activity . . . of the masses by the mechanical action of armed force." Moreover, "the working class, which is still very unenlightened, sees in the trade union a sort of commissariat, office of administration which decides and does all on its own initiative.[23]

Lozovsky warned the Bolsheviks: "Those of us who were elected at the Third Conference of July consider it to be our duty to protect this independence against all comers, even against the Soviet power itself."[24] Whether he was fully aware of it or not, he had warned that an independent and powerful trade union movement and a Bolshevik minority dictatorship were incompatible.

Lozovsky was joined in his plea for trade union independence by David B. Ryazanov, a Bolshevik who was to become the great conscience of the November Revolution. Ryazanov took a stand against Lenin and for strong independent unions, which he resolutely defended from that moment until he was silenced by Stalin in the 1930s. He warned: "As long as the socialist revolution has not merged with the socialist revolutions of Europe and of the rest of the world . . . the Russian proletariat must be on its guard . . . it must maintain its trade union organization." [25] Like Lozovsky's, his warning conveyed a foreboding note about future developments in trade union affairs. It is clear that both men understood the imperatives of minority rule, and both preferred the alternative of independent, democratic unions. It would be rash to say that this would not have worked.

Taking the floor in rebuttal, Zinoviev, a leading Bolshevik, a brilliant orator, and an ambitious man, raised the basic question: Why should unions want independence in a worker's state?

What, indeed, is this independence, and from whom do you desire to be independent? Is it from your chosen Government, your

Workers and Peasants Government . . . that you would be independent? We also want independence, but it is with the bourgeoisie that we wish to break. We have overthrown the power of the middle classes, and now when the workers and peasant masses have succeeded in giving the power to the proletariat and when your own unions form a part of the Government, what is the use of talking of independence?

He went on to identify independent unionism and the right to strike as a stab in the back to the Soviet regime:

This independence may have a meaning for the adherents of the right wing who . . . wish the unions to be independent . . . in order that they might help and sustain those who are actively opposing the Workers and Peasants Government and those who, in the name of the sacred right to strike, are striking against the working class. . . . I am sure that among the militant trade unionists there is not one single person who will allow the middle classes, our most deadly enemy, to stab us in the back; and yet these allow this to be done in the name of the right to strike and of freedom of association.[26]

Zinoviev put his finger on the heart of the question of independent unions. Neutrality or independence, this was the question; and in the eyes of the Bolsheviks, the practical implication of independence was nonsupport of the system. Politically this was seen as dangerous and counterrevolutionary, for the regime could not stand without labor support. Independence indicated not only reserved support but also opposition from the unions. Its implications for industrial relations were as severe; it meant that relations between the unions and the state would be marked by friction. The conflict could lead only to strikes, economic stoppages, and the undermining of state policy. Under no conditions could the state tolerate a threat to its security. Under no conditions could revolutionaries put up with a policy which posed a threat to the Revolution. Unity was necessary during moments of such travail, and all, including the advocates of independent unionism, would have to subordinate themselves to the common good—the good of the Revolution. This they could do only if they abandoned their policy of independence, refrained from calling strikes, and submerged themselves in working for the common good. If not, they would have to pay the full price for disobedience and freedom of opposition.

The Bolshevik argument was effective. Zinoviev identified the Bolshevik Revolution with the March Revolution. His opponents attempted to counter by arguing that independence under Bolshevik rule or during the period of industrialization did not mean neutrality on the question of the Revolution; that, on the contrary, only by maintaining independence could one defend the principles of the Revolution. But this reply was ineffective, for, as the Bolsheviks replied, how does one defend the Revolution without defending the workers' state when the Whites are preparing to counterattack?

The Bolshevik resolution subordinating the unions to the government carried by 182 votes, marking the complete rout of the opposition on perhaps the most fundamental question before the Congress.

The resolution began with the statement that the political victory of 1917 represented a "victory over capitalist ways of production," that the Soviet Government had become the organ of socialist reconstruction, and that "revolutionary socialists have never considered trade unions as mere instruments of the proletariat's economic struggle for bettering the conditions" of the workers. In Points 4 and 5, subordination of the unions was affirmed. Point 4 declared: "The idea of trade-union 'neutrality' . . . has been and remains a bourgeois idea," and is "treason to the interests of the working class." Point 5 resolved that: "the trade unions must support fully and loyally the policy of the socialist Soviet Government directed by the Soviet of People's Commissars." [27]

There was to be no equivocation on the crucial point of political support for the Bolshevik regime. On the other hand, there was an element of compromise to this resolution.

In Points 6 and 7 it was stated that the unions would play a major role in regulating economic production. Further, the merger of the unions and the state apparatus "would" take place "after [the unions] have gone through the process of the socialist revolution which is now taking place." The emphasis on the future and against a decisive role for the unions in the present contained a concession. It was a vague concession made on Bolshevik terms, but this was the entire issue of the workers' state: Who would rule, the unions or the Soviet apparatus? It was an issue that would plague the Bolsheviks for years to come.

The highly controversial issue of factory committees and trade unions also came up. Again it was the question whether decentralized factory committees or centralized unions would be the dominant labor institutions. It too was subjected to intense debate. But now the political lines shifted. The Mensheviks, the Bolsheviks, and Lozovsky united to form a winning coalition in favor of centralized unions. So effective were they that they steam-rollered their anarchist and syndicalist opposition.

Against an anarchist charge of unions as "living dead" institutions which should be replaced by the factory committees and a system of workers' control, Lozovsky, in his trenchant style, retorted that "merely because there will be a thousand instead of ten factory owners in a particular enterprise does not make it socialistic." And further, this solves "absolutely nothing," but "produces an extremely harmful illusion that the transfer of . . . the factory to a . . . group of workers solves the problem for the given group of workers." This he decried as an anarcho-syndicalist illusion, for no "social question . . . which concerns the . . . means of production can be separately decided at each individual factory." [28]

Ryazanov, who was then chairman of the First Petrograd Council of Trade Unions, joined hands with Lozovsky in a full frontal attack on the committees. Ryazanov warned: "Without . . . a whole network of organs which control the activity of each . . . individual cell in each factory . . . we will have only a pillage of . . . the economy which we want to socialize and organize into a whole. . . . We will have a mass of atomized cells." [29]

The adopted resolution sounded the death knell for the committees. Of its three main points, the second opened the coffin: "with the development and strengthening of the . . . trade unions, the factory-shop committees must become the local branches of the corresponding trade unions." Point three closed it: "the Congress considers that the most satisfactory way in which the working class can carry out all the economic and organizational tasks mentioned above is to accept the leadership of [the trade unions] which have been organized on an industrial basis." [30]

As Ryazanov, in his evaluation of the victory, later said, the decision to subordinate the factory committees to the trade unions was "a death sentence" for the committees, for they "yielded to the trade unions the whole domain of leadership." [31]

Thus the major battles were won by the Bolsheviks. And to cap their victory a Bolshevik majority was elected to the new All-Russian Central Council of Trade Unions. Lozovsky, who had been acting head of the Provisional Board, was replaced by Zinoviev. Zinoviev, in turn, quickly became involved in other activities and was succeeded by Tomsky, a Bolshevik worker who was to become Lenin's primary agent in the labor movement. Shmidt, the future Commissar of Labor, was elected secretary.

Thus, two months after their seizure of power, the Bolsheviks won at this Congress what they had failed to achieve at the Third Conference: control of the executive apparatus and policy-making agencies. They had realized a major objective: adoption of their

policy and capture of the command posts of the Russian labor movement. If they did not have or feel sure of mass support; if they were
opposed by trade union leaders of other socialist parties, still control was in their hands. They were in a position to effect policy and
shape the character of the movement. And if they were not sufficiently powerful to run the movement freely or to push through
their policies in unadulterated form, they could, through control of
the central machinery, prevent labor from becoming a serious obstacle to their minority dictatorship and program of social reform.

Beyond question, the Bolsheviks had profited from labor's late
emergence. But victory had its price; notably, that the compromise
element in many decisions raised more questions than it answered.
The entire question of labor policy, including vague references to
unions' functions, was left unsettled, as was the main question of
the relationship of the unions to the state organs—the distribution
of economic and other powers, the equality or subordination of one
to the other. Thus, although the Bolsheviks defeated the advocates
of independence, the question of the unions' relative power and
position in Soviet society was by no means closed.

THE SECOND TRADE UNION CONGRESS

Less than a year later the issue of union power forced its way to
public debate again. The issue was raised at the Second Trade
Union Congress, which convened in January 1919. Like the First
Congress, it was dominated by the Bolsheviks. This time, however,
they had a 60 per cent majority of 748 voting delegates. At the Second Congress the power of the unions was discussed in terms of the
integration of the unions with the state and the right to strike in a
workers' state.

At this Congress Lenin pushed the integration theme to its logical conclusion and called for the "nationalization" and "statization"
of the unions. He based his argument upon the relative importance
of unions to the state, as ideological and organizational bulwarks of
the regime, both in the period of War Communism and in the
future society. He said: "It is not enough to proclaim the dictatorship of the proletariat . . . it is necessary that the trade unions
merge with the organs of state power and that the unions take over
the entire large scale economic construction." He further justified
the merger on the grounds that:

> After the political revolution the trade unions must take up a central
> position in politics and in a certain sense they must even become

the main political organization. They become the founder of the new society. . . . The Socialist revolution can only be accomplished by the active, immediate, and practical collaboration of millions of individuals in the Government of the State . . . the trade unions must educate the masses and lead them to share in the government of the country. That is why the nationalization of trade unions is inevitable.[32]

Once again the opposition protested the transformation of the unions into public agencies on the grounds that the unions, under this relationship, would have to ignore their membership and thus negate the entire meaning of their existence.

Now, in the face of laughter and scorn, Lozovsky warned that to nationalize the unions was to destroy them. Unions transformed into agencies of the state, he counseled, become objects of hatred among the uneducated, famished masses who already blame Soviet institutions for their suffering. Unions that were not independent, he further warned, would become institutions resting on force and substituting coercion for consent. In the hope of strengthening his case with the delegates, he reminded them of the experience the government had had when it nationalized the executive board of the railwaymen's union. This had been done to rationalize the administration of the railways. An unexpected by-product of the move was the development of a serious conflict of interest for the officers, who were torn between commitments to the state and to their membership. This had led to the alienation of the membership. Lozovsky warned: "The experience of Vikjeda during the past year has demonstrated that nationalization of the unions turns them into bureaucratic organizations."[33]

Later he tried to find a common meeting ground with the delegates: "When I speak of independent unions, I do not in any way say independent of socialism, independent of the socialist struggle. No, the *unions must work in the closest contact with the soviet people*"[34] [my italics—J.B.S.].

Martov, too, angrily addressed the assembled delegates, putting to them a hard question. "How strange indeed," he mocked, "that in the socialist state we are told that the workers' organizations should not be independent . . . should they not be independent of the party holding state power in its hands?" Scornfully he challenged, "But we socialists, not sharing new truths of Russian Communism, raise first of all another more important question. . . . The question is whether the state power can really, and not on paper only, depend on the workers' organizations, the trade unions and other organizations of workers—this is [the issue that is] hushed up!" [35]

The Congress ignored these warnings and rejected the pleas for trade union independence. But, once again, the delegates revealed ambivalence, for the resolution they adopted did not make clear whether the unions were subordinate to the state. It rested on the twofold notion that unions were to participate directly in state functions in the present, but were, when mature organs, not to participate directly. The resolution states: "The task of socializing all means of production . . . compels the trade unions to take a more active . . . part in the Soviets, by direct participation in all state organs, by organizing mass proletarian control over the activities, by carrying out separate tasks which might confront the Soviet government through their organization, by cooperating in the reconstruction of various state departments, and by the gradual substitution of them by their own organizations by means of fusing the organs of the union with those of the state." But the resolution ended on a note of reserve. It stated: "It would be a mistake . . . in the present stage of development of trade unions with the, as yet, imperfect state organization, immediately to convert the unions into state organs . . . or for the unions arbitrarily to usurp the functions of the state." [36]

Once again an effort was made to resolve the question of union power and the dictatorship. Lenin pushed the theme of integration, and a majority of the delegates, over 50 per cent of whom were Bolsheviks, passed resolutions rejecting independence and neutrality. But the delegates—in a spontaneous expression—passed further resolutions which enhanced the position of the unions in the realm of economic power. Again, the delegates—all basically committed to the principle of strong labor unions—proved themselves to be either unwilling to cut union powers or unable to resolve the question of union-state relations. Thus, although union independence was further narrowed, the question of union power remained fluid.

THE RIGHT TO STRIKE

The right to strike was seen as the *sine qua non* of a free trade union movement. Denied by the Tsar, the right to strike, like the right to organize, was held to be a matter of principle, and the legislation of 1917 legitimatizing strikes was viewed as a major victory of the March Revolution. The question came up for discussion at the Second Congress in connection with the question of the relationship of unions to the "workers' state." If anything illustrates the dilemma the Bolsheviks faced, it is their stand on the right to strike. Zinoviev, Tomsky, and the rest claimed a commitment to building a strong trade union movement; yet, in the name of the Revolution, they saw the right to strike as a threat to Party dictatorship.

Strikes cut two ways. They may do much to improve organized labor's bargaining position, but they may also do violence to economic performance and the national welfare. Beyond question, they are a potential menace to a government striving to maintain law and order and increase industrial production. In Russia, strikes were a problem for all sides. A rampage of strikes swept the country from March 1917 throughout 1919. The workers struck over any grievance without hesitation. No one—trade unions, Soviet leaders, or Bolsheviks—could control them. Production was thrown into a state of chaos and the existence, first of the Provisional Government, then of Bolshevik rule, was jeopardized by these widespread and constant strikes.

The Bolshevik position on strikes matured only after the November Revolution. Prior to November, their policy was based upon a mixture of principle and expediency. They supported the widespread strike waves of July, August, and September which were undermining Kerensky. However, once the Bolsheviks came to power and strikes were called to overthrow them, or became a threat to economic production, this position was modified.

In November 1917 the Moscow Council of Trade Unions passed a resolution sharply stating the new policy. It read: "The unions consider that while a proletarian government is in power, a political strike is to be considered as sabotage against which the most determined measures must be taken." It added that to cross picket lines was not scabbing or "blacklegging, but a means of fighting sabotage and counterrevolution." [37] Implicit in this position was the declaration that the right to strike was sacred as long as it was directed against the bourgeoisie, but that a strike against the socialist revolution and the working class was an act of treason.

In January 1918, at the First Trade Union Congress, Tomsky, a loyal Bolshevik trade unionist who was relatively close to Lenin but who, surprisingly, had been assigned no major role or office in the immediate period of November and December, began to make his Party loyalty felt. (Significantly, neither John Reed, Sukhanov, Chamberlain, or any major commentator on the November Revolution mentions Tomsky by name, though he was in Petrograd at the time.) Tomsky expressed the point of view that was to become the general policy on strikes throughout the nation. He said, ignoring the strikes of 1914,

> Even before . . . October . . . the general conditions of industry forced the trade unions to give up strike action. . . . Now, when the proletariat has assumed the political and economic leadership of the country and removed the bourgeoisie from the management of industry, the struggle of the workers for the improvement of their position has naturally had to take on new forms. . . . The sectional interests of groups of workers have had to be subordinated to the interests of the entire class.[38]

At the Second Trade Union Congress, Tomsky developed the implications of nationalization, saying: "At this moment when the trade unions regulate wages and the conditions of labor, when the appointment of the Commissar of Labor also depends on our Congress, no strikes can take place in Soviet Russia." [39] But Tomsky also spelled out the political imperatives of the right to strike. In commenting on the Menshevik resistance, he said that when seven-eighths of the workers fight for socialism, it is intolerable that one-eighth, the Mensheviks, should go against them. He added:

> We do not insist that these unions obey us blindly, but merely that they follow the general plan. When we ask them to work in the interests of the dictatorship of the proletariat and to promote proletarian discipline, it is not that we have any personal spite against the Mensheviks as such. But we must root out all those who, having recognized at the First Congress the necessity of collaborating with the Soviet Government, still persist in organizing strikes against that government. The unions which foment strikes . . . must suffer for it.[40]

Strikes, numerous at the time, were gradually brought under control—but not without the frequent use of force and the Cheka. Strikes were never outlawed, however, and to this day they remain a legal right, though only on paper.

The policy which the Bolsheviks adopted had some interesting implications. The first assumption was that collective bargaining and the strength of unions did not rest on the right to call a work stoppage, but on its political relationship with the state and the Party. In all cases the burden of responsibility for avoiding and terminating strikes was now transferred to the trade unions, the very institutions for which the right to strike was vital. The trade unions were left in the impossible position of having to deny the one power that would give them strength and enable them to protect their membership. Furthermore, the unions were placed in a position in which the leadership was forced to side with management against the membership, in which the unions, rather than the state, were responsible for forcing the workers to go back to work. The net effect was a severe restriction of union power and over-all undermining of the position of the unions vis-à-vis the workers and the state.

Thus the outcome of the First and Second Congresses was the denial of trade union independence; the transformation of unions into "socialist state organs," that is, public institutions, socialist in substance; and the unqualified affirmation that the trade union movement, representing two and one-half million members, had a vested interest in the regime and stood in firm, undeviating support of the Soviet system.

All told, the decisions of the First and Second Trade Union Congresses were fundamental. They established the basis of trade union policy and determined the framework within which the unions in the future would have to build, operate, and fight—and this was on Bolshevik terms.

Yet not all had gone well for the Bolsheviks. The end result was not completely as they would have had it. Regardless of the fact that they had won on the key issues and that policy was more or less as they had written it, the very issues over which the battles had been fought, and the bitter tone of the struggle, had not always been for the best from the Party's point of view. In a peculiar, negative way the opposition, even in losing, had also structured the relationship; the Party would have to operate within the context of the terms on which it had demanded that the issues be fought.

The Bolsheviks had opened a Pandora's box. They had won badly needed support, but they had "unleashed" the serious and disturbing questions of union power vis-à-vis the state and the Party. In addition, the level of disagreement with the dissenting Mensheviks, syndicalists, and other unionists was still very high, and the defeated opposition was in a position wherein the cost of agreement with the Bolsheviks was almost higher than the cost of breaking free. Thus, the price of victory on Bolshevik terms was a deeply divided and split labor movement.

In the final analysis, the Bolsheviks had won a major victory and could breathe more easily. In a major sense, the threat of a labor movement advocating independent trade unions, which would have jeopardized their regime, had been successfully met. They had won the needed support of the labor movement, and essentially on their own terms. Clearly the Bolsheviks' position was stronger than before, and in a way their levels of expectations were higher than ever.

3 ✿ Round Two: The Affiliated Unions

The Moscow worker is as different from the Petersburg proletarian as a hen from a peacock. But even he, as familiar to me as the Petersburger, is not altogether benighted and homespun. Here at the [Second] Congress, however, the hall was filled with a crowd of a completely different order. Out of the trenches and obscure holes and corners had crept utterly crude and ignorant people whose devotion to the revolution was spite and despair, while their "Socialism" was hunger and an unendurable longing for rest. Not bad material for experiments, but—those experiments would be risky.[1]

Comrades, we [the railwaymen's union] cannot carry you [Bolsheviks] to Moscow. We are neutral. We do not carry troops for either side. We cannot take you to Moscow, where already there is terrible civil war. . . .[2]

And just take note of this, comrades [said the representative of the railwaymen's union to the Bolsheviks]. Without us you couldn't have coped either with Kornilov or with Kerensky. I know you've just sent some detachments of *saboteurs* to tear up the lines leading to the capital. But without us, you know, you couldn't even do that. We could fix all the damage in twenty minutes. We tell you we're not going to help you, but will fight you if you don't come to an agreement.[3]

"Yes, now you see what these Bolsheviki have done. They have raised the counterrevolution against us. The revolution is lost."
"But won't you defend the revolution?"

"Of course we will defend it—to the last drop of our blood. But we won't cooperate with the Bolsheviki in any way."

"But if Kaledin comes to Petrograd, and the Bolsheviki defend the city. Won't you join with them?"

"Of course not. We will defend the city also, but we won't support the Bolsheviki. Kaledin is the enemy of the revolution, but the Bolsheviki are equally enemies of the revolution."

"Which do you prefer—Kaledin or the Bolsheviki?"

"It is not a question to be discussed!" he burst out impatiently. "I tell you, the revolution is lost. And it is the Bolsheviki who are to blame." [4]

He who is not with us is against us. People independent of the march of events—that is a fantasy. Even if we grant that such people did exist once, at present they do not and cannot exist. They are no good to anyone. [5]

Even before their First Trade Union Congress victory, the Bolsheviks turned on the individual unions—whether affiliated or not affiliated with the newly-created national labor movement—seeking to bring them into line or to destroy them. The overriding issue was union support for the consolidation of power. The Bolshevik campaign against the individual unions reflected Bolshevik strengths and weaknesses in the labor movement. The unions for the most part resisted, and a bitter struggle ensued which lasted throughout the civil war.

THE DECLINE OF WORKER SUPPORT

At first, the rapid rise of worker support was a major factor influencing the Bolshevik campaign against the unions. In the fall of 1917 the Bolsheviks felt strong enough to take on the Menshevik-controlled unions, particularly those in which worker support for the Mensheviks was falling away. Indeed, the Bolsheviks felt obliged to dislodge the Menshevik leaders in these unions even if the workers were not ideological Leninists, and a sizeable "war" was waged to do so.

By mid-1918 the situation had changed; the Bolsheviks had a different reason for attacking the unions. By spring the Bolsheviks had passed the apex of their popularity and a precipitous but uneven decline in worker support was well under way.

The causes of this turnabout were many: food shortages, unpopularity of the Brest-Litovsk Treaty, civil war, growing unemployment due to demobilization and economic exhaustion, crushing of trade unions, abandonment of workers' control, use of the Cheka to crush strikes, incompetence of Soviet administrators, complete disorganization of life, plundering and profiteering, suppression of civil liberties, arrests and executions without trial, and general heavy-handedness of the regime. The workers expressed their disillusionment in retaliatory acts: strikes, quitting jobs, absenteeism, sabotage, indifference, pilferage. So sharp was the fall-off of support that workers had to be cajoled and forced to make the great sacrifices the regime considered necessary. And during the civil war many had to be conscripted and forced into battle. The *subbotniki* (Saturday) movement, as will be seen later, was by no means enthusiastically embraced by the vast masses of workers, as the Bolsheviks themselves acknowledged. This worker disaffection was well-known to the Party. Lenin, in a conversation with L. S. Sosnovsky in January 1918, two months after the seizure of power, referred to "our" workers as tired, as having "slackened, grown weak" since the November days.[6]

THE AFFILIATED UNIONS

Bolshevik weakness in the labor movement had one other dimension. Of the roughly 28 All-Russian and 900 local unions, few except the metal workers' and textile workers', two of the largest, supported the Bolsheviks. This was evident at both the Third Conference of Trade Unions and the First Congress of Trade Unions, and in the battles and congresses which will be described below.

Thus, the Bolsheviks' position was precarious, but for two entirely different reasons. First, during the early November period when the Bolsheviks enjoyed strong worker support, it was clear that a schism existed between the Union leadership and union membership. The membership leaned heavily in the direction of the Bolsheviks and the leadership of most unions opposed them. To strengthen their position, the Bolsheviks declared "war" on the unions.

Second, the decline in worker support which began early in 1918 forced the Bolsheviks to step up their attack, since less than ever could they afford independent or hostile unions. The political differences over the seizure of power, the dissolution of the Constituent Assembly, and the political role of unions now made the unions a greater threat than formerly. Given the fluidity of the political situation, the silken thread upon which their entire regime hung was becoming frayed and strained.

A BOLSHEVIK MINORITY

A complete picture on a union-by-union basis is difficult to establish. The rapid growth and the changes in union structure and membership; the complexity of union organization (All-Russian, city, regional, industrial, craft, and so on); the splits within unions between leaders per se, between leaders and members, and within the general membership itself on all levels makes the picture so confused as to defy Djugashvili clarity. But if patterns are discernible, the following appears to present the basic case.

As mentioned, the Bolsheviks enjoyed the support of one of the most important unions—the All-Russian Metal Workers' Union. At its founding congress in January 1918 there were 75 Bolshevik delegates, 20 Mensheviks, 52 nonparty, and a handful of Left Socialist Revolutionaries. The Bolsheviks also had the support of the All-Russian Textile Workers' Union. At its founding congress, also held in January, 52 per cent of the delegates were Bolsheviks. And as the credential commission report of the First Trade Union Congress indicates, the Bolsheviks were backed by only seven other All-Russian unions, against the Mensheviks' twelve. Bolshevik strength was especially strong on the oblast and local levels of these unions affiliated with the A.R.C.C.T.U. and attending the First Congress.

On the other hand, the Petrograd Printers' Union, the Moscow Chemical Workers' Union, the Union of State Employees, the Postal and Telegraph Union, and the Railway Workers' Union were hostile to the Bolsheviks, for the most part on both the leadership and membership levels. Further, Menshevik-led unions—and this means most —were officially cold or hostile to the Bolsheviks. So too were most white-collar and highly skilled craft unions. Yet one cannot say that "blue-collar" unions were pro-Bolshevik, as Lenin claimed; the position of the chemical workers' unions, among others—such as those in premanufacturing industries like peat cutting and lumber—indicates the reverse. The leaders and members of these unions, for the most part, seem to have been either highly opposed or indifferent to the Bolsheviks. Wage scales introduced under Bolshevik aegis tended to pay workers who were indifferent to Bolshevik encomiums at a higher rate than those the Party could count on. The workers of the premanufacturing industries were paid at a relatively high rate. The differential wage rates favoring workers furthest removed from Bolshevik reaches speaks for itself.

All told, the number of unions categorized as All-Russian, Menshevik-led, white-collar, civil servant, craft, and premanufacturing —a majority of the unions—were hostile to the Bolsheviks. Bolshevik strength in the lower executive and local levels does not offset this fact.

MYTH AND REALITY

It therefore appears paradoxical that union-Party and worker-Party relations have been predominantly interpreted as harmonious. Yet this has been the view most frequently advanced—that the unions and workers, despite some quarrels, stood staunchly behind the Party, helping it to secure power and defeat the Whites.

There is, of course, something to be said for this interpretation, which is ideological in essence. But the real picture is far from one of unity and harmony. Real enmity existed between labor and the Bolsheviks, and battles were fought for high stakes at great cost, often with disastrous consequences. Union support did come, but it was obtained by destroying opposition and creating new unions, remaking them in the image of the Party and controlling them from above. As for the workers, coercive measures were applied to produce the desired conformity. The men responsible for the dominant view, whether intentionally or not, have created a myth which has contributed to substantial confusion and misunderstanding of the Revolution.

A WEB OF INTRIGUE

The Bolsheviks resorted to any means in their concerted effort to penetrate and capture the unions or destroy their autonomy. In few cases did they gain control of unions by garnering rank-and-file support and winning democratic elections. Wherever and whenever possible they built up membership support and then relied on it to oust union leaders, to justify ordering elections or withdrawing charters. The hiatus that existed in the November period between the leaders and the members was fully and shrewdly exploited. In many instances the charge of "unrepresentative leadership" and "antidemocratic" unionism was leveled against the entrenched Menshevik leadership to lend substance to the Party's attacks; but primarily the Party relied on the national machinery captured at the First Congress. The Party controlled the A.R.C.C.T.U. and relied essentially on its executive powers. It chartered rival unions, withdrew recognition of hostile unions, ordered new elections, and recognized only Bolshevik victories. In addition, it leaned heavily on coercion, raids on union headquarters, seizures of treasuries and membership files, arrests of hostile union leaders, deprivation of civil liberties, and perhaps most cruel of all in light of the hunger of the civil war period, confiscation of ration cards of leaders and members alike.

The unions, caught in a web of cooperation and intimidation, fell one by one. Some yielded quietly and quickly; others were bowled over with little chance to protest. Still others went along only after staunch opposition. All in all, the fight was over quickly; by 1919–1920 the Bolsheviks were well established in most unions.

THE CASE OF THE ALL-RUSSIAN
RAILWAY WORKERS' UNION

The national Railway Workers' Union, allegedly the largest and most effectively organized of Russian trade unions, posed a major problem for the Bolsheviks from the very first hours of the November coup. The actions of this union forced Lenin to face his first real dilemma: the consolidation and use of state power to crush a powerful, democratic union in order to build a workers' state.

This national union, structured like most, was a federation of affiliated craft unions of railway employees. Some units remained outside the All-Russian union, but most joined. On the other hand, the national union combined clerical, technical, manual, skilled, and unskilled workers. Its cross-representation was unusual for Russian unions in 1917–1918, and it was closer to an industrial than a craft union. Although it met in a national congress, the management of its affairs was entrusted to an executive committee: the All-Russian Executive Committee of Railwaymen, or Vikzhel. Of the approximately 40 members on this committee, the majority were reported to have been moderate socialists (Mensheviks, Independents and Socialist Revolutionaries), two Bolsheviks, two Internationalists, and one a nonparty Bolshevik sympathizer.[7]

As a railroad union, capable of striking the entire rail network and paralyzing the country, it occupied a powerful political position. Its power was originally demonstrated during the Kornilov revolt, when the railwaymen, under orders from Vikzhel, switched Kornilov's troop trains onto spur lines or sent them rolling rapidly away from Petrograd, leaving the general without his troops. They were about to do the same to Kerensky and General Krasnov. This was obviously a union whose support it was best to have, or at least one not to be trifled with.

Now, on November 11, 1917, in their very first days of power, the Bolsheviks felt the heavy hand of Vikzhel threatening their coup. At the very end of the final session of the Second Congress of Soviets, just before the question of the composition of the new government could be put to a vote, a Vikzhel representative rose and demanded the floor. Kamenev, the presiding chairman, suspected that something was amiss and refused to recognize him. The man insisted; he appealed to the delegates, and a major disturbance broke out in the hall. Finally, after "extensive consultations" behind the dais, Kamenev agreed to allow the delegate to read a declaration drafted earlier by Vikzhel.[8]

The declaration stunned the delegates. It was an ultimatum to the Bolsheviks. The Vikzhel representative ("speaking very excitedly," states Sukhanov) first reviewed the railway union's services to the Revolution and its support of the Soviets, saying the railwaymen had always been "one of the most revolutionary proletariats."[9] Then he stated that at a meeting on November 8, Vikzhel—in view of the dubious legality of the Congress and in the absence of a central authority—"took a negative view of the seizure of power by a single political party" and felt that the power ought to be socialist, revolutionary, and representative. Also, "pending the formation of a revolutionary socialist government responsible to the whole revolutionary democracy," Vikzhel would assume charge of the Ministry of Communications and supervision of the railways. He concluded by stating that only orders from Vikzhel would be obeyed by the railwaymen, and that the union would not permit transportation of troops except when authorized by the former Executive Committee of the Soviets or the plenipotentiary body to be formed by the city duma and other revolutionary organs. Finally, he asserted that if any repressive measures were taken against the railwaymen, the union would cut off supplies from Petrograd.

To counter this, Kamenev vigorously affirmed the legal rulers of Russia to be the Soviets and not the Bolsheviks. A pro-Bolshevik representative of the railway workers charged that Vikzhel no longer represented the workers, who were in fact repudiating it. Nonetheless, Vikzhel, in control of the railways, held the better bargaining position. The Bolsheviks, whose popularity with the rank-and-file railwaymen was by no means clear, agreed to negotiate. At the same time Vikzhel joined forces with the moderate socialist-Duma officials, who together formed the Committee to Save the Country and Revolution in the hope of preventing civil war, securing the convocation of the Constituent Assembly, and bringing about a "democratic peace."[10]

For two days, however, under Lenin's advice, the People's Commissars stalled. On November 11, while street fighting swept the heart of Petrograd, Vikzhel, which had remained a participant in the Second Congress proceedings, called for a coalition conference in a concerted effort to end a civil war of socialist against socialist. Vikzhel delivered its ultimatum: an immediate general railway strike by midnight if the fighting did not cease.[11] It also sent delegations to Kerensky and to Moscow, where another uprising had broken out, in order to stop the fighting. At 5:00 P.M. that evening the Central Committee, which could stall no longer, yielded. The Central Executive of the Soviets designated Kamenev, Ryazanov, Rykov, and Sokolnikov as their representatives for talks with other socialist parties on the formation of a coalition government. However, to prepare for all contingencies, Lenin and Trotsky looked to their military support, securing assurance that the troops were not being taken in by coalition peace talks.

The interparty negotiations, held at Vikzhel headquarters, lasted for three days in almost continuous session. Finally a tentative compromise was reached. A new government responsible to an assembly consisting of the various existing organs—the old and new Soviets, the Petrograd Duma, the trade unions, the army units, and so forth—was created. At 2 A.M. on November 14 the conference adjourned and each delegate reported back to his party. For the Bolsheviks the compromise marked a major defeat. They were to surrender power to a new government, with a majority of members hostile to the Bolshevik position. Kamenev reported and recommended acceptance. The proposal split the Party. It was totally unacceptable to Lenin and Trotsky, who repudiated the efforts of Kamenev and the negotiation team. Trotsky bitterly dismissed the proposal with the statement: "It was hardly worthwhile to organize the uprising if we cannot have a majority [in the new government]." [12] Lenin said it was time to put an end to Kamenev's politics, that negotiations with Vikzhel were not worthwhile and should be used as a diplomatic move to mask troop movements. He felt that if help could only be sent to Moscow the victory would be complete.[13]

Lenin and Trotsky were opposed by Rykov, Zinoviev, Nogin, and Miliutin, though for different reasons. Rykov contended that the price of breaking off negotiations would be the alienation of those groups whose support was needed for victory. Zinoviev was for continuing negotiations without accepting the proposed conditions. Lenin, losing his temper, said in rebuttal that it was time to put an end to negotiations, and went so far as to say that Vikzhel was on the side of the Kaledins and Kornilovs. Later he added that the

Central Committee had asked Vikzhel to send troops to Moscow and Vikzhel had refused. But whatever the case, the charge was irresponsible, and if Lenin believed it, the fact provides an insight into the man and his understanding of the situation. Lenin also made another extremely revealing statement. After having said that the majority of the workers and peasants in the army were with them, with which few could argue, he then added that "no one has yet proved the lower classes are against us." [14]

A vote was taken. Four voted for breaking off negotiations, against a majority of ten in favor of continuing. On the surface Lenin had lost, but the adopted resolution amazingly reflected his point of view. The Party resolved that its members would be allowed to attend negotiations, but that the Bolshevik delegates "must show the impossibility of such an attempt and the futility of further negotiations on the subject of forming a coalition government." [15]

At a November 14 session of the Central Executive Committee of the Soviet, the Bolsheviks presented conditions so extreme that the Social Democratic Internationalists and Socialist Revolutionaries, still members of the Second Congress, voted to break off negotiations, emphasizing that the Bolsheviks were more interested in dictatorship and civil war than in a democratic coalition.

But the disagreement within the Party cut deep. An articulate minority had opposed Lenin on the seizure of power, raising essentially the same points about dictatorship, alienation of worker support, and civil war that the Mensheviks had been raising. They had fought for coalition talks and now refused to be stilled. On November 16 Lenin moved to silence them with a threat of expulsion for having violated Party discipline. The opposition, however, refused to bow and on the following day raised the issue of press censorship, first introduced on November 9. The motion was voted down and Lenin's critics then resigned from the Council of People's Commissars and the Central Committee. In a simultaneous move, the Left SRs resigned from the military revolutionary committee and the military staff. Lenin had escalated the cost of disagreement. The possibility of a coalition government was further than ever from being realized.

The breakdown in the Vikzhel-commanded negotiations did not completely end efforts to create a socialist coalition. Although the original meeting of socialist parties scheduled by Vikzhel for November 17 did not take place because of the absence of the Bolsheviks, Vikzhel was able to reschedule the meeting for midnight, November 19. At that time the Socialist Revolutionaries and Mensheviks were not present and the meeting was adjourned until their representatives arrived. The meeting came to order at 2 A.M. Zinoviev, exploiting the confusion and masking the Party's objectives, stated that if no agreement were reached at this meeting the Bolsheviks would drop the subject.[16] The Bundist Erlich then stated that it was quite impossible to enter into any government as long as the liberty and safety of the people were in jeopardy.[17] Further, the Mensheviks were willing to join a government, but clearly the Bolsheviks were not. The meeting concluded at 4 A.M. without any concrete agreement.

With the collapse of this attempt it was decided by all parties that negotiations would be carried over to the Special Congress of Peasant Soviets, which was to meet in Petrograd between November 23 and December 8, at the very time when elections to the Constituent Assembly were to be held. Before the Congress got under way, however, another attempt was made to negotiate. An All-Army Committee at staff headquarters, acting on its own, tried to appoint a national government. V. M. Chernov was designated as minister-president. Representatives of Vikzhel attended the session and gave their consent to Chernov, offering to put the railroads at the disposal of the new government. Chernov wired the proposal to the central committee of the Socialist Revolutionaries, which also consented. But before preparations could be completed, Gotz and Auxentiev, who claimed they had been appointed by Kerensky to form a new government, arrived at staff headquarters and forced Chernov to abandon his effort. Petty politics triumphed over the opposition once again.

When the Congress of Peasant Soviets opened, the question of a coalition government was again picked up and became the dominant issue of discussion. At this Congress the Bolsheviks appeared to be at a clear disadvantage, with only 37 delegates against 195 Left Socialist Revolutionaries and 65 of the Right. In the early sessions a majority did seem to favor a coalition "composed of all socialist parties from the Bolsheviks to the Socialist-Populists inclusive."[18] But at the critical moment of electing a new executive committee, the split between the Left and Right SRs proved a more crucial issue and the congress fell apart. The Left SRs then initiated separate negotiations with the Bolsheviks, whose position had been enhanced by victories in the Petrograd elections for the Constituent Assembly. On November 28, agreement between the Bolsheviks and the Left SRs was reached, and three Left SRs joined the Council of People's Commissars. At the same time an informal agreement was reached with Vikzhel. A former member of Vikzhel was appointed Commissar of Ways and Communications. In turn, Vikzhel recognized the new "coalition."

VIKZHEL'S COMPROMISE

Vikzhel's recognition of the government was a major victory for the Bolsheviks. As Hendelman, the Socialist Revolutionary, said at the November 11 meeting of the socialist parties, future historians will most likely say that the "railwaymen saved the revolution" or the "railwaymen ruined the revolution." [19] He was right; they were the only power that had successfully forced the Bolsheviks into coalition talks. Now, with this decision, they were actually contributing to the preservation of Bolshevik rule, the very government they had been trying to bring down. Surely they could not believe by any stretch of imagination that a coalition with just three Left Social Revolutionaries was democratic and representative. Why then did they do it?

There are of course a number of possible explanations. One which has been suggested is that of inept leadership and political naiveté.[20] This, of course, may hit the mark. But the fight they had waged did not indicate ineptness and naiveté. Also improbable is the explanation that they had a change of heart at the last minute and joined with the Bolsheviks. Third, and quite plausible, is the possibility that the protracted negotiation and intransigence of all sides so disheartened them that they decided this was the best settlement they could get at the time. Also, the Bolsheviks were winning, and short of more bloodshed and a civil war between socialists— which they were on record as firmly opposing—this was the best way to obtain the minimum acceptable settlement. A fifth, and to my mind the most likely explanation, is that the elections to the Constituent Assembly had just taken place and Vikzhel could not have helped being impressed with the fact that the Bolsheviks had won the overwhelming support of the industrial centers, although they had lost the election. While the worker vote was discouraging to Vikzhel, there was the compensating fact that the Bolsheviks had promised to abide by the results of the election. Now that they had lost and a new and representative government appeared to be in the offing, Vikzhel's November demands were no longer so imperative. Further, a new, although limited, coalition would compensate for the nonrepresentative element of Bolshevik rule during the short period left before the SRs would assume power. Thus recognition had its compensating qualities. Adding weight to this argument are the facts that Vikzhel still commanded the railways and the new Commissar of Ways and Communications was a former member of Vikzhel; thus Vikzhel retained a veto power, or so its members thought. On these two last points they were rather naive, as events were soon to prove. Nonetheless, all the preceding speculations are possible and probably the truth is to be found in some combination of them.

THE BOLSHEVIKS RETALIATE

It was not long before Vikzhel found how wrong it had been in accepting Bolshevik assurances. In less than a month the Bolsheviks, probably in preparation for the dissolution of the Constituent Assembly on December 21, took steps against Vikzhel. A representative of the military revolutionary committee, with a company of soldiers, took possession of the railway telegraph and all the entrances to the Ministry of Railways and refused to admit members of Vikzhel. From then on admittance to the Ministry was by a pass from a Bolshevik commissar. At the same time the Commissar of Railways threatened to hand over to the revolutionary tribunal those who decided to strike.[21]

If this act did not end Vikzhel's uneasy agreement with the Bolsheviks, the Bolshevik dissolution of the Constituent Assembly did. Sitting in session at the same moment was the First All-Russian Congress of the Railway Workers' Union. Under the leadership of Vikzhel it passed (by a small majority) a vote of confidence in the Assembly. Once again it openly challenged the Bolsheviks; this time, however, it delivered no ultimatums.

The Bolsheviks now struck at the union directly. A minority of the delegates attending the Congress were pro-Bolshevik and voted against the Constituent Assembly resolution. This minority, under Bolshevik encomiums, walked out of the congress and convened one of its own. As recommended by Lenin, it created a rival union. Its 40-man executive committee, Vikzhedor, consisted of 25 Bolsheviks, 12 Left Socialist Revolutionaries, and 3 Independents. The new congress and its executive committee at once received official recognition from the Council of People's Commissars. A member of Vikzhedor, Rogov, became Minister of Communications, and Vikzhedor was assigned complete control of the railways. The struggle between Vikzhel and Vikzhedor began in earnest and lasted throughout 1918; yet, while it was going on, Vikzhel and the Communist Party, paradoxically, cooperated in fighting the civil war.

During 1918 the question of administration of the railroads also came to a head. The record of Vikzhel in this regard is difficult to assess. Compared to other unions, the railwaymen were well disciplined, as again the Kornilov and November incidents indicate. During the pre-Vikzhedor period, chaos had existed on the railroads; yet Vikzhel is acknowledged not to have suffered the disorganization that other unions experienced. Against this picture of Vikzhel's relatively disciplined membership is the fact that the Bolsheviks did experience enormous difficulties with the railroads. Part of their problem was the dislocation produced by World War I and the civil war—shortage of materials, exhaustion of equipment, administrative disorganization. But part, as Shlyapnikov's following assessment indicates, was due to labor difficulties. "For instance," he said in a memo to the Party, "trains nowadays often go unlighted, without observing any of the regulations with regard to signals, . . . while the cars are never cleaned. . . . The usual excuse is that no kerosene or candles are available. However, I have ascertained that both these commodities are available but are being pilfered in the most shameless manner." He went on to say that the railway crews, not being interested in the exploitation of the railways, would sometimes refuse to man the trains. Thus, Shlyapnikov asserted, "both cars and locomotives may be available but there are no engineers and no conductors: . . . *they either pretend illness or else simply refuse to go.*" He stated that when a substitute for a sick member of the train crew was needed, the stationmaster was unable to exercise his authority for *no sooner would he find a replacement than the substitute would tell him that he would not go without the consent of the committee.* It was impossible to get the Committee together on the spot so the train could not be dispatched. Then Shlyapnikov gave an example: "The station of Tver has locomotives available but . . . for a number of days, twenty-seven engineers were sick and consequently twenty-seven locomotives were tied up. . . . You can easily imagine what a traffic jam resulted at that junction point."

He went on to describe the disorganization and demoralization that prevailed in the railway shops. He told of the station at Klin where the "roundhouse has been converted into a club" and the engines were "being repaired in the open air. It is known that the repair shops release very few cars and locomotives." Then he drew this conclusion: "In a word, from the moment the railway employees were guaranteed a minimum wage they ceased to display any minimum degree of efficiency." He referred to the "complaints" heard in Moscow from "the class-conscious elements" that they "must at any price get our railwaymen interested in the exploitation of the roads." He suggested that this might be done in the shops by introducing piece-work and the crews might be paid per *verst*. He believed this to be "the only painless method to raise the efficiency of the railway employees." [22]

But the problem Shlyapnikov describes is not to be attributed entirely to the selfishness of the workers. The refusal to man trains or release locomotives, the pretense of illness, the insistence on consent of the committee for substitutes, the impossibility of assembling the committee so the train could be dispatched—all smack of political opposition as much as the chaos of workers' control and the selfishness of the workers.

Significantly, the measures to which the Bolsheviks resorted were intended to serve a double function. First, as is generally asserted, they were introduced to solve the problem of labor discipline and restore the lines to working order. Second, they were geared to weaken further Vikzhel's political power. The January transfer of complete control of the railways to Vikzhedor marked the beginning of this latter step. This move qualified the legislation introduced on January 23, entrusting railway administration to a Soviet elected by the railwaymen of the line; and general control over all railways to an All-Russian Congress of Railwaymen's Deputies. But these steps did not carry the Bolsheviks far enough either way. Administrative chaos actually worsened. Finally, on March 26, 1918, one-man management was re-established for the railways. The Commissariat of Communications was given "dictatorial powers in matters pertaining to railroad transportation." The unions' powers were limited to the election of members to the commissariats. The elections, however, were made subject to approval by the Council of People's Commissars and the A.R.C.C.T.U.[23] One of the Commissariat's first moves was to dissolve the workers' committees, singling out the Murmansk line—a Vikzhel line—in particular.

With great embarrassment Vikzhedor enforced one-man management, dissolution of the commissions, and cuts in overtime, which had also been introduced. As could be expected, the effect on the rank and file was negative. Vikzhedor, which had been unable to make much headway against Vikzhel, was further weakened by having to underwrite these measures.

In June another crisis occurred. In protest against wage rates on the railroads, Vikzhel, still stronger, threatened a railwaymen's strike. Though it was averted, the C.P. saw itself unable to counter with Vikzhedor and helpless against the railway employees union, just as in November 1917. Finally on November 28, 1918, as a response in part to the civil war and in part to the politics of the railwaymen, the railways were placed under martial law. Military commissars were appointed for the railroad on each front. All employees were mobilized, ordered to remain at their posts, and placed under military discipline.[24] The Bolshevik policies of military rule crushed Vikzhel and all opposition. When in February 1919 another Congress of the All-Russian Railway Workers' Union was called, the Vikzhel forces were too weak to fight. The outcome of the Congress was the election by show-of-hand vote of a 30-man executive committee, consisting of 17 Bolsheviks, 8 Independents, and 5 Internationalists. None were Mensheviks or Socialist Revolutionaries, the parties which had dominated Vikzhel. For all practical purposes the fight, one of the most interesting and serious between the Bolsheviks and a national union, was over.

THE CASE OF THE STATE EMPLOYEES' UNION

The second taste of labor opposition came from the state employees. On November 9, 1917, two days after the seizure of power and just as the Bolsheviks were feverishly fighting to consolidate their impressive but incomplete victory, a strike in all administrative departments was called by the newly-created Union of Unions of State Employees. This strike, intended to bring down the Bolsheviks, coincided with the efforts of the very active though divided moderate opposition parties organized as the Committee to Save the Country and Revolution, and with those of the railway workers union, the military kadets, Kerensky and General Krasnov.

During the next few days, the strike spread rapidly among the government agencies. The employees of the Ministry of Agriculture, after enumerating Bolshevik violations of the March Revolution such as freedom of the press, assembly, and speech, resolved not to recognize the organs of its government. The employees of the Ministries of Labor, Post and Telegraph, Food, Finance, Foreign Affairs, and State Bank did the same. The employees of the Ministry of Education, declaring themselves unable to work under the threat of a club, resolved not to return until a legal government was formed. By December 28 more than 30,000 teachers in the City of Petrograd were on strike. They were joined by the employees of public libraries and people's houses.

The Bolsheviks countercharged. The strike of state employees represented the protest of the "wealthy class" of workers and was by no means a labor vote of no confidence in the seizure of power. Given the fact that most were civil servants and better off than wage earners, this was partly true—but not entirely, for some, like the telegraph workers, were blue-collar workers. Also, given the friendly nature of the alliance between the Committee to Save the Country and Revolution and the railwaymen's union (as well as several other unions, including the printers), the charge is open to question.

The Bolsheviks fought with all means at their disposal, though haltingly at first, reflecting their lack of a single or carefully calculated approach to the problem. Shlyapnikov, the Commissar of Labor, displayed the utmost restraint when, on November 9, he "requested" all employees to resume work, stating that those who did not "will be regarded as having resigned." Trotsky and Menzhinsky, Commissars of Foreign Affairs and Finance respectively, were "hawks." Trotsky used force without compunction. In his memoirs he almost chuckles when reporting that he enlisted the aid of a Baltic fleet sailor to use physical force to bring "order" in the Ministry. Nor did he hesitate to arrest or physically coerce those he presumed to be strike leaders.[25] Menzhinsky assumed a similar stance on November 12, warning the employees of the Ministry of Finance and the savings banks that all who continued to strike on the next day would be arrested.[26]

But the results were mixed. The strikers and the Committee were unable either to win mass support or to oust the Bolsheviks. But the Bolsheviks were unable to end the strike. By the end of November, as resistance continued unfailing, all Party Ministries resorted to the same policy—they threatened to apply force. A typical statement was that of Avilov, Commissar of Post and Telegraph. In a November 27 order he declared that all employees and officials who did not recognize his authority, and that of the Council of People's Commissars, were to be dismissed immediately and deprived of pensions from that day. All those of military age were henceforth removed from the exemption list and all officials occupying state dwellings were to vacate them by the second day after the publication of the order. And then, to divide the strikers, he added that the vacated quarters were to be placed at the disposal of those who remained in service and of others who wished to join. In a housing shortage of major significance this was no ineffective technique for dealing with the strikers.

But these were not the only techniques upon which the Bolsheviks relied. On December 8 the military revolutionary committee declared the strikers to be outlaws, "enemies of the people." The official pronouncement concluded: "He who will not work with the people has no place in the ranks of the people. Blacklist all saboteurs! Boycott the criminals!"[27]

The strike continued for several weeks but gradually collapsed.

The failure of the Committee to Save the Country and the Revolution to win popular support against a minority dictatorship took the heart out of the state employees. Slowly, individuals drifted back to work and joined those who had never "gone out." On January 26, 1918, the executive committee of the Union of Unions met to discuss ending the strike. They entertained the idea of ending the political strike but continuing an "economic one," but after lengthy discussion the motion was voted down. The executive committee then decided to refer the question to the local unions, in effect forfeiting any bargaining position they might have retained, and really forcing each local union to scramble for its own settlement. With the Union of Unions' decision, the employees of the various ministries voted to go back to work, one by one. The employees of the Ministry of Agriculture called off their strike on January 27. On February 7 the post and telegraph employees voted by 141 to 32 to end the strike.[28] Each attempted to enter into negotiations with their respective commissariats.

The Bolsheviks yielded absolutely nothing. On February 14 *Pravda* carried the decision of the Council of People's Commissars not to have any negotiations with "saboteurs." It refused to recognize or bargain with either the Union of Unions' executive committee or the individual unions; rather, it insisted on dealing with all strikers individually and as "saboteurs." The Council then authorized each commissariat to employ "such individual saboteurs as are needed and willing to submit and support the Soviet Government."[29] The action of the various commissars differed, with the Commissariat of Food taking the harsh stand: "under no circumstance [would it] take back the saboteurs" and "all vacancies [were] to be filled by honest laborers from the free proletariat."[30]

Simultaneously with their efforts to cope with the strike by cajoling and threatening the strikers, the Bolsheviks attacked on an entirely different level. They organized a rival state employees' union. They hoped that by labeling the striking union a bourgeois and paper union they could destroy it. The dual-union tactic did not produce any immediate results, although some headway was made, particularly with minor clerks and maintenance personnel. Until February 1919, the anti-Bolshevik union remained the larger and dominant union. In May 1919 the A.R.C.C.T.U., acting to destroy its opposition once and for all, ordered a unification congress. At this congress, the Second All-Russian Congress of State Employees, under conditions less than democratic, a Bolshevik majority was elected to the union central committee—composed of 12 Communists, 3 Internationalists, and 6 Independents. That this was a farce is evident. The opposition union had lost strength as the Bolsheviks organized and as the failure of the strike became evident, but had not weakened so much that it could not have, under democratic conditions, elected a stronger slate to the executive union offices. In a way this is all irrelevant. Protests on the destruction of the state employees' union had been registered at the Second Trade Union Congress in January 1919, but the matter was settled; this was their end.

THE CASE OF THE PRINTERS' UNION

The Printers' Union was a somewhat different case, but the pattern was the same. The A.R.C.C.T.U. used its authority to set up a rival union to capture the union's machinery and to isolate the Menshevik leaders.

The fight, which lasted from 1917 to 1921, started shortly after the November coup, when the printers declared their opposition to the Party's seizure of power. It reached a high point in December 1917 when the Menshevik-led union came out in opposition to Bolshevik censorship of the press. Opposition by this union was serious; it occupied a strategic political position and was esteemed for its history of political leadership and opposition. The Bolsheviks met the challenge in every way they could, slowly pressing it down.

Early in 1920, after more than two years of harassment, the union, considering the possibilities of improved relations less likely than further deterioration of their power, chose to retaliate. The union chose an A.R.C.C.T.U. decision on a city-wide wage scale as the issue over which to fight. At the same time, it asserted its independence and political neutrality. And in some cities where the Bolsheviks were weak or had fallen, branches of the Printers' Union attacked the Bolsheviks in the press.

The Party retaliated. The A.R.C.C.T.U. organized and chartered a "red union" in an attempt to wrest control of the printing trade away from the Mensheviks. Once this Bolshevik-controlled union had gained sufficient strength, it called its own congress and elected its own central committee. At this juncture the A.R.C.C.T.U. ordered a merger of the two unions.

The printers gave a graphic picture of the tactics employed. In an article entitled: "The Independents and the Press," they stated:

> Communists sometimes use threats of arrests against the workers to oblige them to leave their posts in the board of the union voluntarily, and in practice this often happens. Sometimes they do it otherwise;

they say that if a Communist is not elected to the Board or Factory Workers Committee, they, the Communists, will arrange so that their workers will receive less food and other necessary things. And sometimes this produces its effect. This affirmation can be verified in many factories in Moscow.[31]

Finally the Menshevik central committee, under considerable pressure, acceded to A.R.C.C.T.U. demands for a unification congress. The calls went out and an election campaign, quickly rigged, was launched. With the hope of a man headed to the gallows, the Mensheviks petitioned the A.R.C.C.T.U. for a postponement of the congress and for new elections, both of which the A.R.C.C.T.U. promptly refused.

At this point the Mensheviks, still enjoying the support of a majority of the printers, decided to boycott the congress and destroy it by withholding their support. This did not, however, deter the Bolsheviks, who convened their "unification" congress and petitioned the A.R.C.C.T.U. for recognition. The A.R.C.C.T.U., aware that the Bolshevik congress represented only a minority of the printers, did not hesitate to charter the Bolshevik union as the official Printers' Union. With this act the Menshevik union, though claiming a majority of the printers, was "outlawed" and denied recognition as a union. Nevertheless, it continued to live, function, and fight.

Responding on another level, the Party denied the Menshevik Printers' Union the right to a participation vote at the Second Congress of Trade Unions, though the union sent nonelected delegates. The basis of the refusal was the dispersal and reconstitution of the union.[32] Although the silencing of the opposition was protested on the floor by some delegates, Bolsheviks included, the Menshevik delegates made no headway, and in fact were taunted with a charge of treason: "that your independence goes so far that you go along with Kolchak, that you consider it necessary to support the shooters of communists in those cities where you act with our enemies. Let us admit that." [33]

Matters finally came to a head in the spring of 1920 with the visit of a British trade union delegation to Moscow. The Mensheviks sought out the delegates, cited their grievances, and called on Britons to attend a mass rally called by the Moscow central committee of the Menshevik Printers' Union. This action alone irritated the Bolsheviks, but to make matters worse, V. M. Chernov, who had been in hiding, appeared at the meeting to address the British delegates.

This was more than the Bolsheviks could take. Troops were sent to seize the union headquarters, 40 Menshevik leaders of the union present were arrested, and the central committee was dissolved. Still the printers fought back. They went out on strike, demanding the release of those arrested; but of course they stood little chance of winning. The Soviet government broke the strike by eliminating the remaining leaders, threatening the rest, and confiscating their food rations. The printers succumbed, stating: "the privation of food is, under the present conditions, the most terrible measure against starving people that was used." [34]

OTHER PROTESTS

There were other protests, some of which occurred late in the spring of 1918, even from quarters friendly to the Bolsheviks. At a meeting held on March 20, 1918, attended by 83 delegates representing 25 of the more important Petrograd industries, a declaration protesting Bolshevik trade-union policy was adopted. It opened with the statement:

> The workers have supported the new government which calls itself the government of the workers and peasants and promises to do our will and to work for our welfare. All our organizations stood back of it and our sons and brothers shed their blood for it. . . . Four months have passed and we find ourselves without faith and without hope. This government which calls itself a Soviet of Workers and Peasants has done everything to oppose the will of the workers. It has blocked every attempt to hold new elections to the Soviets, it has threatened to use machine guns (against workers), and it has broken up meetings and demonstrations. [35]

At a special meeting on March 27, 1918, at which 170 delegates spoke for 56 Petrograd factories and workshops, a resolution passed by an overwhelming majority condemned the Bolsheviks for denying the trade unions their independence, for "turning them into bureaucratic organs of the Soviet Government." A report demanding independent unions, presented by a worker named Kimmerwald, summed up their grievances:

> The disgraceful peace, hunger, incompetence displayed in connection with the evacuation, the complete disorganization of factory life, all these fell as a heavy burden upon the workers . . . who are deprived of their professional organizations and have to face unarmed all these misfortunes. The trade unions have lost their inde-

pendence . . . and . . . are no longer fighting in defense of the workers' rights.[36]

On April 29, 1918, a minority group of trade union leaders, including Lozovsky, issued a statement containing in effect the same message, but providing a more complete picture of the methods the commissars were employing against the unions.

> Since the November Revolution we have witnessed innumerable instances of how big, small, or even microscopic commissars have used every kind of oppression, including bayonets, in their dealings with recalcitrant proletarian organizations. Here are a few instances: the Soviet government closed the quarters of the Union of Employees of Credit Institutions, arrested several times its board of directors, closed the cooperative store which supplied the families of the employees of [the credit institutions] in order to force the starving employees formally to recognize the Soviet Government. In Rybinsk the executive committee [of the Soviets] ordered an "inspection" of the local Soviet of trade unions. . . . To fight opposition tendencies of certain trade unions new unions of the same trade and sharing the point of view of the Soviet Government were set up. The authorities then decided which union is more adequate for the interests of the workers.[37]

The statement ended with the assertions that membership in the unions was decreasing and that the majority of trade union leaders believed the independence of the trade unions to be an essential to correct the "sad results" produced since the November Revolution.

MENSHEVIK RESURGENCY

As Leonard Schapiro states, by 1920 there was little love left for the Bolsheviks among the six million or more members of the trade unions which represented the great bulk of the Russian industrial class.[38]

It is not possible, for lack of data, to estimate accurately the extent of the rift. All that can be offered with certainty is the fact that Mensheviks, pro-Mensheviks, and other anti-Communists estimated the total anti-Communist following among the industrial workers in 1921 at 90 per cent or over 99 per cent. Zinoviev acknowledged that he believed the opposition to be this extensive. Even Trotsky, who ridiculed such an estimate as a "monstrous exaggeration," conceded that the anti-Communists were "very numerous."

He was constrained to justify the Party dictatorship on the grounds that it "was more important than some formalistic principle of workers' democracy" because it defended the fundamental interests of the working class "even during a period of a temporary wavering in its mood." [39]

But the situation was worse than that. The Menshevik decline of 1917 appears to have gone into reverse gear, with support for them climbing rapidly after 1918. Their persistent presence at trade union congresses, against all odds and in spite of the tactics resorted to by the Bolsheviks to pack the congresses, is evidence of their staying power. Perhaps even more revealing is their growth in popularity among the ranks of the workers. The tables had turned; the Mensheviks were now in the position that the Bolsheviks had been in during the late summer and fall of 1917. Menshevik popularity grew as that of the Bolsheviks waned. Lenin was feeling their bite, and little could have rankled him more than making concessions to the Mensheviks about the impracticability of building socialism in a backward Russia after the bitter years of War Communism.

As the indications of abandoning War Communist policies and of introducing a new economic policy became increasingly clear, Lenin's personal hostility toward the Mensheviks increased. They had been advocating a policy of economic retreat and recovery for some time. His identification of them with the counterrevolutionaries became more frequent. Finally, in the spring of 1921 Lenin underwrote a massive attack on the Mensheviks, and in April, shortly before the Tenth Congress, he wrote: "the place for the Mensheviks and the SRs . . . is in prison." [40]

What adds a macabre touch to this judgment is that, in a way, the Mensheviks and the Bolsheviks were moving toward each other when Lenin signaled the final assault. For a short while in 1918 the Mensheviks enjoyed the status of a "legal" party. That October, in a manifesto known as the "October Thesis," the Mensheviks had undertaken a conciliatory step by recognizing the November seizure of power as "an historical necessity." They stressed their rejection of any violent overthrow of the Bolsheviks, emphasizing their position as that of a loyal opposition. They promised support for the Red Army and the defense of the Revolution, and strongly believed it their duty to help rebuild the country. Yet at the same time they demanded abolition of Bolshevik terror.[41] Miliukov, the Kadet leader, has even gone so far as to suggest that for a brief period there was some consideration of sharing power with the Mensheviks, but that the idea proved barren because Dan, Martov's successor, demanded guarantees for political freedom which the Bolsheviks were neither willing nor able to agree to. As Schapiro points out, however, there is nothing in Dan's memoirs to corroborate this contention.[42]

All in all, any reconciliation or concession appears most unlikely from the Party's point of view and the subsequent outlawing of the Mensheviks. To have had the Mensheviks at liberty as the Party shifted gear and introduced the New Economic Policy would have reopened the entire question of the Constituent Assembly and of shifting power to the party whose policy was now being introduced. To have had them criticizing the Party and building their strength within the unions just when the Party was fighting a growing labor opposition both within and outside its own ranks would have invited the complete split of the party along worker lines and raised the specter of declining Bolshevik rule.

Thus Lenin was caught on the horns of another major dilemma. He had seized power in the hope of building a workers' state, but in the process of consolidating power he had alienated the workers and waged a destructive war against the unions and labor. He left the labor movement weak, hostile, and divided, and with the Mensheviks on the rise. This was the price of success. He could not rule with them and retain power; he could not rule without them and not be ideologically compromised. He could not sacrifice either without sacrificing both. Lenin had won, but the price of success was failure.

Somehow he had to juggle, to hold out, to hope. This is what he did, but he showed increasing signs of disappointment and resignation to failure. Sickness and death blessed Lenin, for they stole him away before the full fury of his failure could no longer be rationalized away. In a way, his inability to resolve the succession problem points up the agony of his last dilemma.

4 ✹ Industrial Relations: 1917-1921

In the field of industrial relations the Russian Revolution promised a transformation as profound as the overthrow of political absolutism. The Bolsheviks (and the non-Bolshevik Left as well) promised to humanize the entire work process. Labor was to be propelled forward. The worker's welfare, rather than profit, was to be the goal of the entire system. Relations between the factory worker and management were to be revolutionized through the introduction of democratic management; relations between man and machine were to be altered through an adjustment of the work process to the needs and psychology of the human being; worker participation in plant decision-making was to become primary. Ixion, the mythical Greek figure bound by Zeus to an eternally revolving wheel, symbolizing man's bondage to the work process, was about to be unchained.

A crucial question in any industrial relations system is: Who governs?—management, labor, the state, or what combination of the three? This applies on the plant as well as the national level. The final resolution of this question will very much determine the character and values of the system. Throughout the first period of Soviet industrial relations this was a primary problem and it cut across all attempts at workers' control, collective management, one-man management, collective bargaining, and nationalization of industry. Also involved was the question of how much labor penetration of economic management should occur on the shop and national levels. In effect the management question was the decisive one, fundamentally affecting the outcome of union power and the entire industrial relations system in this first period, 1917–1921, of Soviet rule.

MANAGEMENT ON THE MICRO LEVEL

Workers' Control

Workers' control radically transformed industrial relations. It was a revolution in its own right. For the short period of its existence, labor was propelled into the realm of decision-making on the shop level, converting labor into managers or co-managers with authority over input and output, personnel policy, and finance. No other single act increased labor's powers so extensively in the early post-March days. Few other policies could have so changed the industrial relations system, the procedures governing the operation of the work place.

The First Acts—Management

The workers' acts of March are legend, but so is the confusion in industrial relations that accompanied the revolution. No one knew what was going on, much less how to exercise any control. Each group—the Soviets, management, the workers, the factory committees, the Provisional Government—approached problems in its own way and either deliberately or accidently worked at cross purposes with everyone else. Management particularly operated in the dark. The workers were still on strike; their demands grew by the hour. The Soviets remained an unknown quantity as far as their political and economic intentions were concerned, and management had no way of telling how effective the Provisional Government would be or how much support it would offer them. For that matter, management had little power to do anything, but they were not going to give in to labor without a fight—particularly on the question of plant seizures and worker interference with management of the plants.

Finally the Soviets, after negotiating with the Provisional Government and some of management's ranking representatives in Petrograd, immediately issued a call to the workers of Petrograd to return to work. They did not set forth any specific terms, but simply recommended that the workers submit formal demands to the factory owners. The workers acquiesced, but without waiting or negotiating they proclaimed the eight-hour work day. The Soviets immediately backed them up by sanctioning their proclamation.

Management resisted, but to no avail. Strikes broke out in Moscow and spread rapidly throughout the country.

In mid-March the Petrograd Manufacturers Association and the Executive Committee of the Soviets drew up an agreement. It was an historic occasion, marking the realization of long-sought objectives, some more liberal than those attained in other industrial countries. Its principal terms were the introduction of the eight-hour day without a reduction in pay; recognition of factory committees elected by the workers; and establishment of a conciliation commission, consisting of equal representation by both management and labor, for the express purpose of resolving conflicts. In addition, other needed legislation, particularly regarding social insurance, was included in other major provisions. Significantly, however, it contained no provisions on worker rights in the area of administration or collective management. This issue apparently was not negotiated, but it was beginning to be pressed with increasing force.

Sukhanov states that the agreements on working conditions and conciliation procedures were a "bagatelle compared with the . . . eight-hour day." To Sukhanov and many others like him, this marked their major victory. The realization of this major objective of the international socialist movement was the crowning achievement of the first days of the Revolution.

On May 6, 1917, the Provisional Government officially and legally established the committees as the basis of worker representation within the plants. Kerensky, however, was not happy with the committees or the idea of workers' control. The May 6 act legally recognized what could not be avoided, but simultaneously marked an attempt to contain the further advance of workers' control by narrowly construing the rights and functions of the committees. Kerensky's attempt was to no avail. The movement was too popular and was spreading rapidly. Management was unhappy with the turn of events but still did not quite know what to do. The Petersburg factory owners saw the inevitability of major worker gains and other important changes as a result of the Revolution and, to an extent, appear to have been reconciled to them. They made no great fuss over the eight-hour day and the extension of conciliation commission powers during the negotiations. On the other hand, according to Sukhanov: "this did not prevent the patriotic bourgeoisie from starting a vicious campaign against the idleness of the workers and stirring up against them the soldiers who had to sit in the trenches and wait for death, not for eight hours at a time, but the whole twenty-four." [1] This campaign, however, had only a short-run effect, for although armed soldiers came to the factories to force the employees to work, the workers invited them to witness the conditions under which they labored, the low wages they received, and also the fact that many were working more than eight hours to fulfill contracts. On the whole, the workers succeeded in convincing the soldiers that they were not malingering or winning benefits at the expense of the soldiers. Further, as we shall see, many demobilized soldiers who returned to the plants advanced greater and more radical demands than the old established worker element.

For the most part management was divided, particularly on how to reply to demands for workers' control. Some were fighting mad; others were willing to wait on events; some recommended immediate concessions as the "cheapest way out"; and some favored "running while there was still time." In addition, management was handicapped by the fact that it was working on war contracts and legally could neither close down nor apply lockouts.

During the month of August, management called a national conference of employers' organizations to meet in Petrograd to discuss the crisis and arrive at a common set of tactics. They created the All-Russian League of Manufacturers Association. The object of the organization was "to unite the employers in defense of their interests." Lozovsky quotes Bimanoff, chairman of the conference, as saying that the league would work out "guiding rules for the abolition of interference of the factory committees in factory management." [2] Although they agreed on many points, it was seizure of the plants and interference with management by the workers that they saw as the real issue. On this question they were of one mind; they were prepared to do battle—to call lockouts if necessary—to protect their interests.

According to Lozovsky, they were particularly heartened by the failure of the July uprising and it was then they decided on a course of firm resistance. But at this time the workers also increased their demands, particularly the Moscow leather workers, the Don miners, and the textile workers of Ivanovo-Vosnessensk. From July to October the two clashed, and the country was seized once more by a wave of strikes that almost destroyed the nation's productive capacity. This was the situation up to the November coup.

Management Prefers Nationalization

Following the Bolshevik seizure of power, a decree on workers' control (discussed below) was introduced and management was confronted with the issue in its starkest terms, and again expressed its firm hostility to the idea. But now it shifted tactics—easing up on lockouts and adopting a more diplomatic posture, yet remaining adamant against workers' control. Nationalization, in their minds, was preferable to workers' control.

Typical was the reaction of the Ural mine owners. Meeting on November 11, and not seriously believing the Bolsheviks could maintain power for any length of time, the owners stated that workers' control was "quite impermissible." [3] Confronted with the decree and its forcible introduction, they resolved to close each affected enterprise or block its finances. The South Russian mine owners concurred in this decision. The Samara Factory Owners' Association followed suit and decided to shut down all enterprises where workers insisted on the right of control. And most important, so also did the All Russian Congress of Manufacturers' Association, which met in Moscow December 7-9. Their position, however, was slightly more flexible. They were prepared to shut down all enterprises where workers' control interfered with administration; on the other hand, if the movement were merely limited to demands for information they proposed that countermeasures be taken in accordance with local conditions. [4]

Also typical was the attitude expressed by V. V. A. Auerbach, an executive of the metal industry:

> Had this question [nationalization] been presented to us in March 1917 . . . the answer would have been in the negative. But early in 1918, after the introduction of workers' control, when the real masters of the situation were not the owners but the working masses whose main endeavor was to undermine the established order, to destroy both works and production and to terrorize the administration, many of us thought that nationalization was both inevitable and welcome as a measure capable of re-establishing the equilibrium in industrial life and of removing the antagonisms between the administration ("the flunkies of capitalism") and the workers. . . . Besides, many of us thought that all this would be temporary, that the Soviet Government would not be able to manage the nationalized works, and that nationalization would merely enable industry to pass intact through the period of turmoil. [5]

It was this deep and lasting resistance, however, which was to have a decisive effect on the over-all outcome of workers' control. Regardless of other factors, this made the costs of workers' control extremely high, so high as to force the Bolsheviks (despite their own ideological opposition to workers' control) to look to immediate nationalization for a solution to the industrial relations problem. This point cannot be minimized. Workers' control failed to a large extent because of the battle management waged. The paradox is that many managers, at least of those who remained, appear to have preferred nationalization (state control) to workers' control and cooperated with Bolshevik commissars to introduce it. Their motives are not too difficult to understand, as the above quote from Auerbach's memoirs reveals. The issue of who runs the plants—who makes the decisions—is, and probably always will be, the crucial question for managers in any industrial relations system.

On the other hand, these managers were living in a "fool's paradise." To many of the workers, rightly or wrongly, "nationalization," "workers' control," and "seizure of the plants" were one and the same thing. Once a plant was nationalized, they elected their collective managers and forced out the former ones. Where management was ousted, and this appears to have been the prevalent case, a hard and fast battle had to be waged by the Party and the commissariats to protect and reinstate its specialists and administrators. Ultimately these specialists and administrators were returned to their former positions, but only after Lenin had waged a hard campaign in their behalf, which in turn created deep fissures within the Communist Party. Yet the managers preferred nationalization, and this reveals much about the depth of their convictions on the question of managerial prerogatives.

Limits and Confusion of the Decree on Workers' Control

The decree on workers' control was promulgated on November 14, 1917, to establish Bolshevik intent and legalize what was already a fact: worker participation in the control of the plant.

Contrary to a prevailing belief, the decree did not go as far as the workers actually did in controlling the plants. And although the decree underwrote workers' control, which is not to be minimized, it nonetheless severely limited it and foreshadowed further restrictions that would render it meaningless.

Under the provisions of the act, factory committees in all enterprises won extensive but only supervisory rights. They did not have the right to seize and run the plants, which in fact they were doing. On the other hand, the supervisory powers granted them were in the crucial areas of production: output, costs and prices, stocks and finances. Furthermore, the committee enjoyed the right to examine the books of an enterprise and to control all business correspondence. And perhaps most important, the decisions of the committees were held to be binding on the owners of the enterprises. At the same time, however, it was specifically stated that responsibility for the continued operation of the plants rested with the owners, who, again, were to act under the supervision of the committees. This latter clause cut two ways: It preserved an element of managerial prerogative and private property while limiting the powers of the committee. The intention of the government was to legitimatize workers' control of industry and property, but at the same time to limit it.

December Instructions: Owners Have Managerial Rights

The decree had little bearing on reality, and chaos continued to reign. In December a new set of instructions was issued which further restricted the powers of the committees. On the decisive question of administering and seizing the plants the new instructions went into greater detail, *stating that the owners, not the committee, held managerial rights.* The committees were specifically instructed not to take part in the administration of the enterprise; they were not responsible for its operation. And they were instructed not to concern themselves with financing; any such question was to be passed on to state economic institutions. Regarding seizure of the plant or employing compulsory measures, the committees might raise the question with appropriate agencies but they had no right themselves to seize and administer an enterprise.

The Confusion of Not Having Bargaining Machinery

On the fundamental question of industrial procedure the instructions contributed little to the clarification of industrial relations. The original decree underwrote workers' control as the contextual base of industrial relations, but at the same time it curtailed labor's jurisdiction; management and labor were implicitly seen to be in a bargaining relationship, each sharing a field jointly with the other but operating from conflicting ends. But no bargaining machinery, no procedure for settling conflict or making agreements binding—enabling each side to fulfill its functions—was provided in either the original legislation or the December instructions.

Thus the provision was hopelessly vague. It generated a conflict situation: Management and labor would bargain (since labor was not to interfere with plant administration) but no mechanism for bargaining or enforcing agreements was provided. It was an impossible arrangement; it could not work. Yet the intention of the entire decree was to end conflict between management and labor for all time. The unwritten assumption was that labor would preside and management would follow orders, but the paradox was that labor's area was restricted while management's was made more discretionary. This point about the ambiguity of the act is of decisive importance, for it reveals the confusion of the Bolsheviks and their hopeless naiveté, their inadequate control of industrial relations even after they began to assert their strength in the industrial arena.

Political Control

In the November decree the political question of factory committee power vis-à-vis trade unions and political organs was also dealt with. In this decree, plant committees were subordinated to local councils of workers' control, which in turn were made agencies of Soviets. To ensure an element of trade union control, the unions were made members of the local councils. But in the new December instructions, trade union control over the committees was strengthened; the respective trade union in an industry was specifically stipulated as the next higher authority for each factory committee. Further, the union administration had the right to supervise the work of the committees and their subordinate commissions.

State control of the committees was also strengthened. Workers' control organs were subordinated to the Supreme Council of the National Economy and to other state organs regulating the national economy. This provision proved to be of decisive importance in the next phase, for with it the hegemony of the state apparatus was established over worker organizations on the plant level. Thus, on both levels, workers' control was further curtailed.

The Bolsheviks undercut workers' control, which is evident from the picture of chaos presented above, and it reflects in turn the deep political disagreement over workers' control. (Lenin and many of the leading Bolsheviks never fully accepted workers' control, in the full syndicalist sense of the term, as ideologically desirable.)

Operational Problems of Workers' Control

On the other hand, the workers themselves contributed substantially to the failure of workers' control. Though the technicians and directors were not in all instances chased out by the workers, the standard pattern was for the committee to begin its activity by assuming complete control of the factory or shop. It interfered with the acts of administration, annulled its orders, and reworked (frequently upsetting) the entire economic equilibrium of the factory, as if the factory or shop belonged to the workers.

The first problem was that the workers were utterly ignorant of the complexities and techniques of administration and they wreaked havoc with plant production. Frequently the workers fought among themselves over how to manage the plants, who the managers were to be, and how its "spoils" were to be divided. In many instances the most active members of the committees were ex-soldiers, who had become declassed and had replaced the so-called "conservative" workers, while in other cases the plant seizure was effected by workers who arrived from other plants and out-fought the local workers.

Naiveté was also a factor, and it was phenomenal. In one case the factory committee, having opened the safe of the appropriated plant, was baffled to find not cash, but just books.[6] Because of their ignorance of market conditions, functions of banks, and so on, the majority of workers, especially those in the provinces, were quite sincere in their belief that as soon as "control" began there would come to the surface lots of money which the "sabotaging" entre-preneurs were supposed to be hiding away. In some instances the situation got so out of hand that workers sought out their former managers and pleaded with them to return.

Sometimes, where managers had been expelled, the workers developed a sense of "property" and acquired the habits of small proprietors: seeking favors from the state for their factories and attempting to compete with other plants. In the Donetz basin metal works and mines, the factory committees refused to deliver iron and coal to each other on credit, and the iron was being sold to the peasants without considering the interests of the state.

In quite a number of enterprises the committees sought sub-sidies for their plants. There were also a number of smaller and technically backward concerns which had to be nationalized at the insistence of the committees because they were being so badly administered, and had become a heavy charge on the national budget.[7] In some instances, where the managers were not chased out, the workers entered "into contract" with the entrepreneurs, soliciting money and raw material for the enterprise from the gov-ernment. Collaboration appears to have been frequent when both sides viewed with distaste the orders of the government. For ex-ample, in the munitions industry both agreed to ignore orders to shut down plants or combine factories. There was also one notori-ous incident where the government decree prohibiting night work for women was ignored with the common consent of both parties.[8]

The second reason for the failure of workers' control stems from the worker himself. His interests and psychological predisposition were alien to that of management. The worker approached the prob-lem of management from the point of view of a man whose level of education was very low, who was neither trained to be an admin-istrator nor encouraged to see the operation of the plant complex as one integral part of the output process. As a man whose whole life was determined by his job, he could not see the question of labor as one of costs, which like all other costs had to be factored in with resources, machinery, and overhead. He was inclined to see it in very human terms: employment or unemployment, a decent life or privation and hunger for himself and family. His perspective and interest, as against those of management, were not only different but incompatible. With the advent of the Revolution the worker saw an opportunity to gain for himself what he had been denied. He could not and did not operate as a manager.

Third, there were of course cases of pure selfishness. Instances occurred where the workers, having assumed control of a plant, indiscriminately voted themselves wage increases, or worse, appropriated funds or sold stocks, even selling the plant itself for whatever they could get. Arsky, a Bolshevik economist, reported that workers were carrying away plant machinery, considering these objects their own property. This avarice, however, also smacks of hungry men in a situation where money is being replaced by barter, and this was of course happening. There was some sobering up. There were voices urging control not only over the bourgeoisie but also over the workers, but for the most part chaos reigned.

There were other, less subjective, reasons for the failure of workers' control. Operationally, workers' control was highly fragmented, with various plants, operating on the shop level and autonomously, sometimes acting at cross purposes with others and with the national government. It offered little or no command over the national economy. This was disastrous. Workers' control offered little that could provide the order and discipline necessary to run the plants. The unions waged a fierce campaign to establish their domination, thus substantially undercutting workers' control, diluting its power within the political arena. The introduction of a system of limited nationalization and the creation of the Supreme Council of the National Economy, which presupposed an entirely different system of industrial control, undercut workers' control still further. In this regard the masses were nonplused by the disciplinary attitude of the state. Primitive communism made more sense to them than Communism running the factories.

Significance

Workers' control marked a break in the managerial monopoly of the decision-making process. Labor had won a major victory. Industrial relations had been radically transformed. Even if workers' control amounted to limited participation for the fleeting moment and was undercut by the Party, it marked a revolutionary gain for labor and would have permanent effects on labor thinking.

Politics aside, it was a noble experiment. It would be erroneous to say, as might conceivably be inferred from current theories of worker protest, that workers' control represented only the very high level of protest so frequently evident in the early stage of industrialization when the worker stands opposed to the entire industrial process. Perhaps so, but workers' control also had a philosophic base and an ideological content. Even at its peak it was much more than pure and simple protest. And although the meaning of "workers' control" has remained ambiguous—alternating between "direction," as Lenin understood it, and "hegemony," as the syndicalists viewed it—it represents a moral ideal of some men, not all of them utopian, who would like to interject equity (the end of arbitrary and capricious power and treatment) into the work place.

To be sure, workers' control is open to the charge of utopianism. Its greatest weakness is that it is contrary to fact; workers' control depends on the real world of industrial relations for its concept of the future, and this is a methodological fallacy of the crudest sort. Yet what remains impressive is the moral argument behind "workers' control." This is the desire to introduce equity and democracy in the work place, to end the distinction between "citizen" and "employee" that reduces an employee to the status of a commodity and denies him his dignity and sense of satisfaction in an activity that is basic to his existence and happiness. The contention of the proponents of workers' control is that this distinction is unhealthy, the danger is that a man cannot enjoy dignity and freedom in only part of his life without being threatened with political schizophrenia.

To recognize the force of this argument is not to deny that much has been done to introduce equity in the work place in many modern industrial societies; and, as many have pointed out, trade unionism in democratic nations has realized great accomplishments. We are incomparably better off with the gains that have been made within the framework of collective bargaining, and even as limited as have been the objectives of trade unionism, they have served to offset the undemocratic and psychologically negative features of the industrial process. Being much more piecemeal in orientation, and without challenging the organization of the work process itself, unionism has worked and worked well. Yet, when all is said and done, the "social engineering" approach to trade unionism, which leaves untouched an antidemocratic plant structure, leaves much to be desired; and if workers' control is impractical or not yet sufficiently tested, perhaps it is in its hortatory value that its usefulness is to be found.

COLLECTIVE AGREEMENTS: UNIONS AND MANAGERS

In January 1918 the first collective agreement was introduced. The contract marked an attempt to delimit the authority of management and labor, which was lacking in the workers' control provisions, and to bring order out of chaos. It was introduced at a time of incessant worker demands for wage increases. One of its chief aims was over-all wage stability and the closing of a wages gap between privately owned and nationalized enterprises. The contract, however, led neither to order in industrial relations nor to wage stability. Although at first enthusiastically sponsored by the government, use of the contract faded out with the adoption in December 1918 of the Labor Code, which fixed wages. Though the collective agreement was reintroduced in 1920 in modified form, the disappearance of private employers and the central determination of wages and labor policy reduced it to a triviality.

The Contract: Characteristics

According to the rules for the adoption of collective agreements, issued by the Council of People's Commissars on June 29, 1918, and applicable to all agreements, contracts were to be concluded between the unions and the employers (private or public). A collective agreement was to contain: names and addresses of contracting parties; the date when the agreement became effective; names of organizations entrusted with its implementation and with settlement and dismissal; regulation of working hours, rest periods, overtime, leave; wages and classification of workers; output quotas and methods of attaining them; the type of organization determining method of work (assessment, technical and other commissions); rules for the use of living accommodations, canteens, clothing; rules for apprenticeship (age, duration, pay); validity of the collective agreement; and rules for its amendment and termination.

Ratification steps were: Collective agreements drawn up according to the above regulations were submitted by the union to the employers association or, in its absence (euphemism for private enterprise which could not organize), direct to the employers, who had to either accept it within seven days or propose negotiations. The draft agreement was then sent to the Commissariat of Labor for registration and approval; only this made the agreement legal.

The Commissariat was required to obtain an opinion from the local union or the All-Russian Council of Trade Unions, but not necessarily from both. In cases of nonacceptance by the employer, or in cases of disagreement, final decision rested with the Commissariat of Labor. If one of the contracting parties was a state enterprise, the agreement was concluded jointly by its delegates and the local representatives from the Economic Council of Goskontrol and the Commissariat of Labor.

Collective agreements did not exist long enough on the industrial relations scene to determine the character of Soviet labor relations in any but a negative sense. The experience was brief and did not serve either to bring order to industrial relations or to end wage drifts, and thus collective agreements were viewed in a negative light. They did tend to limit union powers since all contracts had to be approved by the Supreme Council of the National Economy, but the Bolsheviks did not pioneer much in the way of a new industrial relations system.

One-Man Management

Collective management had been introduced simultaneously with workers' control and nationalization as the former owners and managers of the plants fled or were expelled. A Plan of Instruction was adopted in March 1917 at a conference of representatives of nationalized enterprises and institutions. It stressed the principle of "collegial administration" and "broad" democracy, which was defined as the right of all members of the factory organization to elect managers and the "right of recall" of elected factory managers.[9] The number of managers varied, particularly after bourgeois specialists were brought back, but five was more often than not the rule.

Collective management, however, did not work. The inexperience of the workers was a prime problem; the worker-managers did not know how to perform managerial functions, despite good intentions in many instances. Collectivity itself was a problem. There were just too many "cooks." Contradictory decisions, buck passing, managerial paralysis because of power struggles, and serious misunderstandings between workers and managers were too often the outcome of "democratic management." Instead of harmony and efficiency, the result was an administrative pile-up which further undermined an already tottering production system.

There was another side to the problem. From the very start the war had placed a premium on production, which was the key to military victory as well as social reform. Without increased production, neither could be realized. But production was declining, not rising. This was the basic problem over which the Bolsheviks were stumbling.

Under the pressure of all these events Lenin was forced to face the very hard and real question of what to do. What was the least expensive way out? Since his problem was one of declining plant efficiency under collective management and his need was for increased output, he could not both increase production and retain collective management. Retaining collective management would mean, in effect, making no headway in over-all economic production in the short run—that is, while the diseconomies of collective management were being worked out. There was no question that he had precious little time, and that this was a price he could ill afford to pay.

On the other hand, to yield on the ideological question of collective management meant alienating workers and Party unionists. This was a threat of a different sort, but a very serious one. In terms of costs, it first entailed violating a socialist principle and turning against the very people in whose name Lenin was leading the revolution. Second, if he alienated the workers, productivity might continue to decline. He not only would make no headway, but would also lose ground at the expense of political support of the worker. There would be little or no economic gain. Here too the price was high.

This was his dilemma. Which of the two courses of action would cost him the least? Lenin's decision was to abandon collective management and reintroduce one-man management plus the system of traditional authority patterns in the plants. Lenin was responding to the problem of war demands but he was also taking a great step in the direction of socialism by technocracy in a Saint-Simonian sense.

Of interest in this particular situation is that Lenin, a man who has been called a "hard-headed realist" by most political observers, appears to have made a quick and "all or nothing" decision on collective management sometime in early 1918. Though it took him a while to win, he apparently made up his mind quickly. There is no evidence that Lenin gave serious thought to revising the system of collective management. It does not appear that he worried about the possibility of further estrangement of the industrial proletariat and consequent decline in output because of their opposition. He did not listen to Tomsky and the others who opposed him. In what was really good Calvinist fashion, he called for discipline and sacrifice for the realization of his objective. After making the decision he appears to have felt little inner turmoil over the question—as did many of his colleagues. He called it a temporary retreat but apparently felt confident this was the only thing to do. This reaction is extremely revealing about the man and his reasoning.

Lenin won, but his victory was not total. A compromise resolution, introduced by Tomsky in opposition to Lenin's stand, was pushed through at the Ninth Party Congress. (The political aspects of this fight are described in the next chapter.) Even though it was a compromise, Lenin essentially won the fight, for one-man management was soon introduced on a wide-scale basis. Like the earlier decision on workers' control, the judgment to reverse course on collective management cannot be minimized. In its own way, it too was a revolution. It too structured the entire field of industrial relations for years to come, and its consequences had drastic implications for labor.

At face value, there was a return to the traditional pattern. Labor's jurisdiction was cut back to the area of wages and conditions, though continuing to cover powers marginally more extensive. The major decisions of management were now closed to labor, which would henceforth confine itself to the welfare of its members.

But the decision carried with it a far greater setback. With participation in executive decisions ended and strikes all but theoretically outlawed, labor was at a great disadvantage. It could no longer enforce its decisions. Labor's maximum moves now could hardly disrupt management's plans; moreover, management could ignore labor commands with impunity. Management had regained its independence. Labor had lost its position of superiority without even retaining one of equality. Few upsets could have been so decisive as the one that came with one-man management. Ironically, it had occurred with the consent and cooperation of the A.R.C.C.T.U., and under Tomsky's personal guidance (though in all fairness to Tomsky, he did not realize labor would come out so badly).

The price Lenin paid was high and unintended. As labor and management antagonized each other, their relationship proved to be increasingly unstable. While the Party proved willing to look the other way as long as output was increased, management became increasingly independent and even engaged in "illicit" acts. Managers violated or ignored trade union instructions and labor laws. They skimped on funds allocated for labor and safety devices; did not pay overtime; shifted manpower within the plants at will; hired outside the established procedures; and of all things, resorted to blacklists.

Labor fought back but to little avail. Could management's

abuses, the use of blacklists, testify more to the tremendous ground labor had lost on the shop level? Significantly, the source of their setback was politics, not failure in collective bargaining. It was the Party and its decisions that determined the changes in industrial relations. Political unionism, the alliance between the unions and the Party, not only did not help labor but actually undermined it. It was a political alliance in which the basic objective was won by the cooperation of two parties, but one of the parties was destroyed by the victory.

The last corollary of labor's loss of power in the industrial relations field was that labor's power relative to the Communist Party was also weaker. The Party was less inclined to listen to unions who could not deliver the goods than to managers who could.

The loss of power was of decisive importance for a labor movement which had won a revolution in 1917 and with it the right to enter the domain of managerial decision-making. The significance of the decision to abandon collective management, like the earlier one to sacrifice workers' control, cannot be minimized. The entire system of "industrial control" had been radically restructured for a short time and Russia had been on the threshold of something very new and big, something which might have brought to reality an element of the dream of 1917. Conceivably, it could have had the impact on the Western world in the 1920s and 1930s that centralized economic planning was later to have.

THE MACRO LEVEL

With the November seizure of power the Bolsheviks confronted the herculean problem of organizing and integrating an entire economy. Since they lacked any organizational blueprint, they improvised, utilizing the unions and those institutions whose techniques they could adopt. Roughly between 1917 and 1920, both before and after the state commissariats were organized, the unions played a major role in shaping aggregate economic policy and in performing functions essential to the production and distribution of goods and services. There was little elasticity in demand, for no other institutions were able to replace the unions in the performance of these services. The unions, even if not directly represented on the Politbureau, were a power to be reckoned with; they were able to prevent the introduction of many measures they opposed and to force the adoption of those they considered important. Yet actual control of the economic machine during this period was haphazard at best and realized day by day through local agencies.

Commissariats Challenge Union Control

The unions did not enjoy an unchallenged position for long. The state commissariats, created in 1917, had become increasingly active. Organized to administer the economy, the commissariats spread their administrative tentacles to envelop all aspects of it. But the unions continued to hold their ground, actually taking over control in some key industries. For example, by 1918, the union of textile workers had assumed two-thirds of the responsibility for management and organization of the entire textile industry; the union of tanners did the same in the tanning industry; the union of sailors assumed charge of water transport; the union of railwaymen took over the railroads; the union of the Ural miners were managing that entire branch of the industry, and so forth.

At first, harmonious relations existed between the A.R.C.C.T.U. and the "friendly" unions on one side and the commissariats on the other. All parties worked together to bring order into the economy. Even hostile Menshevik unions cooperated on some questions, of which there are many examples: their combined attack on strikes and unemployment and their efforts to establish a minimum wage, restrict worker demands, regulate employers, re-establish discipline, and stabilize wages in order to check inflation.

In addition, the unions and the A.R.C.C.T.U. played a major role in creating the state administrative machinery. They had had a hand in appointments to the commissariats and had 35 representatives on the Central Executive Committee of the Soviets. In fact, Shmidt, the Commissar of Labor, who owed his appointment to the A.R.C.C.T.U., revealed that the whole Collegium of NKTruda, his commissariat, was composed of representatives from the Central Council of Trade Unions. As for the role of unions, he said:

> The role of the Commissariat . . . must be to give obligatory effect to the recommendations and plans worked out by the trade unions. Moreover, not only must the Commissariat not interfere with the rights of the unions, but even the organs of the Commissariat . . . should as far as possible be formed by unions themselves. Here at the center we act consistently on this principle.[10] [He said further]: In all questions concerning the classification of labor and wages the Soviet authorities have always adhered to the opinion of the trade unions.[11]

Conflict-Ridden Relationship: Unions Assert Trade Union Superiority in Top Decision-Making

It was not long, however, before conflict between the unions

and the administrative commissariats became the dominant characteristic of their relationship. The conflict involved: coordination of
services, the relative authority of each, overlapping jurisdictions,
and the embarrassing fact that they sometimes made contradictory
decisions.

The question was first touched on at the Fourth Conference of
Trade Unions, which met in March 1918. M. Tomsky, chosen to
establish the unions' leading position, yet at the same time to be a
peacemaker, acknowledged that the unions and the Commissariat of
Labor, although working toward the same goal, "sometimes decide
one and the same question differently, introducing an undesirable
dualism into the single economic policy of the working class." [12]

The core of the problem was the relationship itself. The two
shared a joint field but intersected each other's line of command.
Some functions could be shared, but as the commissariats extended
their jurisdiction by introducing regulations in wages, manpower,
and conditions, they narrowed the boundary of union jurisdiction
and pressed it close to the point where loss of functions precluded
union existence. The unions in turn attempted to push the boundary
back, either to a point of mutual indifference or beyond, to a point
of union supremacy. A bargaining situation existed, but since the
questions were crucial to the respective power of each, neither had
nor was willing to trade something which could satisfy the other;
each wanted matters its own way. No move was possible that made
both parties better off; all moves harmed at least one party. Thus
the attempt to define the jurisdiction of each gave rise to further
conflict.

Even when jurisdictional agreement existed, conflict occurred.
Frequently the sources of conflict were vested institutional views
and interests. Policy frequently smacked of what was least objection-
able to all, but still the conflict remained.

There were moments when the A.R.C.C.T.U. felt itself compelled to oppose proposals or operations of the commissariats. A
classic case occurred in 1919 as a system of payment in kind was
substituted for money wages. Responsibility was divided between
the Commissariats of Defense, Finance and Supply. The shift to
payment in kind brought in the A.R.C.C.T.U. To ensure their primary responsibility, the respective commissariats advanced their
own priorities. To ensure regular payment of wages and rations, the
A.R.C.C.T.U. applied pressure and subordinated the services of
supplies and distribution to the general wages policy. The net effect
was intense conflict among all the parties, but a victory for the
A.R.C.C.T.U.

Meanwhile the unions continued to amass functions. Their role in wage determination amply illustrates this. In 1919, a section for establishing tariffs and classifications was attached to the A.R.C.C.T.U. Throughout the civil war this section had played an important part in the administration of wages policy. It classified various trades employed in different branches of production, revised tariffs submitted by various unions, and fixed overtime rates, basic wages payable in kind, and so on. In 1920 the depreciation of the ruble and the over-all insufficiency of wages knocked out standardization of wages. Again the power of the unions was illustrated. Control was sought within the framework of trade union action, first by an order of June 17, 1920 (Article 68), whereby the unions were given the right to raise wages in cases where need was evident. Then, because the situation continued to deteriorate, the A.R.C.C.T.U. finally took over both the setting of norms and the administration of wages.

In the undertakings as well the unions continued to play a vital role. Wage estimate committees operated under management of the local unions, which in turn were entrusted with the enforcement of A.R.C.C.T.U. and central wage authority instructions. Similarly, trade union offices and departments for the regulation of wages were set up in the economic organs. Each local department of the Commissariat of Labor had a wage section to which union officials were attached.

Regardless of its efforts, the Communist Party was unable to cope with the conflict, unable to eliminate or contain it by working through either the A.R.C.C.T.U. or the commissariats. This was a problem Lenin had no more anticipated than he was able to control, try as he might. At times he even contributed to the conflict, making all sorts of demands on all those concerned, or favoring by turns the commissariats and the unions.

By 1919 a full jurisdictional fight was under way. The net effect was a major breakdown in administration, which ultimately led Trotsky to propose the dismantlement of the unions and their absorption into the state apparatus. These were the sources of friction which triggered the political debate of 1920-1921.

The Debate and Point Five

The Eighth Party Congress met just as the jurisdictional conflict was coming to a head. The Congress, held in March 1919, was convened to draw up a new program, to define the role of the Party and its auxiliary organizations, and to stipulate the Party's plans for a postrevolutionary Russia. The problem of drawing up a program, difficult under any circumstances, was compounded by the various fights already in progress, particularly the one between the union Communists and the state commissariats.

The Party program itself reflected the divergent views. In Point 5 of the program, the section on economics, the unions were given the upper hand in a clause which reflected a distinct syndicalist and workers' control bias:

> The organizing apparatus of socialized industry must first of all rest upon the trade unions. The latter must free themselves from their narrow guild outlook and transform themselves into large productive combinations which will unite the majority, and finally all the workmen of a given branch of production.
>
> Trade unions, being already, according to the laws of the Soviet Republic and established practice, participants in all local and central organs for managing industry, must actually concentrate in their hands the management of the whole system of public economy as an economic unit. The trade unions, thus securing an indissoluble union between the central state administration, the public system of economy and the masses are, moreover, the principal means to carry on a struggle against bureaucracy in the economic apparatus of the Soviet state, and afford the opportunity of establishing a really democratic control over the results of production.
>
> [On the other hand, in Point 6, perhaps the key point, the Party reflected a pro-state administrative policy]: A maximum utilization of the entire labor force of the state, its regular distribution and redistribution among various territorial regions and between different branches of production, is necessary for the systematic development of the public economy, and must be the immediate task of the economic policy of the Soviet government. This aim can be attained only in close cooperation with the trade unions. For the purpose of carrying out certain social duties, a general mobilization of all capable of work must be carried out by the Soviet power, aided by the trade unions, on a much broader and more systematic scale than hitherto.
>
> [In Point 7]: The trade unions play the principal part in the work of establishing a new socialist discipline. . . . They must put into practice and try various measures, such as the establishment of control, standards of production, the introduction of responsibility of workmen before special labor tribunals . . . for the realization of this aim.[18]

To the labor leaders, who thought in terms of the primacy of unions in economic organizations, Point 5 was their *Magna Carta*, legitimatizing their claims and their rights to the supremacy of the unions over the state. It is not difficult to see why; from the point that "the organizing apparatus of socialized industry must first of all rest upon the trade unions," it is no great leap to the conclusion that the unions, rather than the state, would play the dominant role in economic management. Nor is it far to the inference that in the future society the state and Party would wither away, and that the trade unions, as the organizers of the means of production, would become the administrators of things, the primary institution of the classless society.

It is not surprising that in two years' time the Workers' Opposition, a Party faction, would base its case on Point 5 of the Party program. What is surprising (as R. V. Daniels notes in his unpublished dissertation) is that Shlyapnikov, one of the principal leaders of this faction, was so carried away with the concept of union organization of the economy that he proposed a remedy based on the principle of separation of powers.[14] He suggested that the Party be granted total jurisdiction over all questions of ideology, that the state be given power over political administration, and that the unions be delegated jurisdiction over administration of the economy. He believed the unions would be the only one of the three institutions that had any degree of permanence, for obviously the other two would wither as quickly as would their functions. For a Marxist, a separation of powers argument was a heretical proposal. Indeed, he was arguing that the unions would become "the administrators of things" in the future society.

The relevant question of course is why Point 5 was included in the 1919 Party program. Isaac Deutscher contends that in all probability Point 5 was a syndicalist slip committed by the Bolshevik leadership in a mood of genuine gratitude to the trade unions for the work performed by them in the civil war.[15] Beyond question the Bolshevik leaders were grateful, but a more plausible explanation is simply that Points 5, 6, and 7 were a compromise. The fight had been going on for a while and the costs were becoming increasingly high at a time when they could least be afforded. Further, by 1919 the fight had reached its crucial point. It was probably felt that there was no one way of resolving the issue without paying the high cost of estranging one of the two parties. To avoid a showdown and compromise the differences between the two, this deliberately ambiguous statement affirming both sides of the argument was introduced; undoubtedly the hope of waiting on events, of letting matters take care of themselves, was a primary motive at the time.

If it was not a compromise one must infer that the Party leaders and members did not know what they wanted or what they were doing; that syndicalism and socialism, socialism and anarchism, appeared to mean one and the same thing; that the promised society was little more than a vague dream; and that any path was as good as the next as long as a "stateless society" and "the administration of things" was secured. This may be so. There is sufficient evidence to indicate that Lenin was vague about his concept of the future society and, in many respects, was close to the anarchists in conceiving of it as a "stateless" society where communal obligation would keep the society functioning. Nonetheless, he was sufficiently sagacious to realize that Point 5 had strong syndicalist overtones and was in contradiction with Points 6 and 7.

In a way all of this was irrelevant, for the 1919 program represents only an attempt to establish the bounds of the relationship on ideological grounds, and plainly symbolizes little more than a statement of intentions, and vague ones at that. In actual fact it was not ideological declarations that determined the relationship, but the functions seized by each and the decisions made by the Communist Party. However, two points remain. First, Points 5, 6, and 7 created more problems than they solved. They left unsettled the question of whether the unions were superior to, coequal with, or inferior to the state apparatus. In addition, Point 5 opened the door to syndicalist sentiments which had remained dormant, though strong, since the abandonment of workers' control. Both issues lent themselves to the debate of 1920 and the rise of the Workers' Opposition movement.

Second, the conflict between the two contenders for jurisdictional powers continued unabated well into the 1920s, with the unions losing ground almost in proportion to the comprehensive development of the state apparatus and the extension of state powers. By 1921 the unions had lost their earlier power to pass decrees on labor questions, fix minimum wages, control labor distribution, settle disputes, administer social insurance, and so forth. This is not to say that unions were completely closed out of the decision-making areas; they were not. Rather, the bounds of the relationship had been altered; union jurisdiction had been pushed back. The locus of maximum union power was narrowed, yet the unions remained viable; that is, they still had functions to perform, and remained a partner in the relationship. Nonetheless, the union-state relationship which had prevailed in the early post-Revolution period had been reversed. With respect to economic power, the unions could not have yielded more nor endured a more catastrophic setback.

Lenin's Ideological Shift

It was during the course of the 1920 debate on the role of trade unions that Lenin revealed an interesting shift in his ideological position. In "The Mistakes of Comrade Trotsky," delivered at the Eighth Congress of Soviets on December 30, 1920, Lenin said:

> But the trade unions are not state organizations, not organizations for coercion; they are educational organizations, organizations that enlist, that train; they are schools, schools of administration, schools of management, schools of communism.
>   The place the trade unions occupy in the system of the dictatorship of the proletariat is . . . between the Party and the state power.[16]

One month later, in an article of January 25, 1921, entitled "Once Again on the Present Situation and The Mistakes of Comrades Trotsky and Bukharin," he further expounded this position:

> The trade unions are reservoirs of state power, a school of communism, a school of management. In this specific sphere the specific and main thing is not administration but "contacts between the central (and local of course)" state administration, national economy and the broad masses of toilers (as our party says in Point 5 of the economic section). . . .[17]

His change of heart is perhaps most clearly underlined by his statement, also from "The Mistakes of Comrade Trotsky": "Trade unions as institutions which were created under capitalism inevitably exist in the period of transition from capitalism to communism, but their future is doubtful." [18]

This was a long step from his views of 1917–1918. His 1920–1921 position marked a clear departure from the official position adopted by the Party in 1918 and 1919: "the trade unions inevitably become transformed into organs of the socialist state . . ."; "the trade unions ought to shoulder the main burdens of organizing production . . ."; "their most urgent task . . . is in participating in all central bodies called upon to regulate output"; and "the trade unions . . . must concentrate in their hands the management of the whole system of public economy as an economic system."

Lenin was developing his transmission belt theory. His change reflected his exasperation with the conflict between the unions and the state commissariats; it also reflected his keen appreciation of the fact that nine-tenths of the union membership were opposed to the Bolsheviks, that under such a condition the conflict between the unions and the state administrative bodies could hardly be resolved in favor of the unions. Once again the long-range impact of the decision to rule as a minority party was fully felt.

CONCLUSION

The first period of Soviet industrial relations ended not with industrial peace but with "protracted conflict" between management and labor, between commissariats and unions. It ended with neither a fixed system of industrial relations nor a well-defined collective bargaining system, but rather with a loosely structured system that seemed to work crabwise in settling disputes and establishing the complex of rules, practices, and regulations (both substantive and procedural) essential to the effective operations of an industrial relations system. The immediate effect of this rather tenuous and inefficient system was to force the Party to resort more and more to direct state control and coercive measures.

But if the approach to industrial relations was unsettled, a new form of unionism was developing. In essence the system rested upon a political alliance between the unions and the Party. The primary effort was to secure objectives by means of de-emphasizing short run labor goals for the Party's larger economic and political objectives. Unions were to think in terms of over-all economic growth and not confine themselves to victories for their members in particular industries. Collective bargaining was de-emphasized. So too were strikes. Instead, efforts were to be concentrated on controlling distributive shares and winning gains through political action and greater union penetration of decision-making on macro and micro levels. That is, the objective was to operate as a political coalition with both parties surrendering something less significant for something more significant. Both theoretically would gain.

What was further significant was that the coalition was marked as much by conflict as by cooperation, and what was impressive was the level of cooperation that was maintained as the Communist Party shifted away from favoring labor to a preference for management and the Soviet administrators.

It is interesting, however, to note that Soviet political unionism and greater economic penetration by labor (though the latter trend was reversed from 1918 on) did not contribute to the unions' political or economic power. Nor did it help labor secure increased distributive shares. To the contrary, labor lost. The political coalition which existed between the Party, its unions, and the Soviet administrators did not in fact constitute a case of each party giving up something less significant in return for something more significant. The coalition won, the Party and management won—but labor lost. It is further significant that the over-all objectives of the coalition were secured while one of the parties to the coalition lost.

On the larger question of unions as a dependent or independent power able to effect changes, the answer appears to be clear in the Soviet case during this period. Union power was dependent once an alliance with the Party was effectively established. Even as a countervailing power, the unions, under conditions of dictatorship and severe economic problems, were not able to swing the weight they might have if they had been independent of the Party, able to bargain with a free hand and to strike if necessary.

5 ✿ The Union Question Internalized: Political Fragmentation

Capitalism has been crushed; but socialism has not yet been built up. . . . the misunderstandings with which we are faced are not all accidental—they are the result of the historical split of the trade unions. . . . class interests stand higher than craft interests. Those workers who are not capable of making such sacrifices we regard as selfish men and cowards, and exile them from the proletariat.

We must confess that we find administration a difficult matter. The proletariat has decreased in number. . . . What we require is more discipline and more single man responsibility and more dictatorship. Without these it is idle to think of victory. We have an army of three million, but the 600,000 Communists must serve as the vanguard of these three million.[1]

By 1920 the battle over the affiliated, recalcitrant unions was ended. The opposition had been overcome and, although worker estrangement was increasing, the unions had been "statized." However, during 1919, when all was over but the final death throes of several opposition unions, the Communist Party itself was racked with major convulsions over the trade union question. By destroying the independent unions the Bolsheviks had believed they would solve their troubles with the trade union movement. But to a large extent they had merely suppressed some issues and created new ones. They not only had to solve the same national problems but do so within the framework of the Party itself. The political problem was complicated by the fact that the labor issue remained a sensitive one and the need to maintain the minority dictatorship precluded the luxury of free discussion within the Party. Thus the transfer of the union question to the Party itself not only culminated in a serious fight, but also in the denial of Party democracy. It ultimately proved to be one of the most expensive moves the Party could have made. It was a reflection of the earlier decision to "go it alone." The price of the minority dictatorship was dictatorship within the Party itself.

LABOR OPPOSITION

In 1918 opposition to Party policy emerged within the Party-union fraction, converging around the Communist trade union leaders. The opposition reflected a number of factors: (1) The emergence of the unions as an "interest" group within the Party, due to fragmentation of interests and proliferation of functions within the Party as it was transformed from a revolutionary to a ruling organization. The trade unionists emerged as a group which had a common interest with the Party but also a vested interest in union power. They operated from a pro-labor position on policy ques-tions, and this frequently led to conflict with other interest groups. (2) Substantive union objection to Party policy on industrial management and labor conscription. (3) Dismay over the loss of worker support and the growing gap between the Party-union leadership and the rank-and-file workers. (4) Annoyance with "excessive party interference" in union affairs. (5) A strong desire for peace. With the cessation of hostilities the unionists wanted a change in policy. They wanted the "harsh" measures of War Communism abandoned; they wanted more concessions for the industrial worker. Further, with peace they began to think in terms of redressing the balance between the state ministries and the unions and realizing Point 5, which a number of them clearly took quite literally. (6) Economic exhaustion and the ensuing disagreement over how to solve this problem.

To grasp the magnitude of economic devastation in postwar Russia is difficult but essential for throwing into relief the labor issue which confronted the Party. The dreadful state of industry was in part depicted by Rykov in his speech to the delegates of the Third Trade Union Congress in April 1920.[2] Describing the damage done to the Donetz basin in Southern Russia, which had shifted hands during the World War and the civil war, he stated that because of the lack of fuel not a single furnace was in operation in the entire basin. Due to flooding of the Donetz mines, their output was about 300,000 tons a month, about 10 per cent of the prewar level. Industry was paralyzed because of the general destruction in the valley and the inability of other industries to obtain material and fuel. The entire output of steel was less than 5 per cent of the prewar level. Of all the textile spindles, only 6 per cent were operational. Production of consumer goods was one-quarter of the prewar level. The whole problem was compounded by the almost complete breakdown of rail communications. Tracks, bridges, and trains had been dynamited; rolling stock had not been renewed and had barely been kept in repair. Agriculture had fared better, paradoxically, because of the primitive state of its technological development, but was in very poor shape nonetheless; it was subsistence farming at best. The war, the primitive communes, and the requisitions had lowered agricultural production to a point where prewar industry or the urban labor force could not be sustained.

Professor S. N. Prokopovich stated at the Eighth Congress that the total number of workers in 1920 was only 46 per cent of the prewar level, that the productivity of the average worker had fallen to 30–35 per cent and total productivity to 14.5 per cent.[3]

Nogin, at the First Congress of the Supreme Council of the National Economy, which met in May 1918, indicated how serious was the decline in the real wages of the workers.

Wages in Petrograd, which have been rising rapidly, are now 947 per cent higher than in 1914. The average daily wage [on a comparative basis] of a Petrograd worker in the early part of May is:

	rubles	kopeks
1914	1	7
1915	1	15
1916	2	94
1917	5	33
1918	11	20

The cost of the average ration of a manual laborer during the same period was as follows:

	rubles	kopeks
1914	0	26.1
1915		32.4
1916		41.0
1917		85.8
1918	20	5.0

This meant that the increase in the cost of living in 1918 in relation to 1917 was 2,289 per cent. He said that clearly the Petrograd worker was in no position to purchase enough food to enable him to do the work required of him.[4]

THE ORIGINS OF LABOR OPPOSITION

In its most strident form, the labor opposition may be attributed to the issue of one-man management, but labor dissatisfaction had begun to make itself felt around 1919. The emergence of a labor opposition was very significant. Until 1919, Communist trade unionists like Tomsky, Shlyapnikov, Shmidt, and Lutovinov had been among the most loyal supporters Lenin could have asked for. As Schapiro points out, it was these men who had won him his victories in the unions, who stood up and fought the crucial battles, not with the Whites or the bourgeoisie, but with the Menshevik and other trade unionists and comrades of the Left. Without their support at the First and Second Congresses, workers' control, union independence, political neutrality, and the right to strike could not have been passed. Lenin could not have survived without their willingness to be utter Machiavellians, to use A.R.C.C.T.U. powers to disperse and destroy opposition unions, and to face stoically the charges of Brutus-like treachery leveled at them by the Mensheviks.

Few unionists had resisted Lenin's earlier policies. Shlyapnikov, Lozovsky, and Ryazanov were among the most prominent dissenters. Shlyapnikov, one of the few real workers in the ranks of the Party in the pre-1917 period, objected to the refusal to form a coalition government with the other moderate parties, but he was too troubled about his loyalty to his old comrade Lenin to resign his post as Commissar of Labor, as did the others. He merely confined himself to a protest.[5] On most labor questions he went along with Lenin and personally molded labor policy on strikes, neutrality, and so on. Yet even there one can see ambivalence, for when it came to ordering the strikers to cease and desist, his formulation of the order and his approach was that of a "soft." As events were soon to prove, he was capable of resisting Lenin and he did have strong views on the role of labor, views which were heavily syndicalist in essence.

Sukhanov did not think very highly of Shlyapnikov. This is what he said of him:

> A party patriot, you might say fanatic, prepared to approach the entire revolution from the point of view of the well-being of the Bolshevik Party; an experienced conspirator, a first-rate technical organizer, and a practical trade unionist, as a politician he was quite

incapable of grasping and generalizing the essence of the conjuncture that had been created [the March Revolution]. If he had any political ideas they were the clichés of ancient party resolutions of a general nature, but this responsible leader of the most influential workers' organization [metal workers' union] lacked all independence of thought and all ability or desire to appraise the concrete reality of the moment.[6]

Lozovsky and Ryazanov also doubted the wisdom of Lenin's policies. They had fought him on the question of union independence, and Lozovsky, who was able to muster impressive support for his views because of his prominence in the labor movement, was expelled from the Party on the eve of the Congress at which the fight occurred. D. B. Ryazanov was not much of a threat. A word is in order about this unusual rebel whose dissent was most consistent and persistent on the labor question throughout the period 1917–1928. Born in Odessa in 1870, the son of Jewish parents, he joined the populist movement at the age of 15, became a founder of the Social Democratic Borba group, and in 1905 became a trade union organizer. After being arrested and imprisoned several times, he was exiled from Russia during the World War. He returned in 1917 and joined the Bolshevik Party in July of that year. He was one of the few leading and articulate Bolsheviks to see the need for independent labor unions to perform under the Soviets essentially the same role as under the Provisional Government. It must have been particularly galling for him that he was not only unable to pick up much support in the Party fraction, but was spoofed time and again by Party leaders as "idiosyncratic" and not to be taken seriously. Sverdlov did it, so did Trotsky. Ryazanov repaid the compliment by calling them "old ladies," but they were more effective than he in making the label stick. He was thus isolated in the trade union movement, and, like the petrel that he was, he was left to fly his lonely, stormy course alone.

But others, like Tomsky and Shmidt, although not entirely free from doubts or able to see their way clear beyond the immediate objective, were loyal. They were for the "November Revolution" and had little sympathy for those Mensheviks and trade unionists who were opposed to it.

The labor opposition to Lenin was significant in a second, more important sense. It was this elite group that Lenin depended on. It was upon their shoulders that Party strength and success in the union movement rested. It was upon this "thin red line," to borrow a phrase from Wellington, that the Party's continued control of the union movement hinged. If they had fought Lenin, or if he had alienated them, the result could have spelled political disaster.

NOT OF ONE MIND

Though an interest group, the trade union Party fraction was not of one mind, and it fragmented rapidly. The divisions reflected personality clashes, petty jealousies, union politics, and the development of power machines. There was also sharp cleavage within the union leadership ranks over policy alternatives. Beginning in 1919, two main groups began to emerge, a "left" wing led by Shlyapnikov and a "right" wing led by Tomsky. In that same year Shlyapnikov and Lutovinov, the latter another prominent trade unionist, were so concerned about the drift of Soviet policy that they organized a faction called the Workers' Opposition.

This group paralleled the emergence and activities of the Democratic Centrists within the Party, a faction led by Sapronov and Ossinsky which staunchly protested the rise of a bureaucracy within the Party, the monopolization of all policy-making by the Politbureau and its committees, and the quashing of discussion among the local Party unions and the rank and file.

The Workers' Opposition reflected the same type of protest, but it was almost completely trade unionist in composition. It emerged out of the discontent that developed when the policy of employing bourgeois specialists became official; it also reflected the growing dissatisfaction with the diminishing part played by the workers in the control of industry. It deplored the bureaucratization of the Party and excessive control by the center, and reflected the growing fear that the impulses of the leadership were less in the direction of a "workers' dictatorship" than of some bureaucratic compromise. And finally, it reflected the increasing hostility to the policies which Leon Trotsky was advancing.

TROTSKY

By 1919 Trotsky had become active in the labor field. Much disturbed by the extent of economic devastation and by the debilitating conflict between the unions and state administrative organs, which he saw as a principal obstacle to the resolution of economic chaos and stagnation, Trotsky began to play an increasingly important role in labor affairs.

In December 1919 Trotsky submitted to the Central Committee

a set of "theses" on the economic transition from war to peace. Intended for closed discussion, they were inadvertently published in *Pravda*[7] by Bukharin. Couched in strident terms, Trotsky stated that army methods should be applied to civilian labor; labor armies should be formed and run in military fashion. Upon hitting the streets, the *Pravda* article provoked a long, loud cry of protest. Rykov, Larin, Ryazanov, and Gol'tzmann deferred in strenuous terms. As Deutscher points out, it was not long before Trotsky was referred to as the Arakcheev of War Communism.[8]

Shortly thereafter Trotsky proposed that the conflict between the unions and the commissariats be resolved by the absorption of the unions into the state; that the unions be converted from "trade" (*professional'ni*) unions into "production" (*proizvodstvennii*) unions and be made administrative branches of the state; and he again advanced his labor mobilization measures. He explained: "To difficult periods in the life of peoples and classes there correspond harsh measures. . . ."[9] And as the proponent of "harsh measures," "shaking up the unions," and merging them into the state apparatus, he was the *bête noire* of the trade unionists.

The left wingers were particularly antagonized by Trotsky's proposals which, they believed, violated the very principles of the October Revolution. They were, however, intrigued by his idea of "production" unions. It smacked strongly of Point 5 and union hegemony over the state apparatus. Shlyapnikov appears to have used it as a point of departure for developing his own 1919 position—of a separation of powers between the unions, the Party, and the state apparatus—which had strong incipient syndicalist overtones.

It would appear that Shlyapnikov was not aware of the full implication of his position; namely, that the Party would be relegated to a subordinate power position. Under his proposal the unions and not the Party would provide the real political leadership. Needless to say, this idea had little appeal to Lenin.

At the same time he revealed no desire to undermine the Party dictatorship. At a meeting of the Communist fraction of the A.R.C.C.T.U. in the spring of 1919, Shlyapnikov proposed a resolution that included a statement urging the unions to assume the leadership of the growing mass dissatisfaction and endeavor to remove the causes of it. But at the same time he said the unions should "fight with all our might against the tendency [to] strike by explaining [the] disastrous" effects on the dictatorship.[10]

Against Shlyapnikov and Lutovinov, Trotsky had at least one firm supporter of importance in the upper Party-union echelons.

Gol'tzmann, a prominent trade unionist, temporary head of the metal workers' union and rival to Shlyapnikov, was definitely on Trotsky's side. So was Andreev, a figure who was to play an important role after the 1919 Trade Union Debate. Gol'tzmann was attracted by Trotsky's idea of labor armies. He saw in them the possibility of converting to peace without severe unemployment and manpower dislocation; but more important, he saw in them the possibility of creating a worker "officer corps" for industry. Managers trained from the ranks of the workers would be placed in charge of industry—a "worker aristocracy." It would have the additional advantage of being an alternative to collective management just when it appeared the Party was in need of abandoning the earlier system, and would give the workers a share in management without impairing efficiency. It was, in Gol'tzmann's eyes, a happy compromise. The worker and the expert would "co-determine" managerial policy. For a short while after Gol'tzmann advanced his idea of a "worker aristocracy," Lenin waxed enthusiastic about it. As an alternative to collective management, he thought it might satisfy the unionists at a time when it was important both to placate them and to abandon collective management. Labor opposition to the whole idea was strong and fairly well entrenched. It smacked of "Trotskyism" and also represented a possible threat to the entrenched positions of the worker-union managers. To others like Shlyapnikov it possibly smelled of a "sellout" on Point 5. At any rate, Shlyapnikov preferred his scheme of a functional division of labor, which he believed could work and would offer a more desirable and permanent solution.[11]

TOMSKY AND THE RIGHT

But Gol'tzmann represented only a minor trend in the over-all fragmentation of views among the union-Party leadership. The main opposition to Shlyapnikov and the Left came not from Gol'tzmann but from Tomsky. A worker himself, Tomsky was Lenin's loyal Number Two person in the union movement. He was the man who, next to Lenin, was most responsible for making Soviet trade union history in the early period. Two things are especially interesting about Tomsky: the quality of his leadership ability and the sense of loyalty to both workers and Party that gave him his peculiar schizophrenic quality.

It is intriguing to note that in November 1917, Lenin, although he had known Tomsky very well from the early days and was aware that he was in Petrograd, did not assign Tomsky any position of importance in the Party, the coup, or the Soviets. Why? It cannot be explained by his being fully occupied with his leadership duties in the unions. He was only second in command under Zinoviev in the trade union movement, and did not become its head until Zinoviev was transferred to another assignment. In 1920 Tomsky was paid the compliment (perhaps a dubious one) by Lenin, that "he so thoroughly allied himself with the trade union movement that he faithfully reflected the feelings and thoughts of the mass of workers." [12]

In 1917, however, Lenin needed support in the unions and Tomsky was one of his key assets. Thus one can only speculate as to the reason why Lenin did not give him a leading role. Unfamiliarity and suspicion must be ruled out. It is possible that Tomsky was totally occupied with his own union responsibilities, or even with some secret mission, though the latter appears to be most unlikely. It is more likely that Lenin was not particularly impressed with Tomsky as a political leader, viewing him as a man of limited capabilities, and was thus willing to advance him only as his need for a loyal "blue collar" Bolshevik developed. What is also interesting, though it hardly settles the question, is that neither John Reed nor N. Sukhanov ever mention Tomsky as either an important Bolshevik figure or trade union leader. Their silence about him makes the case more intriguing, but it also tends to add weight to the inference that he was not seen as one of the more able and important Bolsheviks.

The question of Tomsky's dual loyalty is intriguing, for it reveals the classic problem of a man torn by two sometimes conflicting allegiances. There is little doubt that in his own mind Tomsky was unequivocally devoted to the workers and their movement. For this very reason he believed it was necessary to join the Bolsheviks, support their no-strike and piece rate policies, and then even help destroy opposition unions. Yet at the same time he was so deeply committed to the workers that he resolutely fought Trotsky on labor discipline issues and opposed Lenin at crucial times in order to force some concessions from the Politbureau. And, as is well known, in the late twenties he fought with Stalin over the critical question of intensive industrialization, holding to his traditional stance of supporting the worker.

In 1919, when the trade union question was being discussed, it was again Tomsky's sense of loyalty to the workers that played a part in his break with Shlyapnikov and the A.R.C.C.T.U. Tomsky was convinced that Shlyapnikov's ulta-leftist proposal of "production unions" was out of touch with reality. He believed that the workers—who were receiving only seven poods of bread per person as against the peasant's seventeen—were exhausted, fed up with War Communism, and in need of concessions and a breathing spell. To Tomsky, anyone who believed, as Trotsky did, that the worker could be forced to work, was doomed to fail; anyone who, like Shlyapnikov, believed that "production unionism" was the remedy for the severity of War Communism was naive. Tomsky favored concessions.

Tomsky was certainly among the first to advocate the abandonment of War Communist policies, and apparently did so before Trotsky became an advocate of free trade and quasi-N.E.P. policies. Perhaps the only difference between them is that Tomsky never formulated a program and did not wage as hard or effective a campaign for his views as did Trotsky. Tomsky was not that type of person; he was neither thinker nor leader. He was more an organization man inclined to work silently within established channels for his objectives.

Yet it was his dual loyalty and his limitations as a political leader that combined to undermine any clear position he might have held, and led him to play into Stalin's hands and later commit suicide once he realized he had failed both the workers and the Party.

It appears that Tomsky was totally unaware of the succession fight. Either he was the utter Machiavellian, but isolated from the real inner chambers of power, or he was absolutely gullible because of his deep sense of loyalty to the Party. No doubt his enmity toward Trotsky and the left wing proposals blinded him. He was particularly dense about Stalin and at first did not believe the charge that Stalin was striving to make himself the dictator of the Party. Yet later, when he himself fought Stalin, he did so in the name of the workers. Even then, it appears, he did not make full use of the union machinery or power, though admittedly at that point the unions were rather weak, having lost substantial rank-and-file worker support. What overshadows all of these points is again the question of Tomsky's relative stature as a man. One cannot help speculating as to what the outcome might have been had someone of Trotsky's cast, a first-rate political leader, been heading the trade union movement. Perhaps events would have gone the other way, with Stalin going down to defeat rather than rising to victory because, in part, of the absence of any real opposition from the man who controlled the only organization with a mass political base.

THE FIGHT OVER UNION POWER BEGINS

By early 1919, when Lenin began to press for the reintroduction of specialists—thus raising the larger question of labor in management—the Party unionists almost to a man expressed distinct unhappiness with his proposal.

With a touch of irony, it fell to Shlyapnikov to lead the fight. Though now the advocate of "production unions" and the logical person to object to the further diminution of union powers, Shlyapnikov had, while Commissar of Labor in 1918, delivered the *coup de grace* to workers' control of the railways with a biting indictment of the waste and inefficiency of worker management. Now in 1919 it was Shlyapnikov, chairman of the metal workers' union and member of the A.R.C.C.T.U., who was outspoken in his criticism of Lenin's proposal to end the chaos of industrial management and take the logical step following abandonment of workers' control.

LENIN COUNTERATTACKS

Worried about union resistance and in need of their support, Lenin counterattacked. Astute politician that he was, Lenin approached the union opposition anticipating the need to split or neutralize it in case of resistance. He was well aware of the areas of disagreement and the personality clashes within the ranks of the key men. He knew how one or two could be won over, others persuaded to accept what a third was only likely to tolerate, and still others divided or contained. Once more Lenin proved his shrewdness.

First, Shlyapnikov was suddenly ordered off on a diplomatic mission to Norway by the Central Committee. Lutovinov, who was very close to Shlyapnikov but not beyond the reaches of gullibility, stated that Shlyapnikov had not been exiled by Lenin. (Many others, including Lozovsky, who opposed Lenin on the specialist question, were exiled "on the widest scale." [13] Lenin forcefully denied the charge.) Conveniently, however, Shlyapnikov was removed from the scene just when he was beginning to make trouble.

At the same time, Lenin began to promote Tomsky, Gol'tzmann, and Rudzutak. Tomsky was the logical choice, given his opposition to Shlyapnikov and Lenin's estimate of his sensitivity to worker moods and his willingness to cooperate. Gol'tzmann, who had little support but reflected the Leninist mood, was, significantly, appointed as Shlyapnikov's replacement as head of the metal workers' union. But Gol'tzmann's rise to fame was a faint flicker. His pro-Trotsky leanings led him astray in these early trade union debates.

Jan Rudzutak, on the other hand, was an interesting selection. A Latvian peasant before the Revolution, he rose quickly in the Party and union apparatus after 1917. Lenin thought highly of him and a personal friendship developed between the two. Rudzutak got to know Lenin in a way that very few ever did. Rudzutak was talented and could come up with a solution that just fitted Lenin's needs. In 1920–1921 he was to do just that. He gave Lenin his solution for the trade union problem and formulated a policy position on the trade union question which became a major part of the platform of "The Ten."

Not only did Lenin promote these men, but he also exploited the fact that at this early date most labor leaders, though in sympathy with Shlyapnikov, were not prepared to do battle with Lenin, and certainly not full-scale battle over Shlyapnikov or the issue of "specialists." Rather, they were inclined to accept Lenin's leadership, abide by Party discipline, and listen to those who counseled "party" support and compromise on the grounds of winning the war and having faith in Lenin. Thus Lenin maneuvered, counting on personalities, union politics, and loyalty to the Party and himself, not to mention luck and circumstance, to help him win his battle.

ONE-MAN MANAGEMENT

The real battle was not fought until the issue of one-man management was posed. This was soon followed by the fight over labor armies. The reintroduction of specialists in industry had not produced the desired results. Production had not gone up enough and there was still too much confusion in the ranks of management. So Lenin took the next step, the predictable one, once the reintroduction of bourgeois specialists and managers was an accomplished fact. He now demanded the abandonment of collective management and the reintroduction of one-man management. On this issue the divided and confused labor fraction united.

This was the issue that made the unionist Party members wonder what their sacrifices had been for. If the collective boards elected by the workers were abandoned for one-man managers, if the pre-Revolutionary hierarchical system of authority and discipline were reintroduced, what had they won? If single managers were to be reinstated—the very people whom they had so hated before the Revolution—why had they fought? If these people were to run the plants, again enjoying the same element of authority as formerly, if the workers were subordinated as before, where was their power? If the unions were in a subordinate position, sacrificing policy-making positions on managerial levels, what were they?

The entire question struck at the heart of their aspirations and victories. Lenin was now calling on them to modify their position and to accept his. At this point, for a majority of the unionists, the cost of agreement was higher than disagreement and the war was on.

LENIN'S EARLIER MANEUVERINGS

In the face of the failure of collective management and a threatened breakdown of production, Lenin and other members of the Central Committee had begun to press for the reintroduction of a unified system of command in the plants. Discipline and centralization had been the rule in the Party, and Lenin, who was not committed in any absolute sense to collective management, saw a very real need for it in the work place as well. Actually Lenin had first tried to circumvent collective management informally. It was transformed into a "commissar manager system." Although there were many variations, in form and practice the standard policy by 1918 was to have a commissar surrounded by five colleagues with whom he was supposed to consult on major issues. The catch was that the commissar had the right to appeal their decisions, not by taking his case to the plant rank and file but by carrying it to the Supreme Economic Council, which was frequently responsible for his appointment in the first place.

While resorting to this technique, Lenin also began to legislate in the Soviet and Party Congresses for one-man management and plant efficiency. Immediately following his introduction of one-man management at the Second Congress of the Council of the National Economy in December 1918, Lenin suffered one defeat after another. In characteristic fashion he persevered. He tried again in 1919 at the Seventh Congress of Soviets, but this time dropped the issue in the face of forceful opposition. Sapronov's remarks typify the attack against the proposal.

> Comrades, the *collegia* are composed of five men, three workers, two specialists. If you switch over to one-man management then whom will you place in it? The worker? But he alone cannot cope with it. The specialist? It will not do; he will work not for the revolution, but for the counter-revolution. [Also]: We will not reject the use of specialists, but they must be only under the control of the

proletariat. They must administer together with the workers and under their control. Therefore, not in any case may one-man management be permitted.[14]

In the early months of 1920 Lenin picked up the issue again. This time he approached the Bolshevik fraction in the A.R.C.C.T.U. He addressed them in January, but failed to sway them. He tried again in March, but the second meeting was worse than the first. The fraction not only rejected his appeal and another by Bukharin as well, but adopted an alternate thesis defending collective managment which had been presented by Tomsky. The fact that it was Tomsky cannot be minimized. One of Lenin's most loyal and dependable supporters was now prepared to break with him on this question. Little else could reveal how deep was the fraction's objection to Lenin's proposal. Further, the fact that it was the leader of the fraction who introduced the resolution was meant to convey the message that it was not a personal break but a solid uprising of the overwhelming majority. Tomsky's resolution read:

> The basic principle in the development of the organs regulating and administering industry, which alone can ensure the participation of broad nonparty masses through the trade unions, is the present existing principle of collegial administration in industry, which is inclusive of the presidium of Vesenkha down to factory administrations.[15]

To make Lenin's life more difficult, the unionists had the support of two other Party groups. The "Democratic Centrists," headed by Ossinsky, Sapronov, and Maximovsky, argued that collective management was democratic and one-man management was not; it smacked of prewar authoritarianism and was a real threat to the Revolution. Circumstances, in their opinion, did not warrant a retreat. The second group supporting the unionists came, surprisingly, from the extreme right in the Party. It was a group of management leaders headed by Rykov and Miliutin, who were ideologically committed to the concept of collective, democratic management as an integral aspect of plant management at this time. Under the guidance of Rykov and Miliutin the Third Congress of the Supreme Council of the National Economy, which met in January 1920, rejected Lenin's plea for one-man management and affirmed collegiality as the basic form of management. In addition, Party conferences in Moscow and Khar'kov *guberniia* also voted down resolutions in favor of one-man management.

LENIN IN A BOX

Opposed on all these levels—by the Party fraction of the A.R.C.C.T.U., a strong fraction in the Council of the National Economy, the Democratic Centrists and left wingers in the Party, the water transport workers' union, and at least two area Party congresses—Lenin still refused to yield. He carried his fight to the Ninth Party Congress. It was at this meeting that he succeeded in overcoming all opposition. He finally won on the issue of one-man management.

In preparation for the Congress, the Party-union leaders, maneuvering for a real fight, decided to try to extend union political and economic jurisdiction. They submitted two draft resolutions to the Orgbureau. The first called for extension of the A.R.C.C.T.U.'s authority over all Party members and *fraktsiia* (fractions) in unions. The second proposed that the union, as "the most competent organization available for administering the economy," should be given more responsibility in economic matters. The proposals were radical indeed. Politically they meant the creation of a party within the Party and imposition of union discipline on all Party members, since virtually all Party members were trade union members. Economically, they meant union control of the economy. Had they been approved, each union would have had its own disciplined organization of substantial size within the party and also would have had Party recognition of the primacy of the unions over management and the state economic organs.

The Orgbureau, however, rejected the resolution and passed one of its own, which reaffirmed the disciplined subordination of the unions to the Party.[16]

THE NINTH CONGRESS: LENIN'S VICTORY

At the Ninth Party Congress in 1920 the issue of one-man management was debated in full. For the Leninist caucus, Trotsky submitted a draft resolution calling for the introduction of one-man management. He then appeared as chief expounder of continued labor conscription and the drafting of civilian labor into labor armies. Trotsky played the role of the *enfant terrible* at this Congress and he did it with zeal.

He urged the delegates to underwrite a program of disciplinary measures for labor, "the severity of which must correspond to the tragic character of our economic situation." Embellishing upon this theme, he remarked that "labor deserters" ought to be put into concentration camps or organized into punitive batallions.[17] Compulsory labor, he said, was the order of the day. Though it would not exist under full-fledged Communism, during this period of transition from capitalism to socialism it would attain its peak of intensity.

But Trotsky did not stop there. He painted a picture of the future economic order which suggested that militarized labor would have a permanent place in the order of things, thus implicitly contradicting his avowed statement that compulsory labor would not exist in the future society. Militarized labor, he said, was essential for the development of the economy in a single economic plan, which implied a socialist organization of the economy. Thus he mitigated his contention that compulsory labor was only transitional. And in the same vein of harsh and brutal labor measures which he was to develop even further later in the year, Trotsky now uncompromisingly suggested abandonment of wage equalitarianism by calling for the introduction of piece rates, incentives, and "socialist emulation," which would encourage efficient workers and raise productivity levels. To ingratiate himself even further in the hearts of the trade unionists, he picked up the theme of "progressive Taylorism" and "scientific management and work," [18] an idea toward which Lenin himself was stridently moving.

Trotsky's performance at this congress was remarkable, given the nature of the objections of the unionists and the level of opposition he was encountering. Undaunted by it all, he flaunted his position with a brilliancy few of his opponents could equal. Bowled over by Trotsky and the fact that he spoke officially and for Lenin, his opponents offered less resistance than might have been expected. Ironically, it fell to Sapronov, Ossinsky, Preobrazhensky, Tomsky, and Lutovinov to carry the battle against him. Several of these men were later to join forces with him in his quest for rapid industrial development.

Lenin had made the best choice in selecting Trotsky to present this particular point of view. What Lenin did not seem to perceive, however, was the extent to which Trotsky irritated the unionists and hurt rather than helped Lenin's cause. The Trotsky policies, which Lenin was fully supporting at this time, were destined to throw the Party into one of the severest crises of its history.

Counterproposals defending collective management were submitted by Ossinsky and Sapronov on behalf of the Democratic Centrists. In debate, Rykov, head of the Supreme Council, strongly defended collective management. But it was reliable Tomsky and the A.R.C.C.T.U. who played a surprising role. Tomsky, speaking on behalf of the A.R.C.C.T.U., introduced a compromise resolution. One-man management was to be admitted, but only in small industries and individual militarized enterprises, and only with the consent of the trade unions. In all other instances collective management was to be maintained.

Thus both aspects were affirmed simultaneously, and it appeared to be a workable compromise. Significantly, in his attack on the counterproposal Tomsky did not attack Lenin. Ignoring his earlier challenge, he defended Lenin, stating that Lenin had hesitated two years before supporting such a measure. Nor did Tomsky attack Trotsky, the sponsor of the resolution on one-man management now before the Congress. Instead he blamed the entire matter on Krassin, a minor figure who could hardly have guided the measure through without the support of some of the primary figures in the Party.

Why he followed this line of attack is difficult to say. Tomsky and a majority of the Party fraction evidently felt that Lenin had a majority and could not be beaten. This, they obviously felt, was the best "package" they could walk away with. Yet it is difficult to believe they saw no other way out, no other way to reach Lenin, since they objected so much to these changes in policy. What is interesting is that Lenin convinced Tomsky, as he had in the past, for it was Tomsky who guided through the compromise among the unionists and drew up the compromise resolution. Be that as it may, their shift ensured the passage of a resolution on one-man management. Lenin won through Tomsky, not Trotsky.

However, all had not gone well in the unionist fraction. Not everyone had agreed to the compromise. Rather, the split that had been growing between the Left and Right now yawned even wider, leaving those on either side as clearly opposing factions. Shlyapnikov was conveniently not present at the Congress, away on his long trip to Norway, and the mantle of leadership of the Workers' Opposition group thus fell on the shoulders of Lutovinov, who performed creditably under adverse conditions. Lutovinov and his fellow leftists, as could be expected, were closer to Sapronov and the Democratic Centrists than to Lenin, Tomsky and a majority of the A.R.C.C.T.U. As Tomsky moved more and more in the direction of an accommodation with Lenin, Lutovinov began to state in concrete terms the views of the leftist-oriented unionists: "In our opinion, the production unions can be the only responsible head of each branch of industry, and the A.R.C.C.T.U. the responsible head of all branches of industry—it cannot be otherwise!" [19]

Thus, Lutovinov reasserted the line of attack that Shlyapnikov had advanced in his thesis of mid-1919. In effect, he and the leftists were demanding not a compromise but the implementation of Point 5, the concentration in A.R.C.C.T.U. hands of the management of the whole system of public economy as a single economic unit. Lutovinov, unlike Tomsky, was moving decidedly in the direction of a quasi-syndicalist if not an outright workers' control position. At the time their position was thoroughly inconsistent with that of the Bolshevik leadership. Lutovinov bowed reluctantly but gracefully. He declared that he, and those of a similar view, although absolutely convinced they were right and the Central Committee wrong, would work loyally to secure one-man management, that they would do so "not out of fear but as a matter of conscience." [20]

To cap the victory over the unionist fraction, Tomsky was re-elected to the Central Committee for the second time, and Andreev and Rudzutak, two trade unionists assuming a leadership role in Party-union work, were also elected to the Central Committee. Their election, however, was not unambiguous and did little to cement relations between the various trade union factions. While Andreev was to reveal strong Trotskyite leanings in the course of the next year, it was Tomsky and Rudzutak who provided Lenin with a winning coalition at the Tenth Party Congress.

Lenin fought and won his battle at the Ninth Congress. He had succeeded in overcoming the opposition of the union fraction. Lenin had put to use divisions within the A.R.C.C.T.U. for his own purposes; he had sidetracked one of his most serious opponents; he had elevated the men whom he felt he could reach; and he had not hesitated to impose decisions and individuals upon the fraction. All in all, he had won! But he had not been able to reconcile the many trends of opposition [21] inside the trade unions, nor had he been able to persuade the unions, in any lasting sense, to approve his policy. Lenin was walking a tightrope, but he did not know how precarious his position was. His balance was upset later that year by Leon Trotsky, his former anchorman.

What was evident, however, was that the labor opposition had cost dearly; the issue had spilled over into the Communist Party and sharply divided it. The issue was a logical extension of the decision to rule alone and push through the Bolsheviks' own millenarian program in the face of a backward and exhausted Russia. The minority dictatorship did not mean unity and agreement within the Communist Party. Little had been solved. The issues had merely been transferred to the Communist Party.

6 ✆ The Union Question Internalized: Dictatorship Within the Party

Every independent attempt, every new thought that has not passed through the censorship of our centre is considered as "heresy," as a violation of party discipline, as an attempt to infringe on the prerogatives of the centre, which must "foresee" everything and "decree" anything and everything. If anything is not decreed one must wait, for the . . . centre at its leisure will decree, and then within sharply restricted limits one may express his "initiative."

"The creation of communism can and will be the work of the toiling masses themselves. The creation of communism belongs to the workers." [1]

THE TRADE UNION DEBATE

No sooner was the issue of collective management resolved than the trade union issue flared up again. The end of the civil war gave rise to the question of peace and reconstruction, which in turn gave birth to another round of serious disagreement within the Party. There were many different issues, but it was the trade union question which became the fulcrum upon which all the issues moved. Within the labor question the issue of the Revolution was once again debated. So deep was disagreement over the labor question that, by 1921, Lenin and Trotsky openly broke with one another; the Central Committee found itself divided and paralyzed; and factions developed on all levels within the Party. So badly divided was the Party that Lenin publicly declared he was worried about its future. To settle the question, to re-effect Party unity, Lenin took the final step: He denied the right to caucus within the Party, and thus destroyed the last vestiges of Party democracy.

Tsektran

The impetuous Leon Trotsky was again the *casus celebrati* of the affair. Shortly after Trotsky had proposed the militarization of labor, he accepted, on Lenin's urgings but with great reluctance, a Central Committee assignment to rebuild rail communications, then near total collapse. Trotsky was given wide authority and full Central Committee support to use all methods as he saw fit in a new agency called Tsektran, which combined rail and river transport. With customary vigor he attacked the problem by attempting to apply his labor conscription ideas.

The unionists were disgruntled with the administrative change, but compliant. Stalin, Bukharin, and Krestinsky, but significantly not Tomsky, were assigned the odious responsibility of "selling it" to the A.R.C.C.T.U. Party fraction. Tsektran further subordinated the unions to the state apparatus and had the undesirable feature of cutting across the authority of the A.R.C.C.T.U.; that is, the local communications unions would no longer be under its authority, but rather under Trotsky's. Trotsky did little to mollify the unionists. A Dionysian in his element, he used his powers freely and fully, running roughshod over anyone who stood in his path. He seemed almost to delight in telling the unions that he planned to use his powers as chairman of Tsektran to redistribute and "shake up" officials within the unions. He even went so far as to threaten imprisonment to those who resisted.

The whole affair blew up at the Fifth All-Russian Trade Union Conference, which opened on November 2, 1920. The unionists openly attacked Trotsky on the floor of the Congress for his "shake-up." The mercurial Trotsky was not able to let such an attack pass unanswered. Within six days he had a rough draft of a thesis entitled "The Trade Unions and Their Future Role," which contained his main arguments and recommended a reorganization of the unions. He submitted this proposal to the Central Committee for formal consideration.

Meanwhile Tomsky was reaching the limits of his endurance and was no longer willing to compromise. With the full support of the A.R.C.C.T.U., the communications unions, and several members of the Central Committee (Zinoviev in particular), Tomsky went to Lenin and raised the entire question of Tsektran at a meeting of the Central Committee. Lenin, who had given Trotsky his complete support and had favored the idea of the militarization of labor, gave in under their pressure. He made an about-face and supported Tomsky.

It is possible that Lenin saw the gains he had made and the agreement he had established at the Ninth Congress now being threatened. The weight of the support Tomsky brought to bear, the continued decline of Party popularity among the rank-and-file workers, and the advice he received from other leading Party figures such as Rykov and Zinoviev, possibly convinced him that Tsektran had outlived its usefulness, that labor armies had to be eliminated. The unions in this case had the greater power and he felt compelled to yield. What this does not explain, however, is why Lenin then reacted with such emotional violence toward Trotsky.

In an impassioned speech before the Central Committee,[2] Lenin blamed Trotsky and Tsektran for having driven away the trade union Communists and for having threatened the destruction of the Soviet system. At the same time he introduced a resolution for adoption by the A.R.C.C.T.U. fraction, resoundingly condemning Tsektran. This retort was so extreme that it offended Trotsky, worried Tomsky, and deeply divided the Central Committee. (Lenin later admitted he had attacked in terms that were too violent.) Astounded by the severity of the attack, Tomsky and Zinoviev, with the support of several other Central Committee members, introduced a compromise proposal. They recommended that it should not be Lenin who addressed the Trade Union Conference, but that Zinoviev should speak in the name of the Central Committee; that, instead of a controversial and polemical report, he should deliver a "business-like" one; and finally, that the disagreement should not be discussed outside the confines of the Central Committee. This course of action may have seemed wise, but it was not, considering that Zinoviev was less acceptable to Trotsky than almost anyone else.

Lenin, who by this time was cooling down, acceded. But Trotsky, whose entire position was under attack and who had a great stake in how the affair was conducted, requested permission for the presentation of a minority view at the fraction meeting. The committee members did not think it advisable and Trotsky's request was rejected. Zinoviev's proposal was then voted through by a majority. Opposed were Trotsky and Andreev, as well as two of the framers of the original proposal, Krestinsky and Rykov; Preobrazhensky abstained.[3] With the immediate formalities out of the way they adjourned for the day.

Though Zinoviev was the immediate victor, the issue was still not resolved and the Central Committee met on the following day, November 9. Before it were the alternate theses of Lenin and

Trotsky. There ensued a debate which again divided the Central Committee. Eight favored Lenin's position; four opposed it. Seven favored Trotsky's stand; eight were against it.[4] Thus the Central Committee split, temporarily stalemated and incapable of deciding which of the two extreme positions it preferred.

But even if they could not agree on the basic policy question at the time, they were able under Lenin's guidance to draft a resolution by a vote of 8 to 6 for the Party fraction currently attending the Fifth Conference. Although they straddled the issue they could not solve, the resolution did contain a concession to the unionists. "The degeneration of centralism and militarized forms of work into bureaucracy, red tape, and petty tyranny, etc." was condemned, and "sound forms of militarized labor" were advocated; it was recommended that Tsektran should "increase and strengthen the normal methods of proletarian democracy within the unions."[5]

At the same time, a commission on the union question was set up. It was charged with the task of determining the appropriate means for a wider application of democracy in the unions, wider labor participation in the control of production, and the re-examination of the entire issue of management and the employment of specialists. At face value it was a tremendous victory for Tomsky and the unionists. Lenin was retreating on the question of specialists and the union role in management, and it seemed that the imbalance between the state administrative organs and the unions would be corrected.

The Central Committee then named the men it wanted to fulfill this task: Zinoviev, who was appointed chairman, Tomsky, Rudzutak (a unionist but Lenin's personal representative), Rykov, and finally Trotsky—but no left wingers like Shlyapnikov or Lutovinov. The Committee then instructed its commission that none of its members, with the exception of chairman Zinoviev, would be allowed to publish or speak at any Party meetings on the question of the trade unions.

In some respects these decisions were wise; in others, pointedly Machiavellian. At any rate they were useless, for the commission, by its very composition and its orders, was doomed to fail.

Why Zinoviev was appointed chairman of the committee is hard to surmise, since he was Trotsky's outspoken enemy and had gone out of his way to criticize Trotsky and Tsektran in 1920. This was the first fatal mistake. The second was to appoint a committee which left Trotsky in a minority of one, perhaps two if he could count on Rykov. But given Rykov's record on collective management among other things, he could not be depended upon to side with Trotsky. The last mistake, of course, was to put a lid on discussion of trade union questions by all members of the commission except Zinoviev. This may have made sense, for Tomsky and Trotsky on the same commission undoubtedly would have gone at each other "tooth and claw" in public as well as in private; but again, from Trotsky's point of view it was overly restrictive. The commission was stacked against him and was sure to run roughshod over all he stood for on policy.

Trotsky refused to serve on the commission. His explanation was twofold: First, the trade union question was a deep and ideological one—it could only be solved by work on a long-range mass basis. Second, he could not serve on it unless he were given an equal opportunity with others (a euphemism for Zinoviev) to express his position in the press.[6]

The commission was prepared to go to work with or without Trotsky. An impressive change was then made in its composition. Four auspicious trade unionists were added: Shlyapnikov, Lutovinov, Andreev, and Lozovsky. This gave the unionists a majority on the commission, although amongst them there were some differences of opinion. At face value it appeared everything was beginning to go their way.

Meanwhile, on November 9, Zinoviev attended the Party fraction of the Fifth Conference and presented the Central Committee's resolution. Though the Central Committee had seen it as conciliatory, the unionists at first were not so sure. An intense and acrimonious debate took place, but in the end Party discipline prevailed and the Central Committee's resolution was passed by a majority of 200. Twelve members, however, found they could neither acquiesce nor fight, and they abstained.

As Schapiro points out, this was Zinoviev's first and final triumph as a conciliator.[7] The time had passed for any compromise over Tsektran. Feelings in trade union circles were running at fever pitch. Finally, in the first week of December, the crisis broke. At an enlarged plenum of Tsektran, meeting at the time, the Party representatives of the water and rail transport workers and a large number of others staged a protest walkout. Shortly therafter Zinoviev, either reacting hysterically or as an utter Machiavellian, delivered his "commission's" report at a December plenum of the Central Committee. He called for the dissolution of Tsektran, the dismantlement of Glavpolitput, the replacement of Trotsky's men, and the transfer of transport to the trade unions. Whatever else may be said, this was a flagrant censure of Trotsky and his labor policies.

Lenin responded positively and was supported by Tomsky and Stalin. But once again the Central Committee proved itself badly divided on the question. By a split vote of 8 to 7 Lenin's demand for the immediate abolishment of Tsektran was defeated. Lenin and the trade unionists had lost by one vote.

Again it was Bukharin who stepped into the breach. To avoid a vote of no confidence and reprisals by Trotsky, a "buffer" group emerged consisting of ten members dedicated to a compromise. Under Bukharin's guidance they pushed through a compromise resolution by one vote. It proposed that the unpopular political directorates be abolished immediately. Tsektran, however, was to be left operational until February, when new elections for its executive posts would be held at the congress of rail and water transport unions. Further, all candidates for union posts were to be selected "not only for their political reliability, but also their industrial talents, administrative experience, organizational ability, and practical proof of their interest in the material and spiritual welfare of the masses." [8] Thus the buffer tried to please everyone. They appealed to Lenin by explicitly rejecting, as he did, the reorganization of the unions from above; Trotsky was wooed by a vague approval of production unions; the unions were attracted by a call for more union authority and greater union participation in administration. In short, the buffer group chose to beg the entire question of Tsektran.

If they preferred statesmanship to battle, the buffer group failed, for neither Lenin, Trotsky, nor Zinoviev were satisfied with the resolution.[9] Lenin rejected the buffer as ineffective and called their compromise a "paper resolution." He said Trotsky's boycott of the commission meant the struggle would continue regardless of what the buffer attempted.

The reaction of the water transport fraction seems to indicate Lenin was right. So angry were they that they broke Party discipline and resigned from Tsektran on December 9, in effect destroying any prospect of compromise.[10] With Lenin and Trotsky unwilling to compromise and the buffer unable to carry its own position, the Central Committee remained divided. Thus, the point had been reached where the Central Committee, torn by the union question and by personality problems and factions, found itself incapable of resolving the question or taking any effective action. Meanwhile the union situation continued to deteriorate before them. At this juncture Lenin openly laid the blame on Trotsky and attacked him publicly.

Angry and worried, he leveled the charge of factionalism

against Trotsky, who, by his refusal to serve on Zinoviev's trade union commission, his unyielding attitude on the trade union question, and his unnecessary and tactless antagonism toward Tomsky, Lozovsky, and other trade union leaders, had brought about the split and paralysis of the Central Committee on this very crucial question.[11]

Among the many points Lenin made as he bore down on Trotsky was that Trotsky was not even fully apprised of the realities of the situation, yet still insisted on making extremely harsh and antagonistic demands. For example, Trotsky demanded 50 per cent representation in the management of industry; but, Lenin pointed out, trade unionists in fact already occupied 57 per cent of the most important organs of the Soviet government—72 of 140 administrators of the most important industries had been workers and 63 per cent of the directors and managers of factories and mills were former workers. He admonished Trotsky, saying:

> The most sensible thing right now in relation to this "merging" is to be silent. Why? Because we have actually already done the merging. We do not have a single provincial branch of VSNKh, of the Commissariat of Transportation, where there is not practically a merger. [Then he asked]: But are the results completely satisfactory? There is the rub! . . . as yet we have not completely assimilated the sum total of our experience. Hence, the most sensible attitude in regard to this matter is: silence.[12]

But Trotsky was not to be dismayed or silenced. He charged that the unions, Zinoviev, and the Central Committee, but not Lenin specifically, were the source of the deadlock.[13] The inability to find a compromise within the Central Committee made open discussion of the question unavoidable. Finally, on Trotsky's urgings and by Lenin's agreement, the Central Committee voted on December 24 to present the question for resolution at the Tenth Party Congress. This decision neither solved nor tempered the debate, and it continued unabated for several more months.

At the Eighth Congress of Soviets, meeting in Moscow's Bolshoi Theater, Lenin officially opened the trade union debate on December 30. In a speech entitled "On the Trade Unions, the Present Moment, and the Mistakes of Comrade Trotsky," he ripped into Trotsky in his best polemical form, denouncing his program as an undesirable and unhealthy factional document which was full of theoretical errors.[14] What was interesting about Lenin's attack was that it also reflected a shift in his own position on the trade union question. Advancing a proposition set forth by Rudzutak, he said:

But the trade unions are not state organizations, not organizations for coercion, they are educational organizations, organizations that enlist, that train; they are schools, schools of administration, schools of management, schools of communism.

The place the trade unions occupy in the system of the dictatorship of the proletariat . . . is between the party and the state power.[15]

With this pronouncement Lenin broke away from his earlier position spelled out on November 30, 1920, which had called for the acceptance of the "sound forms" of militarization of labor. Lenin was beginning to develop his theory of "transmission belt" unions.

The debate filled the press and there were innumerable rallies. With the Central Committee announcement, the left wing unionists and Party members openly joined a fracas which had unofficially been going on since the Tsektran crisis in November. By the time the Tenth Party Congress convened in March 1921, eight separate and distinct platforms had emerged out of the debate. Lenin's and Zinoviev's became known as the "Platform of the Ten," with Tomsky, Rudzutak, Kalinin, Kamenev, Lozovsky, Stalin, Petrovsky, and Sergeev affixing their names to it as well. There was also one submitted by Bukharin and Larin, but within a few weeks they and their supporters merged forces with Trotsky. The other prominent unionists who supported Trotsky were Gol'tzmann and Kossior. In addition, Andreev, Dzerzhinsky, Krestinsky, Preobrazhensky, Rakovsky, Pyatakov, Serebryakov, Sokol'nikov, Kon, and several other prominent Party figures supported Trotsky. Another platform was submitted by Ryazanov, Ignatov, and Nogin, though it was more of a personal manifesto than a platform. The Democratic Centrists also submitted a platform, but, like the Ryazanov group, were afraid of a split and eventually withdrew it. Of great importance was the fact that they revealed little sympathy with the one other group which was very close to their position and which also submitted a platform—the Workers' Opposition.

While the debates were still raging Lenin became increasingly agitated about the depth of the cleavage within the Party. He now saw the Workers' Opposition, and particularly their substantive arguments regarding labor's share in management, as a critical threat. On January 19, 1921, he published an article entitled "Party Crisis." In it he warned that "minor differences and disagreements have grown into big ones," and then added: "*We must have the courage to look the bitter truth straight in the face. The Party is sick. The Party is shaking with fever.*" He demanded "the most rapid and surest cure."[16]

Threat of the Workers' Opposition

Lenin saw the Workers' Opposition as the most difficult problem for the Party. It was in fact reopening the syndicalist debate of 1917. The "minor disagreements" he had referred to had grown into "syndicalism"; this, he added, "means the complete rupture with Communism and an inevitable split in the Party if the Party does not prove to be sufficiently sound and strong to heal itself of the sickness quickly and thoroughly." [17] To leave no question as to the magnitude of the threat he made two further points: First he attacked Shlyapnikov's interpretation of Point 5 and his demand for transferring the control of the economy to the unions. He stated: "Syndicalism transfers to the masses of non-Party workers . . . the management branches of industry, . . . thus destroying the need for the Party." [18] His second point really restated the first: "If the trade unions, nine-tenths of the members of which are non-Party workers, appoint . . . the managers of industry, what is the use of the Party?" [19] Thus the issue was posed; for Lenin the question of the Workers' Opposition went to the very heart of all questions. It was: Who would rule Russia, the workers or the Party?

In persuading Lenin to open the debate, Trotsky had suggested it would have the effect of minimizing use of the unions as a vehicle of political opposition. He had also peddled his own argument by adding that if stress were placed on the "production" aspects of the unions in the economy, the Workers' Opposition would lose a great deal of its attraction to the disenchanted elements in the unions and the Party. Lenin had seen the shrewdness of Trotsky's suggestions, thinking that of a choice between the latter's position and that of the Workers' Opposition, he preferred Trotsky's, and had agreed. His object had been to steal their thunder, or, as he said in "Party Crisis," it was to "absorb what was sound in the 'democratic Workers' Opposition.'" Thus, one of the motives behind the Central Committee decision to open the question to public debate had been to temper the growing strength of the Workers' Opposition in the trade unions and the Party.

During the course of the debates Lenin hammered away at the Workers' Opposition and at the entire question of workers managing industry, striving at all times to negate worker control of management. On this question he was joined by Trotsky, who used the opportunity to move closer to Lenin.

Then at the Second All-Russian Congress of Miners, which convened on January 22, 1921, Lenin and Trotsky joined forces. At this congress, Lenin, in white anger, shouted: "Does every worker know how to rule the country? Practical people know that these are fairy tales." Then he asked, "Can you say right now, speaking sincerely, that the trade unions as administrators can always produce a given number of qualified managers? In administrative positions there is a possible need of sixty thousand, a hundred thousand persons. Can they supply them? Everybody who is not carried away and running after formulas . . . will say No. . . ." He added, "If we should say that not the Party nominates the candidates and governs, but the trade unions alone, it will sound very democratic but it destroys the dictatorship of the proletariat." Finally he rejected trade union management of the economy as "syndicalist twaddle." The "whole syndicalist absurdity," he said, "must be thrown into the wastebasket." [20]

When the Tenth Congress met in March, Lenin stated the issue as plainly as he could: "After two and a half years of Communist rule we stood up before the entire world and said at the Communist International that the dictatorship of the proletariat is impossible in any other way but through the dictatorship of the Communist Party." [21]

THE WORKERS' OPPOSITION

On December 30, the day Lenin blasted Trotsky and officially opened the trade union debate at the Eighth Congress of Soviets, Shlyapnikov presented a thesis entitled "The Tasks of the Trade Unions." [22] Before a joint meeting of the trade union representatives and the Communist fraction of the Eighth Congress, Shlyapnikov reiterated his plea for the unions' autonomous control over the economy. He started by reviewing the history of the general positions that had been adopted to determine the role of the trade unions in the Soviet state. Quoting from the First, Second, and Third Congresses of trade unions as well as from Point 5, he emphasized the assertions that the organizing apparatus of industry must rest in the hands of the trade unions; that the trade unions must actually concentrate in their hands the management of the whole system of public economy as an economic unit. He urged the delegates to make these resolutions a living reality. He called on them to introduce the principles of election of all administrative officials by the workers; the responsibility of all administrative organs to the workers; the reorganization of unions along "production" lines; and the establishment of the "direction of the whole national economy [by an] All-Russian Congress of Producers, which unites the production unions and which is elected by the production unions." In his conclusion he said:

> In this way there is created the unity of will which is essential in the organization of the economy, and also a real possibility for the influence of the initiative of the broad working masses in the organization and development of our economy.[23]

Shlyapnikov's thesis of December 30, 1920, was an elaboration of what he and Lutovinov had urged at the Ninth Congress. On January 25, 1921, the program of the Workers' Opposition was published in *Pravda*.

Composition of the Workers' Opposition

To digress briefly, it is of interest to consider the composition of the Workers' Opposition. Its leadership was notable for its lack of top-echelon political figures. This was both its strong and weak points. It reflected a grass roots rebellion and trade union opposition in particular. But the absence of important figures in its ranks also meant it lacked status and power. Few of its proponents had the political abilities essential for successfully carrying through a program on the top levels of the Party. In a way it is not surprising that the Opposition could not attract top-level leaders. Essentially it was a workers' pressure group, pushing trade unions and appealing primarily to workers. Membership was, apparently with few exceptions, working class in social composition. Another reason for its homogeneity was the fact that the group's position was a radical one, and there was a risk and an opprobrium involved in joining a faction which so fundamentally challenged Lenin and the Central Committee.

In another sense, however, the lack of first-caliber leaders, intellectuals, and nonworkers in any significant degree is surprising, for they were giving voice to the very complaints the Democratic Centrists and other leftists were making. They, like the Democratic Centrists, were a focal point for opposition to excessive centralism, to the destruction of the democratic process within the primary Party units, and to the growing Party bureaucracy. They reflected these trends and, apart from the duplication of organization, it is difficult to understand why they did not attract some support and leaders from other elements within the Party who were taking the same risk and were protesting these very same developments. The growing social differentiation within the Party and the wide cultural and political gap between workers and intellectuals, between workers and Party functionaries, and so on, contributed substantially to the relative isolation of the Workers' Opposition. (Union membership was becoming increasingly a mere formality for Party members.) So too did the fact that the Workers' Opposition represented the extreme left wing of the union element and many of these other critics of Party policy did not feel entirely comfortable with the Workers' Opposition advocacy of turning over control of the economy to the unions.

Some intellectuals and left wingers did join their ranks. One of them was the incomparable Madame Kollontai, perhaps best remembered for her outspoken advocacy of free love and equality of the sexes. Imbued with the fervor of democracy within the Party, she joined ranks with these trade unionists around January 1921, giving to their cause the element of prestige and force that was needed psychologically to carry home their attack.

Madame Kollontai wrote a pamphlet entitled *Rabochaia Oppozitsiia,* which contained the economic and political views presented earlier by Shlyapnikov.[24] The pamphlet, the fullest statement of the Workers' Opposition position ever to be printed by them, was published specifically as a document for the Tenth Congress. Its flyleaf states that it was "only for the members of the Tenth Congress of the R.C.P." According to another statement on the cover, the pamphlet was published officially in one and a half million copies for the Tenth Congress discussions, but according to Madame Kollontai, only 1,500 copies were in fact published, "and that with difficulty."[25]

Madame Kollontai made a great issue of the absence of well-known leaders, saying that this was the group's strongest point in its fight against bureaucratism. She declared that the Party was up against a grass roots rebellion which was springing up "simultaneously in all corners of Soviet Russia."[26] She further indicated that its membership was growing quickly, that it had centers in the major industrial cities, and that organizationally it embodied both Party and non-Party workers.

This latter point considerably altered the picture. The recruitment of non-Party members by a political faction altered the game of Party politics and the stakes for which it was played, even if the faction intended to operate within the Party and was only thinking of extending its democratic procedures. Even though the Workers' Opposition lacked prestigious and highly competent political leaders, it was now a force to be reckoned with, particularly with the development of its own local organizations. And with its syndicalist and democratic orientation there was the possibility it could build up sufficient outside pressure to force through the changes it sought. Contrary to a prevailing point of view, the Workers' Opposition was a viable opposition group posing a real threat to the Party.

Madame Kollontai stated her case most eloquently. Acknowledging that the unbearable conditions under which people were forced to live was a major factor in their opposition, she nonetheless insisted that the root of their opposition went deeper. She said: "The basis of the controversy is namely this: whether we shall realize communism through workers or over their heads, by the hands of Soviet officials." She added that the opposition was a "product of vacillation, inconsistencies, and direct deviations . . . from the . . . principles of the communist program." [27]

She then pressed for Party reforms, state bureaucracy curtailment, and workers' control of the economy. She proposed that: (1) a body to administer the national economy be formed from the workers; (2) the transformation of the unions from the role of passive assistance to active participation and the utilization of their creative initiative, this aim to be realized by a series of gradual and orderly measures; (3) the transfer of the administration of industry to the unions take place when the All-Russian Central Council of the Trade Unions found the unions to be qualified for the task; (4) union consent be obligatory for all appointments to administrative-economic posts; the appointed officials to be responsible to and recallable by the unions; (5) the rank-and-file nucleus in unions be strengthened and factory committees be prepared for running the industry so that the above points could be carried out; (6) the entire administration of the public economy be concentrated in one body (without the existing dualism of the Supreme Council of the National Economy and the All-Russian Central Council of Trade Unions), thereby creating the oneness of will requisite for the effective implementation of the plan and the realization of the Communist system of production.[28]

On the problem of bureaucracy and elitism Madame Kollontai proposed three principles: (1) a return "to the principle of election" and "making officials responsible to the masses" (2) "introduction of wide discussion and publicity within the Party on all questions"; "the paying of more concern for the opinions of the rank and file"; and "free speech" for all, including factions, with the right to criticize freely during discussions by making funds available for the publication of faction literature (3) "placing limitations on those who fill offices both in the party and in Soviet institutions at the same time." [29] Elaborating on these proposals, she

said that "bureaucracy . . . is a direct negation of mass activity," [30]
that its harm lies not only in red tape, "but also in the solution of
all problems . . . by means of decisions handed down from the
central institutions, and arrived at by one person or by an extremely
restricted collective. . . ." The worst part of it was that "some third
person decides your fate." [31] Almost echoing the earlier words of
Rosa Luxemburg, Madame Kollontai said that "the task is clear:
to wake up initiative and self-activity in the masses," [32] for "the
creation of communism can and will be the work of the toiling
masses themselves. The creation of communism belongs to the
workers." [33]

This was a criticism that rang of elitism and anti-democratic
politics. She was in effect saying that the general welfare was being
lost to all because a ruling elite pursuing its own interests could
only realize a restricted self-interest—not the interests of the people.
Madame Kollontai's epistle had a direct equalitarian and democratic
ring. Basically she was stating the case for the people who still
thought in terms of democracy and a workers' revolution. It was a
grass roots communism she was purporting. In her eyes this could
best be carried out by the unions themselves. She proposed that
the unions be transformed from passive agencies into active institutions; that the workers, the producers, administer the national
economy; and finally, that the administration of industry be transferred to the unions under A.R.C.C.T.U. guidance and the entire
administration of the public economy be transferred to a single
body.[34] With this last recommendation, intentionally or not, she
formally reopened the question of workers' control, of syndicalism,
the issue ostensibly settled at the First Trade Union Congress.

Lenin now had to contend with a group that was gathering
mass support and advocating worker control of the economy as well
as democracy within the Party, if not the very principles of the
November Revolution. Implicit in its attack was the charge of the
Revolution betrayed. Implicit also was the larger assumption, not
consciously expressed, that a mass democratic system based on the
unions, and perhaps organized on syndicalist lines, would be preferable to the present elitist dictatorship. Few events could have
posed a more direct threat to the Party, to its monopoly of power
and to all Lenin had worked for since November 1917.

Weakness of the Workers' Opposition
The Tenth Congress convened on March 8. It was attended by
694 delegates with voting rights. The Workers' Opposition was represented by 45 to 50 delegates, a mere handful. It is not surprising

that they were in a minority at the Congress, but what is puzzling is why they did so very poorly in electing delegates to the Congress. In the period preceeding the Congress—when they were on the hustings—they had gained a considerable following in Party organizations in Moscow, the Urals, the Ukraine, Samar, and Vladimir. Yet they were only able to elect some 50 representatives. Why? A possible explanation would appear to lie in the following set of circumstances: First, as has been made plain, the pre-Congress debates were fought on all but the bloodiest terms. Lenin and Trotsky waged a tough fight, utilizing whatever machinery they had. They demanded full and unequivocal support, and it would have been difficult for many of the delegates to oppose them.

Second, election to the Tenth Congress was by support of platforms. Elections took place at Party meetings by open vote, and all candidates had to declare themselves. This procedure was originally advanced on January 3, 1921, by Zinoviev and the Petrograd Party machine which he headed. It was generally interpreted as a personal power move in his struggle with Trotsky for control of the Party apparatus; if so it worked, for it drew immediate protests from Trotsky and the Moscow Party organization. On January 21 the Central Committee, with Lenin and Zinoviev in the majority, voted 8 to 7 in support of election of delegates to the Congress by platform. Though perhaps aimed at Trotsky, the procedure had the apparent effect of scaring away and silencing much of the support for the Workers' Opposition. Election by platforms hurt them badly.

Third, in the last week of February strikes broke out in Petrograd, where hunger, unemployment, and a fuel shortage already gripped the city. Strikers' proclamations appeared. The bread ration had been cut by one-third in all major cities and large towns; a fuel shortage had forced the closing of factories, adding to the ranks of the shiftless, hungry, and disgruntled unemployed. Yet in spite of these harsh circumstances, the strikers' demands were political as well as economic. One of their demands, quoted by Alexander Berkman, reads: "A complete change is necessary in the policies of the government. First of all, the workers and peasants need freedom. They don't want to live by the decrees of the Bolsheviki: they want to control their own destinies." [85]

The Bolsheviks ordered crack troops into Petrograd. Just as the tense situation was subsiding, the Red sailors at the Kronstadt naval base, disturbed by what was happening in Petrograd and by the dictatorial sweep of Bolshevik rule, mutinied. The sailors fought under the name of the "October Revolution" for "free elections" and "Soviets, but without Communists." They fought well but it was a futile battle against insuperable odds. The sailors were crushed. Although the rebellion occurred too late to have influenced the elections, it did have the effect of further isolating the opposition. It appears that some delegates who had been attracted to this faction now turned away from it as sharply and completely as did all other groups.

All of these factors lend explanation to the poor showing the Workers' Opposition made in electing delegates. But there is one additional reason. The Workers' Opposition may not have been as strong or as powerful a group within the Party as Lenin and the others had presumed. It is quite likely, particularly with a decline in the number of workers in the Party and with a serious split dividing them into right and left wings, that the Workers' Opposition group consisted of relatively little more than a small minority within the Party, in spite of Kollontai's statement that they were organized in the major industrial centers and Party units and were "growing rapidly."

Lenin nonetheless regarded them as the major threat to the Party, even after the size of their delegation was known, even after he had a private conference with them at the Congress, and even after constant reassurance that (although they were enlisting non-Party support) they had no intention of breaking off from the Party or of forming an alliance with the Mensheviks or any other group. What they wanted was an extension of democracy within the Party and an increase in trade union powers. They were Communists first and foremost, they assured him; they wanted changes but only within the framework of the Party dictatorship.

Judging from all that they said and did, their assurances to Lenin appeared sincere. They were in favor of the Party dictatorship. They wanted freedom of discussion and democratic elections but only within the Party, and apparently they had no desire to extend these rights to any other group or to institutionalize the practice outside of the Party. In many respects this was their great weakness, for implicit in their demands and actions was the larger hope of a Russia organized along democratic lines.

But Lenin saw in the Workers' Opposition the first threat to the Party, and he dealt with it accordingly. At the Tenth Congress he took steps to destroy it. His actions had resounding reverberations upon the nature of Soviet politics.

THE TENTH CONGRESS PROCEEDINGS

The Tenth Congress marks the great divide in the history of the Russian Communist Party. It is from this point on that the dictatorship within the Party was fully and firmly established. It was at this

Congress that the foundations of the Party—as it exists today—were laid. This holds true for trade union policy too. In essence, the resolutions on the unions and on inner-Party democracy constitute the decisive work of this Congress.

Platform of the Ten

The trade union question was eclipsed by the Kronstadt uprising. All united; Lenin and Trotsky joined hands and agreed to smash the opposition. The adoption of the Platform of the Ten, presented by Lenin's faction, became a matter of mere formality.

The Platform, geared to resolve the trade union problem, dealt with the three main sources of friction: the union-state feud, union-Party relations, and union-membership relations.

First, regarding the union-state problem, the major grievances of union repression and the militarization of labor were dealt with by stipulating that the militarization measures were only temporary, that coercive powers were powers unique unto the state, and that unions were not instruments whose primary purpose was to coerce and discipline the membership. Rather, the unions were "schools" whose primary task was the education of the masses to the meaning of Communism and whose primary method was persuasion. The unions were transmission belts, auxiliary organs of the state and distinct from the state, but agencies working with the commissariats to implement policy. The unions were neither equal with, superior to, nor directly subordinate to the commissariats; they were rather quasi-independent and autonomous agencies, responsible to the Party and to themselves for their actions. At the same time they were definitely inferior to the state commissariats, for it was state policy which the unions, as transmission belts, were to help implement.

The subordinate question of union participation in decision-making on the shop level was dealt with similarly. The unions, as transmission belts, were assigned the task of combating excessive centralism and bureaucratism in the state economic organs. They were denied the right to participate in managerial functions and, though they were called upon to help formulate economic plans, they were not assigned a decisive policy-making role.

Second, the problem of union-Party relations was dealt with by a strong reaffirmation of the subordination of the unions to the Party. Here too the concept of unions as "tranmission belts" and "schools of communism" was advanced. The unions were assigned the role of a channel of communication between the Party and the workers and a means for educating and indoctrinating the workers.

Under no conditions were the unions to assert their independence from the Party, assert a policy of neutrality, or assume a posture of equality. To assure Party hegemony a clause was inserted stipulating that the Party had authority over all appointments to trade union posts and could appoint members as it saw fit. The Platform further stipulated that no shake-ups or reorganization from above were to occur; that henceforth all unions were to be run according to the "normal principle of proletarian democracy"; and, to assure union participation in over-all activities, the unions were called on to continue to recommend personnel for Party and administrative posts.

Third, regarding union-membership relations, the policy of obligatory, compulsory membership for all industrial workers was abandoned. Membership in unions was put on a voluntary basis and made an individual matter.

The Platform was adopted by 336 votes. Trotsky and Bukharin's platform received 50 votes, and the Workers' Opposition 18. The Platform symbolically marked the introduction of the New Economic Policy. It marked a retreat from the harsh measures of War Communism.

On face value Tomsky appeared to have done fairly well. He had won a major battle for the right wing unionists, if not the unions as a whole. The unions had forced and won a major fight. Subordination to the Party had been reaffirmed, but cessation of Party interference in union affairs was also affirmed. Trotsky, their major target, had been decidedly defeated. The left unionists too had been refuted; syndicalism was officially a dead issue. Shlyapnikov and his followers were thoroughly discredited within the Party; in all likelihood they would not again pose a threat to the right wing.

But these were superficial gains. While N.E.P. on face value appeared to be a more liberal policy, in reality Tomsky had not fared so well. N.E.P. also marked the introduction of a major shift in trade union policy. Unions were no longer direct participants in economic decision-making or organization, except in a very formal way. Management and the state apparatus were the primary powers in the realm of economic policy and administration. This was a far cry from the intentions of 1917—to liberate the worker and to make him master of the economy.

While all this is very true, it must also be emphasized that the adoption of the Platform signified little more than a gesture to change policy; actual trade union policy and the role of the trade unions was not to be determined until the over-all economic policy of N.E.P. was in fact determined, and this did not take place until

1922. Of greater significance at this Congress was the decision on Party unity, which inaugurated a policy that closed an era in Party history.

The Prohibition of Minority Rights

At the beginning of the Congress Lenin had taken no move to introduce a resolution on Party unity or factionalism. This was surprising, for the pre-Congress debates had been a real free-for-all and very costly. The threat, however, hovered over the Congress, and everyone had expected one. On the second day Lenin, in angry response to the Kronstadt uprising, moved against the oppositionists with full force:

> We need no opposition now, comrades, it is not the time! Either on this side or that, with a rifle, but not with the opposition. . . . And I think that the Party Congress will have to draw that conclusion too . . . that the time has come to put an end to the opposition, to put a lid on it; we have had enough of opposition now.[86]

Shlyapnikov leaped to the floor to reply. With apprehension in his heart but boldness in his voice, he said he would cooperate fully with "any measures designed to restore party health." Then, addressing himself to Lenin, he said: "But do not pick up the stick for a struggle against us. If you do you will undoubtedly crush and destroy us, but in the [end] you will only lose."[87]

Bukharin took it upon himself to answer Shlyapnikov. Standing before the assembled delegates he stated frankly that on March 11 he had intended to introduce a resolution restricting freedom of speech and factional activity, and he left little doubt he still thought it was an excellent idea. Shlyapnikov and Medvedev then seized the floor, for it was clear from the tenor of Bukharin's words that the resolution he proposed to introduce would be aimed at silencing the Workers' Opposition. Attempting to fend off his attack, they declared that until such a resolution were abandoned the Workers' Opposition delegates and their supporters would nominate no candidate for the Central Committee, a threat which was clear to all.

Lenin took Shlyapnikov's reaction seriously. He was convinced of the necessity for having Shlyapnikov and several other members of the Workers' Opposition elected to the Central Committee. At a private meeting with the supporters of the Workers' Opposition in the proverbial "smoke-filled room," Lenin and the Workers' Opposition representatives apparently established some sort of working agreement; at least Lenin succeeded in allaying their immediate fears, for he convinced Shlyapnikov to run for election. Shlyapnikov and Kutuzov were elected to full membership and Kislev was elected a candidate member.[38]

The Congress was scheduled to close on March 15. Its business, however, was not finished and chairman Radek called for an extended session. On March 16, at the very last moment and after many delegates had left, Lenin, without giving any reasons, introduced two resolutions. The first dealt with Party unity and the limits of minority rights; the second, with syndicalist deviations. Both were directed at the Workers' Opposition.

The first of these two resolutions, entitled "On the Syndicalist and Anarchist Deviation in Our Party," condemned the Workers' Opposition as a "syndicalist deviation" and a threat to the Revolution.

> A slight syndicalist or semi-anarchist deviation would not have been terrible; the Party would have quickly and resolutely recognized it and would have set to work to straighten it out. But when this deviation is connected with the . . . growing discontent of the peasantry with the proletarian dictatorship . . . there is no time to argue about theoretical deviations. . . . We will not permit arguments about deviations, we must put a stop to this. . . . The controversial atmosphere is becoming extremely dangerous, it is becoming a positive menace to the dictatorship of the proletariat.
>
> [Lenin proceeded to accuse them of all possible counterrevolutionary activity]: . . . all must know that the Workers' Opposition which hides behind the worker's back, is a syndicalist deviation, it is as well an anarchist deviation, and it contains a petty bourgeois element . . . more than once in the course of the revolution [this petty bourgeois anarchist element] has manifested itself as the most dangerous enemy of the proletarian dictatorship.[39]

Lenin then demanded "an unswerving and systematic ideological struggle with these ideas," and resolved that "the propaganda of these ideas is incompatible with membership in the Russian Communist Party." Thus the fate of the Workers' Opposition was sealed.

The second resolution, called the "On Unity," resolution, dealt directly with the problem of obedience and minority rights within the Party. The resolution stated that:

> All class conscious workers must clearly realize the perniciousness and impermissibility of factionalism of any kind, for no matter how the representatives of individual groups may desire to safeguard Party unity, in practice factionalism inevitably leads to the weaken-

ing of teamwork and to intensified and repeated attempts by the enemies of the Party who have fastened themselves onto it because it is the governing Party, to widen the cleavage and to use it for counter-revolutionary purposes.

In the practical struggle against factionalism, every organization of the Party must take strict measures to prevent any factional conduct whatsoever. The absolutely necessary criticism of defects . . . shall be formulated in the most precise form possible and submitted . . . for consideration and decision to the leading local and central bodies of the party . . . everyone who criticizes must . . . take into account the position the Party occupies in a ring of enemies, and the content of his criticism must be of the nature . . . to rectify the errors of the Party or of individual Party members . . . under no circumstances must [proposals] be submitted . . . to groups formed on the basis of "platforms," etc. . . . the congress orders that *Discussion Sheets* and special symposiums be published more regularly. . . .

The Congress . . . hereby declares dissolved and orders the immediate dissolution of all groups without exception that have been formed on the basis of one platform or another [such as the Workers' Opposition group, etc.]. Nonobservance of this decision of the Congress shall entail absolute and immediate expulsion from the Party.

In order to effect strict discipline . . . and to secure the greatest unity . . . the Congress authorizes the C.C. to apply all Party penalties, including expulsion, in cases of breach of discipline or of reviving or of engaging in factionalism; and in regard to members of the Central Committee to reduce them to the status of candidates and, as an extreme measure, to expel them from the Party.[40]

The epoch-making resolutions were dutifully passed with only thirty dissenting votes, not even the full complement of Workers' Opposition votes. It is of course possible that some defected as the issues crystallized and the price of disagreement rose, but it also appears that some had already left the Congress, as had so many other delegates.

The Workers' Opposition speakers fought on the only grounds left. They bared their souls and pleaded for freedom for dissenting views. They declared they were loyal Communists and had no wish to exist as a separate group, but that they did want the right to speak freely about Party policy, particularly if they felt it went against the best interests of the Party. But apart from Shlyapnikov and the Workers' Opposition speakers, there were no opponents to Lenin's proposal. Significantly, not even the members of the Democratic Centrists came to their defense.

Shlyapnikov, outmaneuvered and stunned, submitted his resig-

nation from the Central Committee. Lenin, shrewd as well as un-
scrupulous, called on the Congress to reject it, knowing Shlyapnikov
would bend to its decision and to Party discipline.

The full significance of the resolutions was fearfully sensed by
many. Radek, commenting prophetically, warned: "[they] can be
used against us!" [41] But discipline, the Party crisis, and belief in
service to a higher cause nonetheless compelled him, and most
others, to vote for its adoption.

The Dictatorship Within the Party

The adoption of these resolutions by the Tenth Congress
marked the great divide in Communist Party history. Minority rights
and the free expression of dissension were outlawed in the most
absolute terms. The resolutions stipulated that interest groups were
outlawed: "under no circumstance must [proposals] be submitted
by groups formed on the basis of platforms." [42] They further stipulated that all criticism had to be in conformity with the Party's
position in international politics. Thus, under the terms of the resolution, no persons—even those in agreement on the basic fundamentals of the Soviet system—could draw up a program, organize
a caucus, offer an alternative position, or organize a loyal opposition. Under the terms of this resolution any basic criticism, any organized opposition, was tantamount to conspiracy, sabotage, or
treason. The significance is clear. If a minority is not permitted to
organize and attempt to become a majority, then there is no real
right to disagree, to dissent, to be free.

Significantly, factionalism prior to 1921 had always been considered to be a legitimate part of the dynamics making up the Party's
politics. Early in his career as a Bolshevik, Lenin had defended
factionalism on the grounds that it made a Party healthy and strong.
On the fly-leaf of *What Is To Be Done,* his pamphlet which essentially expounded all the principles of Bolshevism, Lenin quoted a
letter by Lasalle to Marx in 1852: "Party struggles . . . give a party
strength and life. . . . The best proof of the weakness of a party
is its diffuseness and its blurring of clear-cut differences. . . . A
party becomes stronger by purging itself."

The resolution "On Unity" in turn ultimately posed a fundamental dilemma on the question of political change within the
Communist Party. By prohibiting major criticism, by banning factionalism (the right to disagree as a member of a minority), and by
preventing a minority's democratic accession to power by carefully
designated political processes, the Party precluded peaceful debate
of major issues and peaceful political change. The chief political

means available for political change had been factional conflicts, plots, power fights, and other more or less violent means. This would continue to be the case, but now everyone would go underground; a premium had been placed on conspiratorial and covert action. Stakes were high and all involved flirted with, and many were charged with, treason.

The resolution denied the Party the legitimate means of political change that permits peaceful and responsible change, and that provides a party with internal stability. Paradoxically, the resolution prohibited the very political stability and unity that Lenin had hoped to attain when he introduced it. In effect he created his own succession question. But he did more. With this resolution, dictatorship was firmly and fully established within the Communist Party.

A postscript to the trade union question is in order. Immediately following the Congress, the Party, under Lenin's guidance, reopened its attack against the unions. Tsektran was reintroduced. The Party fraction in the metal workers' union (Shlyapnikov's union) was shaken up, the Workers' Opposition members were victimized, an over-all trade union leadership purge was initiated, and the proponents of democratic politics were subjected to some chastening experiences. All this occurred against Tomsky's apparent victory and the promises of non-interference by the Tenth Congress, but this story will be unfolded in Chapter 9.

7 ❧ An Ethic of Work

LENINISM AND CALVINISM

> The mill was made of marble,
> The machines were made out of gold,
> And nobody ever got tired
> And nobody ever got old.
>
> There was no unemployment in heaven
> There was no clatter or boom
> You could hear the most beautiful music
> As you worked at the spindle and loom.
>
> There was no unemployment in heaven
> We worked steady all through the year
> We always had food for the children
> We were never haunted by fear.

The song, an American one sung also in the Soviet Union, captures an important aspect of the Communist conception of work: Men *work* in the good society; they do not escape from work. Rather, they are free from its drudgery, its "clatter and boom," and they are free from the fear of unemployment and hunger. These concepts are found in the writings of Marx and Lenin, and their ideas, like the song, reflect a spirit of hope but also an element of reservation. Marx and Lenin could conceive of a society without hunger, but neither could conceive of one without work.

Work was, and is, conceived in ethical and millenarian terms in the Soviet Union. In their scheme of things there was, and there remains today, little place for work not related to a moral end. Labor was not merely to overcome scarcity or to secure material comfort or pleasure, but rather to secure socially useful, beneficent, and correct acts. It was for the salvation of the individual and society. Work was seen as an integral part of their Communist creed. It was an ethic and a *Weltanschauung* in itself. An ideal society was constructed and viewed in terms of work, and men were motivated in a spiritual way to realize this ideal. Indeed, they had an eschatology of work. The final deliverance of man centered around work. Work involves death, judgment, and the final state of man and of things.

Interestingly, their concept of work cut two ways. It was for liberating man. In this sense work was to be spontaneous, self-conscious, and self-disciplining. It would enable man to realize himself and his freedom. But it was also for rectitude, for the repression and correction of evil, for disciplining social parasites and nonconformists. In both senses work was compulsory. Men had to work. They had no choice. In the former case, discipline and social service (not hunger, avarice, or compulsion) were to drive them; in the case of rectitude, coercion. Significantly, in both respects their concept of work contained a strong repressive character, a strong ascetic flavor.

The moral tenor of their ethic of work can be seen in the words and deeds of Bolshevik rule. As early as May and July 1917 Lenin clearly articulated a stand in favor of obligatory work and a universal labor service in his address to the All-Russian Congress of Peasants and in his essays, *State and Revolution* and *Will the Bolsheviks Retain State Power?* Again in December, in a letter to Dzerzhinsky, he set forth his position on coercion and expressed his approval of conscripted labor.[1]

His righteous appellation, quite similar to St. Paul's, that "he who does not work, neither shall he eat" (taken from Lenin's *State and Revolution*), represents the dimension of work as rectitude. It was out of moral conviction that he sought to punish the bourgeoisie and those who lived from unearned income for what he considered to be immoral and parasitic behavior. He favored such policies not because of the "needs of the moment," but because he believed in their intrinsic worth. He most definitely applied them to the future society.

In regard to legal acts, it was not until July and December 1918, with the promulgation of the First Soviet Constitution[2] and the Labor Code,[8] that obligatory work and universal labor service were clearly established as the official policy of the regime, reflecting desire as well as need.

Articles 3 and 18 of the Constitution expressed a socialist philosophy of work, man's obligation to society, and the use of labor as a socially repressive tool. Article 3 stipulated that "as a means of destroying the parasitic classes of society work is made obligatory for all." Article 18 stated: "The R.S.F.S.R. proclaims that it is the duty of all citizens to work," based on the principle that "he who does not work, neither shall he eat."

Other politically repressive and socially weighted clauses rested on the principle of class dictatorship. Article 9 stated that "the principle object of the constitution . . . consists in the establishment of the dictatorship of . . . the workers . . . with the poorer peasantry, to secure the complete suppression of the bourgeoisie, the abolition of the exploitation of man by man, and the establishment of socialism." Significantly in this regard, the clause on elections heavily weighted the ballot in favor of the proletariat and thus guaranteed the social dictatorship of the workers, who were in a numerical minority. Consistent with this policy, Article 64 limited citizenship to those performing "productive work useful to society" and denied legal rights and access to office to all others. All those living on unearned income or hiring labor for a profit—private traders, merchants and middlemen, monks and priests, former Tsarist policemen, members of the royal family, the insane and criminals—were denied all fundamental political liberties, including the right to vote, the right to run for or be elected to office, and the right of freedom of association.

In December these ideas, along with those on worker welfare and the emancipation of the worker, were incorporated into the Labor Code. It was proclaimed as the basic statute covering all persons gainfully employed and all institutions employing hired labor. The Code stated that work was obligatory for all, and provided for a universal labor service for all able-bodied persons between the ages of sixteen and fifty. It stated that labor was no longer a commodity for purchase, and formally granted the right to work to all able-bodied citizens, including the aged over fifty who were otherwise exempt from the labor service.

The Code predicated the formula "socially useful" as the measure for appraising work performance; stated that no unemployed person had the right to refuse work; set up state-directed recruitment and distribution machinery for the centralized and disciplined allocation of manpower; established a policy of compulsory job transfer and job assignment; required that every worker and employee over sixteen years keep a labor book containing a record of his employment as a means of regulating turnover, ensuring discipline, and distributing scarce rations. It further contained provisions on: wages in money or in kind, piecework, wage scales, the concept of "reasonableness" as a measure of labor productivity, length of the workday, holidays, machinery and procedure for the adjudication of grievances, length of trial periods, and hiring and dismissing of workers. There were also many other provisions covering factory inspections, labor protection, social benefits, unemployment insurance, and sick benefits.

Thus we can see the tie-in between intentions and acts. We can see the moral tone, the messianic behavior, and the coercive and ascetic character of their concept of work. The main point is that it was their concept of work, as well as the break between the Party and labor, which are keys to the origins of the Soviet system. Although there are great differences between Leninism and Calvinism, like Calvin they turned Russia into their own Geneva, but a collectivist one—a city of glass where every individual lived his life under the supervision of the Party, which represented a minority view and did not hesitate to apply police powers to control the public and private lives of its citizens.

The Bolshevik ethic of work was perhaps one of their most important psychological and ideological motivations. It equals in importance Lenin's theory of Party organization and Revolution, which indisputably governed their behavior. It originated in 1917 and operates today to keep their ideology alive. It lies behind their conceptions of "socially useful work," and the "obligation and duty to work," as well as the anti-parasite laws of today. Witness their harsh treatment of persons who do not conform to the patterns of socially desirable behavior, as in the case of the twenty-four-year-old Josef Brodsky, a promising though dissenting poet, who was sentenced in February 1964 to five years of hard labor and exile. They punished a dissenter but the judgment was that he was not performing socially useful work.

Continuity and Change in Concepts of Work

It would be well to compare briefly the Bolshevik view about work with some of the dominant ideas of earlier periods. Only by placing them in an historical context and examining them in terms of continuity and change can we see the full subtlety, the uniqueness, and the implication of their position.

Greeks, Hebrews, and Christians. To the ancient Greeks, work was simply "a curse and nothing else." [4] Their name for it, *ponos,* has the same root as the Latin *poena,* meaning sorrow. From Xenophon and Homer to Plato and Aristotle, they viewed it as a necessary, unavoidable burden best performed by slaves and mechanics. In their eyes it was "travail," the painful price meted out by the gods for the necessities and luxuries of life. It is significant that work not only was interpreted as a necessary and fateful burden but also was built into their religion and given a moral sanction. Little conveys their attitude of despair more effectively than the myths of Ixion and Sisyphus. Ixion, a Greek king, condemned by the gods to be bound to an eternally revolving wheel, symbolizes man's bondage to the machine. Sisyphus was condemned to push a stone that would forever roll back down a hill, paying the price of a job that would never end.

The Hebrews and Christians also saw work as expiation of sin and incorporated it into their religion. The Hebrews, as the "chosen people," had to pay the price of their sin. The early Christians were both pessimistic and wrathful. St. Paul, who anticipates St. Augustine and St. Thomas, and who set the stage for the Christian position until the Reformation, passes the harsh judgment in his second message to the Thessalonians: "if any of you would not work, neither should you eat." [5] This was not an isolated statement. He saw work as a harsh necessity linked with original sin, for the wages of sin were death.

Luther and Calvin. With Martin Luther and John Calvin a breakthrough occurs, and in the case of the latter, a real revolution in attitude. Work is still seen as necessary, but in a new sense. It becomes a "gospel" for salvation. Work alone suffices, and not for the wealth one gains or enjoys but for redemption. With Calvin the break is carried further than with Luther, whose eyes were on the past and who was perhaps more a bridge between old and new. For Calvin, men are driven to work not so much by external pressure and life's necessities as by an internal compulsion—the need for salvation. Sweat and toil have a new value; they help to establish the kingdom of God on earth.

For Calvin of course good works cannot produce salvation, but they do indicate that salvation has been attained. As R. H. Tawney so succinctly put it, for the Calvinist "the world is ordained to show forth the majesty of God, and the duty of a Christian is to live for that end. His task is at once to discipline his individual life and to create a sanctified society." [6] It is a theocratic state, an omnicompetent state, in which he lives. Government is by the religious community claiming a moral commission. Politics is interpreted in a religious manner, and temporal or lay power is used as an instrument of spiritual power, even if the policies are those of a minority. The Church itself is the governing body; the police enforce its mandates. The activity of government is to prescribe the standards of conduct, through legislation, for the realization of the spiritual ideals of redemption and salvation. Citizenship in turn depends on church membership, and the whole system is preserved from corruption and disloyalty by a stringent, all-embracing discipline.

As Tawney points out, the common observation that Calvin assigned the same place to discipline that Luther had given to faith is correct. Discipline was designed to safeguard the sacrament and to enforce a censorship of morals. It thus differed in scope and purpose from the canon law of the Church of Rome. He made Geneva a city in which every household lived its life under the supervision of a spiritual police.

Calvin represented the new urban middle class revolution, which found its success in industry and made a virtue out of economic activity. He underwrote this spirit, transferring the idea of work to a new plane. His image of work was positive and deeply religious. He states: "With labor will no man now support himself. . . . And yet labor is a thing so good and godlike . . . that makes the body hale and strong and cures the sicknesses produced by idleness. . . . In the things of this life, the laborer is most like to God." [7]

Yet Calvin had a deeply ascetic and repressive view of work. He insisted that under no conditions must men lust after the fruit of their labor—wealth and possessions. He approved of St. Paul's judgment: "If a man will not work, neither shall he eat." He insisted that work be used to rectify evil, to lead man to salvation. Duty and discipline were the implements required to achieve salvation. It is his emphasis on rectitude and discipline and his ascetic view of life that mark him off, that open a window into the world of Calvin for us. The element of discipline cannot be minimized. Discipline was the nerves of religion, "a bridle to curb and restrain the refractory who resist the doctrine of Christ." Discipline was the sinew of his religion of work. [8]

What is remarkable is that he held a view of the Christian society that is quite collectivist and strongly resembles Marx's and Lenin's communist society. In *Institutes* Calvin states: "No member [of the Christian body] holds his gifts to himself, or for his private use, but shares them from among his fellow members, nor does he

derive benefit save from those things which proceed from the common profit of the body as a whole. Thus the pious man owes to his
brethren all that it is in his power to give." [9] Tawney points out:
"As both the teaching of Calvin himself, and the practice of some
Calvinist communities, suggest, the social ethics of the heroic age
of Calvinism savored more of a collectivist dictatorship than of in-
dividualism." [10] The tyranny with which he ruled Geneva has been
"reproached by posterity," yet it would have been "regarded by its
champions as a compliment. . . . For the Calvinist church was an
army marching back to Canaan, under orders delivered once and
for all from Sinai, and the aim of its leaders was the conquest of the
Promised Land, not the consolation of stragglers or the encourage-
ment of laggards." [11]

Although Calvin underwrote the commercial activities of the
middle class, he did not do so wholeheartedly. Calvinism, it is true,
had little pity for poverty; in this respect it differs substantially
from the Marxist view, which also did not approve of poverty but
which hoped to eliminate its misery. But if Calvinism, according
to Tawney, "had little pity for poverty, it distrusted wealth, as it
distrusted all influences that distract the aim or relax the fibers of
the soul"; and, "in the first flush of its youthful austerity, it did its
best to make life unbearable for the rich. Before the Paradise of
earthly comfort it hung a flaming brand, waved by the implacable
shades of Moses and Aaron." [12]

Classical Liberalism. Smith, Ricardo, and Malthus were of a
different mind. They gave birth to "perhaps the most influential
and certainly the most despairing dictum in the history of social
comment, the notion that the income of the masses of the people—
all who in one way or another work for a living—could not for very
long rise very far above the minimum level necessary for the survival of the race." [13] The essence of their message was that hard
work would only produce massive privation and great inequality.
A more dismal interpretation of work had yet to be offered. In many
respects it directly negated the messages of Luther and Calvin. And
if the Greeks saw work as a "curse" and as "travail," the Classical
Liberals made Panglosses out of them all.

Fourier and Saint-Simon. It was not until Fourier and Saint-
Simon that a new revolution in attitude occurred. With Fourier
work took on a joyous and pleasant aura for the first time. Fourier
anticipated the Brave New World. He saw great promise in the
machine and human organization. Not only was opulence possible,
but so was happiness. He believed that if private property were
eliminated and if society were reorganized into small communal

entities (*phalanstères*) predicated upon organization, cooperation, and machinery, men would not only enjoy their work but see it as a festival. These were the keys necessary for solving the problems of scarcity and drudgery. It was technocracy. With it the necessities of life would be guaranteed, the hours required for work cut short. Monotony would be minimized, for fast and ready job substitutions were possible. The individual would be able to work at the task he enjoyed and for which he was best endowed. Services would be performed in rotation by everyone; essential and useful work would pay higher than luxury work. All in all, he believed, harmony would reign and different groups, happy and secure, would compete with each other in jobs that were interesting.

Claude Henri de Rouvroy, Comte de Saint-Simon, also contributed to this mystique about the joy of work. Impressed with the machine and optimistic about man's future, Saint-Simon believed that the entire society should be modeled after the factory. Its direction should be placed in the hands of "Les Savants," the experts and managers, the men of learning who would know how to run the factories. These technocrats would bypass conventional politics. Their task would be made easier by a popular religion predicating science and administration as "a reign of virtue." Above all, he believed that society organized along technocratic lines would culminate in the betterment of the masses, in the "amelioration of the moral and physical existence of the most numerous and poorest class." [14]

Karl Marx. If a breakthrough occurred with Calvin and with the technocrats, so did it with Marx. As Hannah Arendt has observed, it was Marx, more than anyone who preceded him, who drove home the idea that "poverty should help men to break the shackles of oppression, because the poor [had] nothing to lose but their chains. . . ." [15] It was also Marx who gave the first glimmer of hope, a reserved one, that the scarcity problem could be overcome, that affluence and individual freedom could be realized, and that poverty was an unnatural condition of man. Work was a cardinal tenet in his system. It was the clue to man's alienation, to class war, and to social justice and man's realization of himself. The burning issue for Marx was a moral one: Why did men fight? How was it possible to explain man's inhumanity to his fellow man, his willingness to turn his fellow man into a commodity? These were the basic questions for Marx, for they described the condition that angered him, the condition that he felt was entirely unnatural to man and society.

Marx's answer lay in a twofold struggle in which man was en-

gaged: man against nature and man against man. Man was at war
with nature because of the scarcity phenomenon. Man had to work
and struggle to live. What he created by bending muscle and using
his brain was the source of all value. Work was the creative force
in the society. Through work men could find themselves and their
happiness; they could build a better world and realize civilization.
Yet the scarcity principle remained. Man's environment was not
easily mastered; land and supply was limited but demand was not
—thus was man's political problem structured. A man would kill his
neighbor, his brother, his father for a piece of bread. To stay alive
he would reduce himself or his fellow man to an object, a thing.
Out of this struggle of man against nature one could find the source
of change, the history of man's inhumanity to his fellow man, of his
own alienation, and of the class war.

The division of labor represented, in Marx's eyes, man's elemental response to the problem of scarcity. By dividing functions
he took a positive step in the direction of licking the problems of
need and want. He was one step closer to solving the scarcity problem. But at the same time the division of labor had negative results:
It left man a prisoner of one specific function and he thus became
alienated from himself, his fellow man, and society. It also resulted
in the emergence of private property and economic inequality, for
the fact that some functions were of more value than others led to
the introduction of a system of commodity exchange. This led to
unequal wealth, to a short-circuiting of the social condition of
equality as well as the entire social process itself. Man, dominated
by a scarcity psychology, hoarded goods to protect himself against
lean years; land was enclosed; and human hands were hired out
for work. This finally culminated in the class struggle: the conflict
between the "haves" and the "have nots" over ownership of property and the means of production, and a solution of the scarcity
phenomena. It was a conflict over necessity and it permitted no
compromise or reconciliation.

He also saw in the functions of labor the key which would enable man to open the door to social peace and plenty for all. He
was further convinced that the problems of man against nature and
man against man, of scarcity, class war, and alienation could only
be solved in a society which was industrial and communist. Only
when society had been thus transformed could man's alienation
from himself, from other men, and from society be eliminated; only
then could man truly realize himself.

Marx, however, was not as optimistic as Fourier. Marx was
caught in a vise between Ricardo's iron law of wages and the in-

creasing awareness that the industrial revolution could provide affluence for all. Marx was optimistic, and increasingly so, but he could not go as far as Fourier. Neither he nor Engels could envision men running to work as to a festival. As he said in the manuscripts of 1857–1858, written in preparation for *Capital*, "Work cannot become play, as Fourier wants it to." The liberation of work from the fetters of exploitation "does not signify that such work becomes simply play, simply amusement, simply pleasure, as Fourier thinks, with the extreme naiveté of a Parisian grisette. Really free work, the work of a composer, for example, is damned serious work, intense strain." [16]

Engels takes a similar stand. In an 1874 essay entitled "On Authority," he states: "All . . . workers . . . are obliged to begin and finish their work at the hours fixed by the authority of the system which cares nothing for individual autonomy. . . . Wanting to abolish authority in large-scale industry is tantamount to wanting to abolish industry itself, to destroy the power loom in order to return to the spinning wheel." He further noted that a certain authority, no matter how delegated, was imposed with "the material conditions under which we produce and make products circulate." [17] Thus he too was unable to conceive of work as play, though he, like Marx, definitely believed that under a communist arrangement of work much of its travail could be lifted.

There is another and quite optimistic side to Marx. It is best known in his position spelled out in *The German Ideology*. He states:

> While in communist society, where nobody has one exclusive sphere of activity but each can become accomplished in any branch he wishes, society regulates the general production and thus makes it possible for me to do one thing today and another tomorrow, to hunt in the morning, fish in the afternoon, rear cattle in the evening, criticize after dinner, just as I have a mind, without ever becoming hunter, fisherman, shepherd, or critic.[18]

In *The German Ideology* Marx does not see work as pleasant in a communist society, but he does indicate that it need not be so frustrating and unpleasant that it will not be fun to do. In all probability the views he sets forth in *The German Ideology*, rather than his parenthetical comment, represent his most carefully worked out position on the question and the view he was most inclined to be satisfied with. While he was ambivalent on the pain of work, he most certainly believed that it could be made more humane.

Lenin. With Lenin we have a synthesizer. We can see the break with the ancient idea of work as necessity and the Classical Liberal idea of hovering poverty. Yet we can also see the incorporation and blending together of technocratic, Marxist, and Calvinist strains of thought. Indeed, in a very profound way, Lenin, in his interpretation of work, is closer to Calvin than he is to Marx.

The Marxist in Lenin is obvious; the connection need not be belabored. Lenin's ideological frame of reference was Marxist, though he combined in his own philosophy many dominant themes from the ideas of Chernishevsky, Nechaev, and Tkachev as well. He was as much a Russian as a Marxist, if not more so, but clearly he accepted a Marxist scarcity and class war analysis; he saw work as the key to man's liberation from bondage to nature, to the machine, and to his fellow man. Work was the mechanism for creation, value, and the realization of social freedom. This structured his whole approach to an orientation and theory of society.

His embracement of technocracy was complete. It affirms the Marxist in him, but very much links him to Proudhon and Saint-Simon. His whole approach to organizing a socialist and communist society is along technocratic lines. In *State and Revolution* he said: "Accounting and control—these are the chief things necessary for the organizing and correct functioning of the first phase of Communist society." He states further: "All citizens become employees and workers of one national state 'syndicate.'" To Lenin it seemed easy: "all that is required is that they should work equally, should regularly do their share of work, and should receive equal pay." Then he tells us: "The whole of society will have become one office and one factory, with equal work and equal pay." [19] On the other hand, Lenin affirmed the "subordination of the whole of the work of this syndicate to the . . . state of the Soviets. . . ." [20]

Then, too, Lenin saw work in the traditional communist sense. It is performed voluntarily, not for reward but out of habit and as a social obligation for the good of all. In "From the Destruction of the Ancient Social System to the Creation of the New," April 8, 1920, he excitedly set forth his views in one of his most pronounced though not grammatical statements:

> Labor performed gratis for the benefit of society, labor performed, not as a definite duty, not for the purpose of obtaining a right to certain products, not according to previously established and legally fixed rates, but voluntary labor, irrespective of rates, labor performed without expectation of reward, without the condition of reward, labor performed out of a habit of working for the common good, and

out of a conscious realization (become habit) of the necessity of working for the common good—labor is the requirement of a healthy body.[21]

Somewhat more than Marx, Lenin believed the problem of scarcity could be overcome. A communist society was all that was necessary to realize affluence. For example, in "How to Organize Competition" he stated: "there is enough bread, iron, timber, wool, cotton and flax in Russia to satisfy the needs of all, if only labor and its products are properly distributed. . . ."[22] Indeed, there are further statements expressing his optimism. In respect to these points on work, value and technocracy, Lenin is close to Marx. Yet, in spite of his strong Marxist tradition and outlook, Lenin is closer to Calvin than to Marx, in terms of both his outlook and his role in history.

All three—Marx, Lenin, and Calvin—have several things in common, but work is the chief common denominator. It takes on an apocalyptic role, a revelation not only of the final state of things but also of the means for securing that end. For each of these men, life is interpreted in terms of work. Work is a doctrine of salvation, decisive for justice and right. While Marx remains a theorist, Calvin and Lenin actually set up a "theocracy," an omnicompetent state, though there are differences between them and the theocracies they created.

When one sees the emphasis Lenin assigned to discipline, asceticism, and rectitude, a dimension of ideological similarity with Calvin becomes evident. His strong penchant for these attributes, no less than his belief in activism and organization, places him in the same position as Calvin. Lenin urged their adoption as tactics, assigning them the same order of importance and functional role as did Calvin. Like Calvin he believed them necessary for strength against the chaos of his time. But they were not mere tactics; they were qualities that would lay the foundation for a "reign of virtue," both personal and public.

In his personal life Lenin believed in work and discipline. He himself worked hard and lived simply and plainly. His furnishings, when in exile and in Petrograd and Moscow, were incredibly plain, bordering on the monastic. He had tremendous power of self-discipline, as the history of the crises he faced and overrode testifies. In personal affairs he maintained an ironclad silence about his innermost thoughts and feelings that is rare among men. His tastes and habits were austere, his view of life clearly ascetic. Berdyaev has observed: "Lenin did not believe in man . . . but he had a boundless faith in the social regimentation of man. He believed that a compulsory social organization could create any sort of new man. . . ." [23]

Much like Calvin, Lenin saw work as a double-edged sword. It was essential for liberating man. In this sense labor was to produce a self-conscious and self-disciplining man. It was to enable man to realize his freedom or his call in life. But labor was performed, on this level, out of a sense of obligation and for socially useful and beneficial acts. It was a product of an inner drive and compulsion, not a result of motivation for individual pleasure.

It was also essential for penance, for correcting and repressing evil, for disciplining nonconformists. In this sense, labor was conceived in a coercive vein as a repressive force applied externally and perhaps from above.

What is important, though, is that in both senses work was seen by both men as compulsory. Men had to work. They had no choice. On the first level, both men saw discipline and social service as the force that drove man; on the second, rectitude and coercion that checked him. In both respects, the two men held a concept of work which contained dominant repressive and ascetic strains.

Lenin was the first of the Marxists, and perhaps the last, to reintroduce the concept of coercion into the Marxist lexicon of work. As indicated above, he did this immediately following his arrival at the Petrograd Station, before he donned the mantle of responsibility. As early as May he committed himself to a system of obligatory work and universal labor service. He reiterated his position in July, and he did so again in his revelational pamphlet *State and Revolution* and his searching tract, *Will the Bolsheviks Retain State Power?* Before and after the seizure of power he wrote "he who does not work, neither shall he eat."

Of utmost importance was the fact that Lenin extended his concept of repression and rectitude into the future society. It was to be a permanent condition, not a temporary one for him. It was not unnatural to man, but essential for man's condition to realize civilization.

In *State and Revolution,* in the passage where he deals with crime and excesses, he stated: "We are not Utopians, and we do not in the least deny the possibility and inevitability of excess on the part of individual persons, nor the need to suppress such excesses." [24] Yet, on the same page, he indicated that he considered *most but not all* crime to be due to hunger and poverty. Thus he denied and affirmed the orthodox Marxist argument that environment was the source of crime. The point is that he operated from an additional but unspecified premise. It is difficult to say what it was, perhaps it was man's ego, or pride, or a third factor. But he was moving dangerously close to a Freudian ego or Christian concept of original sin. The major point, however, is that he was not very far from Calvin in projecting punishment into his Good Society, into a communist system. In defense of Lenin, he did not believe it would be necessary to coerce or punish most men in the future society, but he certainly did believe in rectitude and discipline in the communist future.

This point warrants serious consideration. Before examining the issue of punishment in the future society, a comment is required about the relevancy of *State and Revolution*. Three criticisms are frequently leveled against this pamphlet to reduce it to the position of "exceptionalism" in Bolshevik thought: (1) it was written in the late summer of 1917 as a propaganda document to incite people to rebellion; [25] (2) as Daniel Bell states: "Lenin simply did not have any notion of the meaning or specific content of socialism when he was forced to confront the issue in 1917"; [26] (3) it is an aberration in light of the policies introduced just six months after Lenin came to power, and hence cannot be taken seriously.

In my opinion, while these judgments are correct, a blueprint is not set forth; they all overlook the crucial point. The value of the document is clearly in its millenarian content, which transcends any propaganda objective or any compromise with circumstance. More important, the concepts of obligatory labor and labor mobilization, spelled out in *State and Revolution*, all have been introduced and have remained cornerstones of Soviet labor policy. Thus, it is of value for its apocalyptic and revelational nature and because it laid the basis for Soviet labor policy. The above statement from *State and Revolution* and those that follow must either be dismissed as aberrations or accepted as indications of his instinctive position on the matter. In my mind there is too much evidence to indicate that it was merely a passing remark slipped by a harried man in a hurry to make history.

In "How to Organize Competition," he said:

> Not a single rogue (including those who shirk their work) [is] to be at liberty, all are to be kept in prison or put to compulsory labor of the hardest kind. . . . In one place half a score of rich, a dozen rogues, half a dozen workers who shirk their work . . . will be put in prison. In another place they will be put to cleaning latrines. In a third place they will be provided with "yellow tickets" after they have served their time, so that all the people shall have these pernicious people under their surveillance until they reform.

In a fourth place one out of every two idlers will be shot on the spot.[27]

Lenin's advocacy of terror and compulsory labor might be explained in terms of the exigencies of the moment, the need to win a war and consolidate power, but the element of repression was also evident in his statement about work in the future society. In "A Great Beginning," he states:

> In the future everyone who calls his enterprise, institution or undertaking a commune without having set an example of real Communist organization achieved as a result of arduous toil and practical success in prolonged effort, shall be made a laughing stock and mercilessly pilloried as a charlatan or windbag.[28]

In discussing preparation for the higher phase of communism, Lenin, in State and Revolution, stated:

> For when all have learned to manage, . . . then the escape [sic!] from this national accounting and control will inevitably become so increasingly difficult, such a rare exception, and will probably be accompanied by such swift and severe punishment . . . that soon the necessity of observing the simple, fundamental rules of everyday social life in common will have become a habit.[29] [Emphasis added—J.B.S.]

Apparently coercion would remain as a permanent condition in the future society. It appeared to be natural to man's human condition and intrinsically worthwhile. There are a number of points from which comparisons between Lenin, Marx, and Calvin might be drawn at this point. A decisive one, however, is that there was a break between Lenin and Marx. It is doubtful that Marx believed that punishment would be at all necessary (or at all evident) in the future communist society, particularly in regard to work. Indeed, Marx disapproved of compulsion. For Marx, work was a creative, liberating force, though not necessarily play; self-discipline, yes, but not rectitude and force. It is this concept of compulsion and punishment (to say nothing of asceticism and repression) that separates Lenin from Marx and places Lenin closer to Calvin.

Although obvious differences exist, the comparison may be pushed further. The Bolsheviks played a role similar to that of the Calvinists. They were a "band of prophets," a "status group"—men cut off from the mainstream of society by their way of life, their values and Zeitgeist, by their concept of society. Yet they were determined not merely to protect their interests but to build a society in the image of their own preconceived views and values. They were radicals, angry, morally indignant men who were committed to the justness of their cause. To use Tawney's words regarding the Calvinists, they brought "not peace but a sword" and a path strewn with revolution.

Like the Calvinists and the Puritans, if not the ancient Jewish Prophets of Doom, they operated in a period of great social and economic upheaval. Like these other groups they responded to the deep change with a political answer. They seized reality and molded it in the image of their social ethic. As politicians of a transition era they strove to secure peace, justice, and security, but not at any price, or for social integration itself. Without hesitation they sacrificed peace, social integration, and liberty in order to secure their view of social justice. It was not inevitable that they resorted to dictatorship and it was not merely their tactics that led them along the path of despotism. It was their social ethic that denied man his liberty and dignity, their fathomless faith that social regimentation and compulsory organization could secure justice and redemption.

THE DESPOTISM OF DISCIPLINE AND TECHNOCRACY

The Bolsheviks were caught on the horns of an output-discipline dilemma. In their eyes, both were necessary to stave off collapse and ensure the realization of the new society; but both raised major political, economic, and ideological problems which were crucial to the success of the regime. It is this output-discipline quandary that has been selected as the basis for further discussion of the problems of a work ethic, social change, and political despotism.

Problems of Labor Discipline, Management, and Productivity

Lenin had been acutely aware of the productivity problem from the beginning. In his early works he emphasized the importance of raising production. In *The Soviets at Work* he said:

> In every socialist revolution—after the proletariat has solved the problem of winning power . . . it becomes necessary to turn first of all to the fundamental problem . . . namely to raise the productivity of labor, and in connection with this, to improve its organization. . . . And here it is at once clear that although it is possible to seize state power in a few days . . . a sound solution of the problem of raising productivity requires at least . . . several years.[30]

Later, in his famous pamphlet on "Communist Saturdays" he maintained that "the productivity of labor is in the last resort the most important, the chief factor in the victory of the new social order." [81]

In many respects the problem of worker performance—of labor output and discipline—imposed one of the most serious limitations on Bolshevik power in this early period. Time and again the Bolsheviks failed to realize their goals. This was in part a reflection of the great economic and social dislocation accompanying World War I, the Revolution, and the civil war. But it was also partly due to the fact that the worker did not support the regime and was not doing his all for it.

Bolshevik policy during these periods smacked of expediency; the Party bowed to necessity. But if one looks at the over-all picture, it is clear they built an element of reality in the image of their ideals. Labor policy was consistent with their precepts of obligatory labor and discipline. The harsh measures mark, in fact, an extension of their concepts of discipline and duty.

Discipline. The discipline problem in its practical form was best stated by Shmidt (then a member of the A.R.C.C.T.U.) at the Second Congress of Commissars in May 1918. He said that the workers, imbued with the idea that the Revolution had liberated them from the evils of capitalism, were very sensitive about discipline and resisted anything smacking of coercion or authoritarianism. As of the moment, he said, no effective form of discipline had been introduced, and such measures were necessary. He acknowledged that trade unions realized their responsibility and were attempting to develop a form of discipline which would rest on comradely persuasion and self-discipline. Under a system of voluntary discipline the workers would feel free from the odious notion that compulsion and repression were being forced on them from above. Realizing that persuasion might not work, Shmidt agreed that dismissal or expulsion should hang—like a Damoclean sword—over the workers' heads as the ultimate threat. [82]

In conformity with this policy, on April 3, 1918, the A.R.C.C.T.U. announced that the trade unions would assume responsibility for enforcing discipline and would play a vital role in developing a new form of labor discipline. It commanded trade unions to "create the indispensable foundation of discipline" and to raise productivity by creating a commission in each trade union to fix norms of productivity for every trade and worker category. They were to use piece rates, pay "bonuses" for productivity above established norms, dismiss violators, and expel from the union workers who refused to submit. [83]

A negative side effect of this policy for the unions and the Party was that, although it marked a bold new attempt to create a system of self-imposed discipline, it made the workers' representative organs responsible for all discipline. Thus the sting and stigma of coercion were passed on to them!

Discipline From Above. The unions failed to secure the sought improvement in worker discipline; the Bolsheviks did not get the cooperation they expected or required. It was therefore not surprising that in a short time the Bolsheviks began to impose discipline from above and to base it on force and heavy penalties.

By 1919–1920 disciplinary measures were introduced to combat absenteeism, tardiness, theft, labor turnover and desertion; they were administered jointly by the union and management and reached a most stringent form. By a decree of June 12, 1919, disciplinary measures were said to be in order if the worker had not put in a full six to eight hours, nor worked diligently and productively. In this decree tardiness meant arriving five minutes after starting time, and absence, fifteen minutes after. The penalty for absenteeism without an adequate reason was the forfeiture of a day's wages. A worker who was late or absent three times in a month was, if the union consented, to be dismissed.[84]

In 1920 a decree issued by the Council of People's Commissars spelled out additional measures to be applied to combat absenteeism, one of the most frequently used forms of expressing discontent. Thirty-two types of illness were listed as the only grounds for sick leave. Penalties for absenteeism were listed and ranged from a wage forfeiture and deductions from bonuses to making up lost time. The most stringent aspects of the decree were contained in clauses stating that noncompliance with disciplinary judgments was punishable by confinement in a labor correction camp, and that absenteeism over three days was to be considered sabotage and subject to court proceedings.[85] Thus the bold step was taken.

In 1920 the problem of discipline was as severe as ever, and the coercive methods as repressive. At this time the concept of "desertion" was broadened and made to apply in cases of noncompliance with registration decrees, concealment of trade or professional experience if the trade or profession were subject to labor mobilization, absenteeism without justifiable reason, possession of false documents, holding of fictitious jobs to avoid work or conscription, or any other form of noncompliance with the labor draft.[86]

Still, throughout the civil war the Party leaders (although relying heavily upon repression) attempted to develop a system of voluntary discipline, imposed by the workers and meant to be free from the onus of police measures imposed from above.

Comradely Court—Voluntary Discipline. A major step in this direction was the creation on November 14, 1919, of the "comradely court." These courts, attached to all trade union organizations on every level in each enterprise, had the authority to deal with all cases of noncompliance and infringements of wage agreements or labor regulations. Composed principally of workers, they sat after work hours. They were delegated authority to censure by public reprimand or to deny the privilege to vote or run for office for six months. They could demote a worker to a lower job slot and reduce his pay for one month. They could also apply the ultimate penalties of dismissal and sending serious offenders to labor camps. The comradely courts did not, however, have jurisdiction over criminal cases.[37]

What was noteworthy about the courts was the attempt to develop a sense of morality at the primary level, but the result came closer to a system of vigilante justice than to democracy. No legal procedures or system of due process were introduced either to protect the accused or to help the court. This in part reflected Bolshevik hostility to formal law; in part, confusion. "Work place" attitudes prevailed; the penalties that could be and were applied smacked more of mob action and party intolerance than of giving each man his day in court or presuming him to be innocent until proven guilty. In *State and Revolution* Lenin revealed a strong element of vigilantism in his interpretation of justice. In considering the prospects of the commission of a crime under Communism—which was probably inconceivable to Marx—Lenin states that since there will be "no special machinery, no special apparatus of repression," like the courts, action "will be done by the armed people itself, as simply and as readily as any crowd of civilized people . . . parts a pair of combatants or does not allow a woman to be outraged." An armed mob replacing a legal procedure is an interesting reflection on the fundamentals of justice and individual rights. Could Lenin possibly have understood the meaning of democracy, which he so firmly declared himself to favor?

The comradely court system did not work. It produced little or no tangible improvement in worker discipline. Why is hard to say, but they were gradually by-passed. Significantly, however, the idea remained alive and a similar system was introduced on a broader basis by Khrushchev during the fifties, as he attempted to develop a Communist system of justice. It is still in use today on a

very wide basis and smacks as much of vigilante justice as it did
in the early post-Revolutionary period.

Communist Saturdays. Perhaps the most interesting attempt
of the period to achieve voluntary labor discipline was that of the
Communist Saturday. Starting on the Moscow-Kazan railway, where
the Communist section volunteered to work a free Saturday in order
to transport troops to the Kolchak front, the movement quickly
spread throughout Moscow and Petrograd and lasted into 1920.
Lenin was enthralled and waxed ecstatic about it as a new concept
of labor, as "communist labor" performed as a social duty without
any compulsion, "as the new socialist discipline." [88] In "A Great
Beginning" he had these words of praise for the movement:

> The unskilled laborers and railway workers of Moscow . . . are
> toilers who are living in desperately hard conditions. They are con-
> stantly underfed. . . . And yet these starving workers . . . orga-
> nize Communist Subbotniks, work overtime without any pay and
> achieve an enormous increase in productivity, in spite of the fact
> that they are weary, tormented, exhausted. . . . Is this not mag-
> nificent heroism? Is this not the beginning of a change of world
> historical significance?
>
> Communism begins when the rank-and-file workers begin to
> display self-sacrificing concern . . . for husbanding every pood of
> grain, coal, iron and other products which do not accrue to the work-
> ers personally or to their "close kith and kin," but to their remote
> "kith and kin," i.e., to society as a whole, to tens and hundreds of
> millions of people organized in a single Socialist state and then a
> Union of Soviet Republics.
>
> Objections to participation in Subbotniks could be considered
> as . . . counterrevolutionary agitation of the bourgeoisie, the Men-
> sheviks, the Social Revolutionaries.[39]

The Party began a drive to organize Saturday work, expand it,
and make it a permanent movement. In July the Central Committee published rules and instructions on the aims and organization
of voluntary work.[40] In addition, the Central Committee issued an
order to all Party organizations commanding them to concentrate
effort on Saturday work.

With this directive a major drive was launched, completely organized and ultimately disastrous. Once the Communist Saturday
became official, pressure was put on the worker to volunteer. He
was threatened with the possibility of being reported to his trade
union for lack of loyalty and conscientiousness. Once the element
of coercion was interjected he "volunteered" out of fear. Furthermore, in a relatively short period of time the campaign took on the

undesirable feature of a drive for unpaid overtime. Under these conditions the program slowly fell apart. What had been spontaneous and voluntary became directed, obligatory, and coerced. What the Party had hoped to nurture, it had destroyed.

Labor Mobilization. On the whole, experiments in voluntary discipline failed. As they did the Party leaders turned more and more to labor mobilization measures to gain their objectives. The measures reflected objective need, but they were underwritten by ideological prescription. The mixture of ideology and circumstance produced a bitter child. In the winter of 1918 the military situation deteriorated badly. In February the Bolsheviks issued the "fatherland is in danger" appeal and introduced measures establishing centralized control of the distribution of food and labor.[41] In March, at the Seventh Party Congress, "draconian measures to contain the crisis" were held to be necessary.[42] Between January and April, to facilitate the state allocation of the labor force, factories were ordered to keep work records. Also, during these months the number of labor exchanges, created as early as January to control mobility, jumped from 50 to 320. By December they were handling half a million unemployed workers.[43]

By May 1918 the Bolsheviks had lost the Don basin coal region, the food belt of the Ukraine, and a substantial share of the iron and steel industry.[44] As the situation worsened the measures grew increasingly harsh. In September, the month in which a state of siege was declared, the unemployed were denied the right to refuse work or appeal compulsory job transfers. They were later warned that the refusal of a job assignment was punishable by three months' deprivation of benefits and relegation to the end of the employment lists; that violation of a job transfer would result in criminal prosecution under the charge of desertion.[45] In October, labor books were declared obligatory for nonworking persons. The books were to replace passports, serve as identity cards, and entitle an individual to rations. They contained data on socially useful work performed. Violations were punishable by a fine of 10,000 rubles and six months' imprisonment.[46]

In November 1918, in response to the September state of siege proclamation, the Executive Committee of the Soviets created the Council of Defense. This Council was granted emergency powers and authorized to mobilize all forces and resources and to adopt all measures necessary for the defense of the country.

Consistent with its orders, the Defense Council conscripted personnel, froze employees to their jobs, and subjected them to military law. Although the Commissariat of Labor stated in December that drafted labor was not a form of punishment and that work conditions would be consistent with regulations, the coercive features of this labor policy were obvious.[47]

The labor exchange boards worked with the Defense Council to secure the state allocation of the labor force during these crucial years. The boards registering the workers had the authority to regulate recruitment and allocation by assigning, transferring, and freezing men to jobs. As the emergency increased and as the need for the controlled flow of manpower became crucial, the boards received more and more discretionary powers.

The single qualification limiting the labor boards' power was a clause which gave them authority to act only in cases of urgent public need and for the allocation of manpower to high priority works. The boards were not authorized to act as independent agencies with a free hand. Before they could assign, transfer, or freeze a worker to a job they had to consult the unions, obtain their consent and have the Commissariat of Labor's approval. However, in terms of the rights of the individual, the power of the registration boards in assigning him to work was unlimited. Neither the approval nor the consent of the individual was required for the board to assign him. Only in the case of a job transfer did the individual have the right to appeal the decision of the registration board. The right to appeal, however, did not apply in instances of urgent public need. Nor did it apply when an entire group was transferred from one organization to another or to a new area. For all ostensible purposes the board's authority over the worker was absolute and final.[48]

From September 1918 to March 1920 mobilization decrees followed one after the other. In October 1918 one decree had introduced labor books, another mobilized men between eighteen and forty-five years for snow clearance on railroads, and still another denied all workers the right to resign without permission.[49] On November 5, 1918, the unemployed were forbidden to refuse work. On November 28 the entire railroad network was mobilized by the Defense Council. On December 11, people living on unearned income were conscripted for socially useful work. On December 19, technicians with academic training and all technical students were ordered to register for a labor draft; on December 20 the order was extended to medical personnel not already employed by the state.[50]

In March 1919, personnel employed on river and ocean transport fleets were conscripted. On April 7 the coal miners were mobilized, placed under military law, and ordered to remain at their work under penalty of prosecution by "revolutionary courts for noncompliance." [51] On April 15 the forced labor camps created under the jurisdiction of the Cheka were ordered to put their captive labor force to work.[52] On May 5, post and telegraph workers were mobilized. On June 26 all those employed in the military supply department, regardless of sex, were mobilized and ordered to remain at their places of work.[53]

On April 12, employees of Soviet institutions were frozen in their jobs in an attempt to curtail labor turnover. They were denied the right to change positions without the consent of their employer on the penalty of a six-month employment ban in Soviet institutions, and on pain of imprisonment or fine for any person engaging them.[54]

On June 25, 1919, the use and requirement of labor books, formerly confined to workers, was extended to all citizens sixteen years and over in Moscow and Petrograd. All citizens in these cities were to possess labor books, which were to be used as identity cards and to entitle them to a ration card and social insurance.[55] This decree cut two ways. On the one hand, it extended the requirement of labor books to many formerly not covered; on the other, it made the labor book an almost universal fact of life since all men from sixteen to fifty, in order to be entitled to rations, were required to carry one. Thus, while all were required to submit to a new restriction, it was at least less discriminatory than before. Although the labor book sharply restricted liberty, paradoxically, as Carr points out, it became a leveler in Soviet society by creating equality between workers and former members of the bourgeoisie.

Between June 1919 and January 1920, when labor armies were created for the first time, the mobilization orders were extended to cover those employed in the timber, coal, oil, and peat industries. In November 1919 and January 1920 the conscription measures were extended to those employees by the railways and the fuel, transport, food, metal works and electrical industries, thus covering almost every field of endeavor and making conscription a near-universal characteristic of Soviet life.[56]

Finally, as the manpower situation reached its crucial point at the end of 1919, protective legislation covering the workday, child labor, and women was waived. On June 3, youths between the ages of fourteen and sixteen years, many of whom were already working illegally, were permitted by the Commissariat of Labor to continue in their jobs, thus legalizing their activity.[57] The only restriction imposed was that these youngsters were forbidden to work in the mines. On October 4 the Commissariat issued a decree permitting women to be hired for night work, though it added the provision that this was only a temporary measure.[58] Finally, on October 23, the Commissariat bowed; overtime was permitted and the appropriate agencies were allowed to introduce the twelve-hour day.[59]

Labor Armies. The creation of labor armies represented the maximum thrust in the direction of a system of enforced discipline. On January 15, 1920, at the moment when Denikin and Kolchak had been defeated and the pressing emergency of the war had been brought to a close, the first labor army was created. The Third Army Corps, operating in the Urals, was assigned temporarily to civilian work. It was called the First Revolutionary Labor Army Corps. It was to be used for procurement of food and forage, transport of timber, and repair of agricultural machinery, agricultural work, and so forth. The Revolutionary Council of the Labor Army Corps was authorized to supervise the work. The Council had jurisdiction over all economic organization in the area. The trade unions were not represented on the Council; rather, it was composed of members of the Revolutionary Military Council, the Commissariats of Food, Agriculture, Transport, and Labor, the NKVD, and the Supreme Council of the National Economy. A representative of the Council of Labor and Defense was chairman.[60]

On January 21 a Ukrainian Soviet Labor Army was created in the area of the Southwest front to enforce labor discipline and to procure food, fuel, and raw materials.[61] Between April and August 1920 the policy was extended to cover civilians employed in water transport, mining, fisheries, and metal industries. All men employed in these industries were conscripted and ordered to stay on the job.[62] With these steps the policy of using conscripted labor, both civilian and military, for the performance of socially necessary work both in wartime and in peacetime, had been carried to its logical conclusion.

There is no doubt that the Bolsheviks bowed deeply to objective need during this period. Yet, at the close of the civil war, a policy of militarized labor was described by the Central Committee as the basis for effecting reconstruction. The Central Committee contended that the deteriorating conditions justified compulsion because a planned supply of labor was necessary. It stated that in the prevailing situation of high labor desertion, absenteeism, and neglect of duties, any means available was justifiable if it eliminated these evils because labor discipline and productivity were now a life and death issue before the nation. The industrial proletariat had to be mobilized; recruitment had to be intensified; the unskilled had to be trained. Labor books were to be introduced for all, as was a general labor service. A socialist organization of labor without compulsory measures, particularly in regard to parasites and peasants, was impossible under the existing conditions. Compulsion could not be eliminated prior to the creation of a highly educated and motivated labor force and a well-developed economy. Until then, compulsion and the militarization of the labor force were necessary; the experience acquired in the administration of the army was to be applied to the labor field; the work to be done and the supply of labor available had to be coordinated in a planned manner.[63]

The entire policy of the militarization of labor, justified politically by objective necessity, suggested the concepts of obligatory labor and socially useful work predicated in earlier ideological statements. In many respects the postulation of this policy can be viewed as the extension of these earlier concepts to their logical conclusion. Leon Trotsky became the archdefender of this policy. It was he who extended the idea of the obligation of labor to a policy which justified compulsory labor. Among the factors and ideas which led him inexorably along this hard, uncompromising path were: the failure of the world revolution to materialize; the imminence of collapse; the fact the Soviets were "face to face with a very difficult period, perhaps the most difficult period of all"; and his view that a "dictatorship is a dictatorship" and "to difficult periods . . . harsh measures correspond." [64]

Trotsky argued, in effect, that the new socialist order rejected the capitalist principle of "free labor," which in essence meant freedom to exploit or to be exploited. Rather, the new order recognized the universal obligation to work as the basic principle of the socialist economy. The workers' state needed labor and had the right to demand it from every citizen.[65] Elaborating further, he said: "the labor state considers itself empowered to send every worker to the place where his work is necessary; and not one serious socialist will begin to deny to the Labor State the right to lay its hand upon the worker who refuses to execute his labor duty." [66]

Trotsky tried to justify his argument on ideological grounds, on the hard facts of life and the necessity of work: "Man must work in order not to die" and "man is lazy and does not want to work, but the social organization compels him." Conscious of the similarity between his position and non-Marxist views, he asserted that the difference between bourgeois labor and socialist labor was that the latter was performed in the interests of society. He argued that they were "now heading towards the type of labor that is socially regulated on the basis of an economic plan, obligatory for the whole country, and compulsory for every worker. This is the basis of socialism," he said, and the militarization of labor is "the indispensable, basic method for the organization of our labor force." [67]

The Third Trade Union Congress. This argument was challenged at the Third Trade Union Congress. Most Party-unionists vehemently opposed Trotsky, but since the Central Committee had endorsed his policy, they listened with ambivalent feelings or with lips forced shut by Party discipline. It fell to the Mensheviks to take up the cudgel of opposition at this Congress. Endearing themselves less than ever to Lenin and the Bolsheviks, the Mensheviks Dan and Abramovich forced the Bolsheviks to publicly debate the implications of their own policies.

Abramovich, in a heated exchange, took up Trotsky's argument on compulsory labor, charging him with a travesty of justice and a fundamental distortion of Marxist ideas. Trotsky, he said, had substituted a formal juridical concept of work for a social one and was reducing to absurdity important distinctions about the compulsion to work and legal freedom. Abramovich added that under capitalism the worker might be forced to work in order to live, but he was not a serf or slave, not bound or owned, but legally and politically free.[68] Trotsky was making a great error if he believed compulsory labor could be productive or that socialism could be built upon it. Abramovich testily pointed out Marx's argument that work would be humanized under socialism. The worker would be free and highly productive; it could not be otherwise. He taunted Trotsky with the remark: "You cannot build a planned economy in the way the Pharaohs built their pyramids." [69] Finally he pleaded: Reject a policy of compulsory labor.

Trotsky, with the wisdom of a Polonius, dismissed the Menshevik argument that forced labor was unproductive. All labor was compulsory, for man did not want to work but was forced to by society and by the basic necessity to live. He further argued that "free labor" was mythical. The world had only known various forms of compulsory labor: slavery; serf labor; the compulsory labor of the craft guilds; and bourgeois labor regulated by hunger, supply and demand, and the compulsion of the employer. He argued that, in the future, labor would be directed by an economic plan for the benefit of the society.[70]

Trotsky further rejected the contention that his policy was dictatorial. He asserted—as did Zinoviev—that the workers were not surrendering or losing power but merely delegating it. His justification was the essence of Leninist policy. He said: "control . . . remains in the hands of the working class, in the person of the Communist Party." [71]

At the time, Trotsky's policy had Lenin's full approval. As I. Deutscher has so devastatingly pointed out, this position on the philosophy of labor represented a radical revision of previous Marxist interpretations. Although Trotsky did not show any sign of being reached by Abramovich's argument at the Congress, or for a long time thereafter, Abramovich had scored. As Deutscher also points out, it was this very argument that Trotsky used against Stalin a decade later.[72]

Thus, with Trotsky's defense of labor armies and the Central Committee's endorsement, the policy of obligatory labor and discipline had been carried to its logical conclusion. An ethic of work had been used to justify coerced labor. It was to be supplemented in the 1930s with even harsher applications by Stalin. But ideologically the Party had gone as far as it could.

Yet the measure did not work. Neither the Party-led unions nor the workers responded positively to it. More important, it did not lead to an increase in discipline. To the contrary, it had a negative effect on output and the policy had to be abandoned. Thus, at the end of War Communism the Party had failed. It had failed not to devise new approaches to the problem of discipline, but to develop an approach, particularly a voluntary one, that would work. To this extent Lenin's and Trotsky's obligatory labor service proved barren.

Management: Workers' Control and Taylorism. An important dimension of the productivity question was that of management. The Bolsheviks were on the threshold of a revolution in industrial relations with workers' control and collective management, but they abandoned these ideas. Actually, from the very beginning Lenin was quite ambivalent. His positions, first on one-man management and then on Taylorism, point up the elements of compromise and ambiguity, but also of consistency of policy. What Lenin did was to transfer the problem to a new level—to give it a new interpretation. Reality was indeed made in the image of an ideal. Significantly, the problems of inefficiency in democratic management had not been anticipated. Regardless of ideological affiliations, most Marxists believed, as had Lenin and Marx, that the problem of production had been simplified by capitalism; that the problem of management was one of "accounting and control"; and that anybody, any cook or unskilled worker, who could "read and write and [knew] the first four rules of arithmetic," could perform the required tasks of management.[73]

After two years of bitter experience, however, Lenin was stating that "the art of administration is not an art one is born with, it is acquired by experience." He said further: "Without the guidance of specialists . . . the transition to socialism will be impossible." To support his plea on what he knew was a very sensitive issue he said:

> Our work of organizing the proletarian accounting and control has obviously . . . lagged behind the work of "expropriating the expropriators." We have to resort to the old bourgeois methods and to pay a very high price for the "services" of bourgeois specialists. . . . Such a measure is a compromise, a departure from the principle of the Paris Commune . . . a step backward on the part of our Socialist Soviet . . . power . . . but one which was necessary because of the backwardness of the masses, the lack of discipline, and because the "Russian was a poor worker," who had to learn to work.[74]

Others, who still believed some form of democratic management was necessary and possible, warned that Lenin's proposal would unavoidably mean a return to industrial absolutism, to the coercive authority of the pre-Revolutionary period which had been so violently cast aside in the March days of 1917. Lenin, Trotsky, and Bukharin met the argument forcefully:

> Individual management does not in any degree limit or infringe upon the rights of the working class or the "right" of the trade unions, because the class can exercise its rule in one form or another, as technical expediency may dictate. It is the ruling class which in every case "appoints" persons for the managerial and administrative posts.[75]

There is little doubt that Lenin bowed to necessity here and that the Party considered the abandonment of collective management a retreat—but let us look at Lenin's concept of workers' control, for it has some interesting implications.

One thing is apparent: Lenin was not at all clear in his own mind about the meaning and significance of workers' control. He was attracted to some features of it, such as democratic management, but he was repelled by such aspects as the inherent element of syndicalism; while referring to workers' control he kept vaguely hinting about running the society in terms of a "plan" which would be the socialist alternative to the anarchistic cycles of capitalism. The point is that his own use of the term, and almost everyone else's, was extremely confused and vague. He reinterpreted workers' control during the debates on that subject, constantly and significantly shifting his position.

Lenin had come to favor workers' control slowly in the late spring of 1917. As Margaret Dewar points out: "there is no evidence of any concerted Bolshevik lead in the early post-[March] period." [76] To the contrary, the Party's principal ideological statements, from Lenin's arrival in April 1917 to the First Trade Union Congress in January 1918, had indicated nothing on workers' control. In his "April Thesis," Lenin had made no reference to workers' control at all. Instead he had advocated nationalization and the transfer of power to the Soviets. At the Seventh Conference of the Russian Social Democratic Labor Party (B), which met at the end of April, the absence of a resolution on workers' control was quite conspicuous.

Workers' Control Gains Favor. The first signs of formal Party affirmation of workers' control were made at the First Conference of Petrograd Factory Committees, which convened late in May. At this conference Zinoviev presented the Party's resolution on workers' control. Lenin confined himself to the discussion, making the innocuous statement that if control were to be effective it must be "control by the workers to whose organizations the factory administration should account for its actions." [77] It is not coincidence that the workers' control movement was reaching a high point in popularity at this point and that Lenin was struggling to establish a foothold in the Menshevik-dominated labor movement. His next major references to workers' control are in *State and Revolution* and *Will the Bolsheviks Retain State Power?* In both, Lenin advocated workers' control but simultaneously affirmed the desirability of nationalization and state control. Thus he sat with one foot in each camp, motivated in part by opportunism and in part by ideological obfuscation.

It was only during the debates on economic control during late 1917 and early 1918 that he apparently clarified his position. Now workers' control was suggested to mean *supervision and regulation* within the context of state control rather than outright control by the workers themselves, as most of its proponents advocated. Lenin said that emphasis should be placed on "administration" and not on "control," that the factory committees were the "organizational nucleus" and "state institutions." [78] Lenin had altered the meaning significantly. "Control," by this definition, would amount to something substantially different from "control" as the syndicalists would have had it. From this point on, when Lenin referred to "workers' control," essentially he had this limited interpretation in mind; of course this was not clear to everyone, particularly the workers and the advocates of workers' control. From here was not a long step to abandoning collective management.

Production Conferences. What is interesting is that the idea of worker participation in management remained a popular one, whereas the exclusion of labor gave rise to heated controversies. In the twenties a hard look was taken at labor productivity, and it was believed by Tomsky and others that some form of worker participation in managerial decision-making might increase the incentives of the workers and restore an element of democratic management of the plants. It was at this time that a new experiment was tried and the idea of workers' control further altered. From the limited concept of "supervision," it became "consultation." In 1924, following the Sixth Trade Union Congress and the Fourteenth Party Congress, an effort was made to stimulate worker responsibility, effort, and interest. Production conferences and committees were created. The primary object was to have management and labor meet collectively to discuss current production problems. It was believed that, to the extent that the two met and consulted, the workers would feel they were not being ignored and exploited; given psychological satisfaction, labor friction, turnover, and strikes would cease and productivity would rise.

The basic idea behind the conferences was one of consultation —discussion for the purpose of common responsibility—rather than worker participation for the purpose of worker rule. Unlike "supervision," under the terms of "consultation" management was not bound to accept the recommendations or decisions of the conferences. In other words, the agreement lacked teeth. Labor had no way of imposing its decisions upon management. This clearly marked an ideological revision of the idea of workers' control. Labor was not without some recourse to make life difficult for management, but it by no means had any power to make policy or to effect basic changes.

Production committees, as agencies for the plant-wide production conferences, were composed of representatives from all departments, plus management. The committees formally transmitted their recommendations to management. If management agreed to implement a proposal, the committee then set a deadline for putting it into effect. Formally, management could not delay in its reply, for there was a time limit on this aspect of the procedure. Also, if management rejected a proposal which the committee considered feasible, the committee could submit an appeal to a third party, the higher economic bodies—the Trust or the Supreme Council. It was management's responsibility to keep a record of all proposals, both those enacted and those rejected. Thus, at least according to the technical provisions, labor could make life for the manager uncomfortable, but in reality management was able to evade the restrictions largely because the production conference was itself little more than a formality.

Although the unions had supported the creation of these conferences in 1924, they had not done so with undiluted enthusiasm. Ryazanov, in his inimitable style, observed at the Fourteenth Party Congress that so long as the unions and the factory committees had no authority, the conferences could not be expected to possess any authority. In his opinion, the whole program was being overemphasized.[79]

Ryazanov was not far from wrong. The conferences proved to be of little value. Outside of the Party leaders, no one was really in favor of them. Management and even the workers did their best to ignore the entire program. In 1926 Ginsburg reported that only 10 per cent of the workers in the country had attended the conferences.[80] At the Seventh Trade Union Congress Andreev bluntly stated that management was openly hostile to the idea of the conferences. He told of managers who appeared completely ignorant of the trade union's right to participate in management, and of others who paid no attention to the production conferences. He further revealed that frequent disputes occurred because management passed over legitimate demands in silence.[81]

At the Eighth Trade Union Congress Tomsky revealed that between 1924 and 1928, while the program had been in effect, no improvement in labor participation could be noted. He said that the conferences met on the average of only three times a year; that attendance was low; and that proposals were not heeded by management, which considered the conferences to be useless and a nuisance for the smooth functioning of the factories.[82]

In the same year, 1928, a special commission appointed by the Leningrad district trade union organization investigated the performance of the production conferences. It revealed that in the Krasny Khimik (the Red Chemical Works), out of 99 proposals suggested by the production conferences of 1927, only six were carried out. In the Baltic Metal Works, out of 35 suggestions, five were carried out. The report indicated similar results throughout Leningrad.[83] A commentator summed up the question: "Do the workers participate in the management of industry?" He answered, "Very insignificantly, if you like, they do not participate at all. . . ."[84]

Thus the concept of industrial democracy had been further revised. Having been launched with the idea of labor domination of management, later shifting to labor supervision over management, the unions had finally been relegated only the right of consultation.

Taylorism

Perhaps the most radical and interesting experiment of the time centered around an attempt to solve the problem of management and productivity within the framework of "Taylorism," or scientific management.

Frederick W. Taylor was the father of one of the most important technological revolutions to sweep the industrial process. He was a man of his age. Born in the middle nineteenth century, he witnessed the transition of the factory system from one in which operations were performed by hunch, guess, and "rule of thumb" into one in which operations were systematically ordered. Taylor, a very nervous and compulsive individual who ordered his own life by attempting to eliminate wasted time and motion in walking, playing, and working, had a major hand in bringing about the revolution of efficiency. A lover of the stopwatch, he was a radical advocate of time-motion and rhythm systems. Operating under the traditional economic assumption that scarcity was permanent and costs had to be minimized, Taylor built his theories on a rationality model which held efficiency to be the price of profit and gain. Taylor, however, carried the cost accounting argument farther than most of his predecessors or contemporaries. Taylor believed that by exact calculation he could break down each act, each procedure, into its components, and then put together the combination of job aggregates and worker motions that would effect the most productive combination. He saw this as an end in itself. As Daniel Bell states, Taylor was aware of the fact that he was subordinating man to the machine, that he was making the worker as much a machine or a part of a machine as it was humanly possible to do. Thus, Taylor became the first advocate of adjusting human psychology to the machine. He said tersely: "One of the first requirements for a man who is fit to handle pig iron as a regular occupation is that he shall be so stupid and so phlegmatic that he more nearly resembles an ox than any other type." [85] He further stated: "What I demand of the worker is not to produce any longer by his own initiative, but to execute punctiliously the orders given down to their minutest detail." [86]

Taylorism vs. Socialist Ethics: Implications. In terms of ethics, Taylor was the *enfant terrible* to the socialists. His radical "scientific organization of work" could only mean the total dehumanization of man by the machine. Ethically, it was a price too high to pay for efficiency. On the question of humanism the socialist judgment of Taylor was clear, or so it appeared.

The problem of efficiency and the socialist ethic raised a perplexing question, for whether they were aware of it or not, the socialists were caught on the horns of Taylor's ox. Going back to Marx, he and most of his followers had great faith in the industrial process. Marx was convinced that the one advance capitalism had contributed to civilization was the development of the industrial process. Through the factory system, man held the key to the problem of scarcity, poverty, and inequality. Marx was convinced that the major problem of capitalism was its anarchistic system of distribution which produced poverty amidst plenty. He believed a socialist system would incorporate the capitalist methods of production and would even extend them, but would reorganize the methods of distribution along more scientific lines. Basically he affirmed the industrial process and the advances capitalism had made in this direction. In this regard, he and his followers were technocrats.

Yet Marx was opposed to the entire industrial process. His strongest objection to it was that it dehumanized man, subordinating him to the machine and turning him into an object. He was not only harsh in his criticism of what happened to the workers in terms of their subsistence conditions, but also in terms of their bondage to the factory system. To him, the enslavement of the worker to the machine was one of the most arbitrary aspects of capitalism. And Engels had had this comment: "The automatic machinery of a big factory is much more despotic than the small capitalists who employ workers ever have been." [87] Both men plainly spoke out their objections. Again in Marx' words: "Owing to the extensive use of machinery and to the division of labor, the work of the proletarians has lost all individual charm for the workman. He becomes an appendage of the machine." [88] His criticism here is of the factory system and the whole principle of mass production. His attacks on poor work conditions—poor sanitary facilities, long hours, and so on—merely dealt with the symptoms. In many respects his indictment is an attack on the entire industrial revolution itself. Marx was angry and upset about the moral consequences of the revolution for both the workers and the capitalists.

Thus it would appear that Marx affirmed and denied the industrial process at one and the same time. Paradoxically, he appears not to have seen the dilemma. He also appears not to have seen that socialists would face the same problem of dehumanization as long as there was mass production and the factory process, resting on hierarchy, rhythm, and order. In other words, a socialist system that provided no alternative to a system based on plant efficiency would offer no solution to the problem of the subordination of man to the machine, particularly if the machine was affirmed as the key to the problem of scarcity. For the most part, Marx thought of solving the problem of industrial dehumanization more by overcoming the division of labor and cutting the workday than by making the entire process humane and democratic. It may be argued, though, that he implicitly believed a form of democratic management would exist under socialism. But if so, he said very little about it. Even if the division of labor problem were overcome, this did not mean that efficiency would not be a prime objective or that work would be pleasant. For Marx there was still the possibility of men not liking factory work. If so, once again the issue of man's alienation from his work was opened. The problem was inherent in the very nature of industrial organization itself. Curiously, Marx never saw it, and significantly he could not conceive of a Good Society without work.

Marx never had to decide which way he would go. Judging by his concern over the alienation of man, the most dominant theme in his work, his ethical position would have prevailed. Marx would have opted for the worker against the machine, against making man into a machine. It is the humanism in Marx that stands out over the technocrat, that makes him such a powerful and attractive critic.

Lenin himself, in his early radical days, had found a scientifically rationalized machine process to be unpalatable. While in prison in 1895–1896, he wrote:

> The factory demands that the worker renounce completely his own will; it introduces a discipline that compels the worker to rise from work and to cease from work at the sound of a whistle; it arrogates to itself the right to inflict its own punishments upon him and to submit him to fines and penalties according to a system it has itself elaborated. The worker becomes a wheel in an immense machine, he must be subservient to it, enslaved to it, deprived of any will of his own, exactly like the machine itself.[89]

Yet, in 1919, in the name of efficiency and science, Lenin said:

> The Russian worker is a poor worker in comparison with the workers of advanced nations. . . . To learn how to work—this is the problem. The last word of capitalism in this respect, the Taylor system

—as well as all progressive measures of capitalism—combine the refined cruelty of bourgeois exploitation and a number of most valuable scientific attainments in the study of motions, in determining the most correct methods of the work, the best systems of accounting and control, etc. The Soviet Republic must adopt valuable scientific and technical advances in this field. . . . We should immediately introduce piece work and try it out in practice. We should try out every scientific and progressive suggestion of the Taylor system. . . .[90]

[And in "A Great Beginning" he said there would be]: A new labor discipline, a new organization of labor, which shall combine the best work of science and capitalist techniques with the mass association of class conscious workers engaged in large-scale socialist production.[91]

Lenin, like Marx, was caught between a socialist ethic and a science of industrial efficiency. His advocacy of Taylorism in 1919 was *not* merely a case of expediency over principle. It was very much a case of having to attempt to reconcile, or else choose between, contradictory values. Lenin may have favored democracy in plant administration, self-imposed discipline, and a liberated worker, but he also revealed a very strong penchant for the rational, scientific, and disciplined approach to methods of management. Carried to its logical conclusion, this meant a whole society organized like a workshop, with no idleness, a society directed by the most competent managers in the most scientific way for the common good. In short, plant efficiency was an end in itself. Lenin was beyond doubt a technocrat. The strange part about it is that Lenin had no concrete grasp of economic rationality; he lacked any real notion of the meaning of pricing, of market resource allocation, or of maximization. Indeed, he had only the foggiest ideas about economics.[92]

It was the technocratic element in his socialist position, as well as objective need, that enabled him to make the choice of production and Taylorism over managerial democracy. In many respects, like Marx, he did not see the incompatibility between the two; believing that if the system were socialist, the plants publicly owned, and the worst features of Taylorism eliminated, the worker would not be exploited or dehumanized.

What Lenin did not see was that his choice marked the complete triumph of mechanization, of Taylorism, over the humanism of socialism. He did not see that in abandoning workers' control and democratic management he was in fact abandoning the one quality of socialism which militates against its radical advocacy of a rational organization of the industrial process, of man and of society.

Once Taylorism was introduced, it was carried to such an extreme that few limits remained to the process of rationalizing the industrial order. The details of the story need not detain us; the point is that the entire system became geared to the idea of maximizing production. The necessary wage and labor adjustments were made so that the trade unions and the workers aimed only at maximizing output and minimizing costs. During N.E.P. the system was extended; wage scales were based on a progressive piece-rate plan, wage differentials or bonuses, and so forth; the entire system of industrial organization rested on hierarchy, the subordination of workers to management, and stringent discipline. The results were absurd from a socialist's point of view, but they were a direct result of a socialism which the Bolsheviks affirmed.

Since time immemorial, work has been a fundamental concern for man. Like few other forces it has had the power of religion over him, motivating him in many ways—physically, ideologically, and ethically. Few other activities with which men have been engaged have moved him as deeply. As Freud remarked, it is work that binds man to reality. Yet what is puzzling is that although it has given him a sense of mastery over nature, of power over the world—and at times a tremendous feeling of self-fulfillment and satisfaction—most social theories have reflected a sense of despair, seeing work as travail, a necessary evil, or an obligation to God rather than a self-liberating and self-fulfilling process. The philosophy of the technocrats does not reflect this feeling of despair, but the consequences of their view are absurd because man is made a prisoner of the process rather than liberated by it. Marxism is perhaps the one exception, but there is a seed of doubt in Marx's mind and he did not see his way clear of the problem. It is difficult to say why the results of these theories have been so dismal, absurd, or ambiguous. Perhaps man has never seen his way clear of work, and all processes of work pose elements of travail. One thing is clear, that neither Lenin nor the Bolsheviks have brought us closer to this sense of self-fulfillment or liberation with their theory of work or their labor policies.

8 ✦ The Party, Unions, and Dictatorship

The Party . . . is . . . duty bound to retain its dictatorship, regardless of the temporary vacillations of the amorphous masses, regardless of the temporary vacillations even of the working class. This
awareness is essential for cohesion; without it the Party is in danger
of perishing. . . . At any given moment, the dictatorship does not
rest upon the formal principle of workers' democracy. To be sure,
workers' democracy is the only method by which the masses can be
drawn more and more into political life . . . this is a truism. . . .

But if we look upon workers' democracy as something uncon-
ditional, as something which stands above everything else, then
comrade Shlyapnikov is right when . . . he says that every plant
should elect its own administration, that every regional congress
should elect its administrative organs and so on, until we come to
the "All-Russian Congress of Producers." From a formal point of
view this is the clearest link with workers' democracy. But we are
against it. Why? . . . Because, in the first place, we want to retain
the dictatorship of the Party, and, in the second place, because we
think that the [democratic] way of managing important and essential
plants is bound to be incompetent and prove a failure from an economic point of view. . . .[1]

SHAKE-UP OF THE UNIONS

Immediately following the Tenth Party Congress, Lenin, in total
surprise to Tomsky and the unions, launched a major attack against
the unions. There had been a general awareness that there would
be major changes in the ranks of union leadership after the Con-

gress, but the broad range of the attack far surpassed all expectations. Lenin was determined to gain control of the unions, particularly before the conciliatory policies of N.E.P. took hold.

Tsektran Reborn

One of Lenin's first moves was to fully reconstitute Tsektran. At a carefully packed Congress of Transport Workers it was pushed through, startling as this may seem considering Lenin's attacks on Trotsky and the lessons learned about trade unions. The communications network was still a horrible mess, but there were other, more temperate, and undoubtedly more effective ways to tackle the communications problem.

Not unusually, only a minority spoke up in opposition to the "resurrection" of Tsektran, and those who did were Mensheviks and SRs.[2] The rest acquiesced to the demands of Lenin and the Central Committee. All of the steps necessary to reactivate Tsektran were taken, but now with a slightly different approach. The political directorates—which had been so harsh, and which had been joined with the union-Party organizations in December 1920—were recreated in October 1921, but as special sections of the Central Committee. Directly subordinate to the Central Committee, they were assigned "direction and control of party work in transportation." Under them was a web of subordinate sections, which remarkably resembled the previous system.[3]

The Workers' Opposition

At this time the members of the Workers' Opposition also felt the mailed fist of the Central Committee. Certainly some suppressive action was to be expected in light of the "On Unity" and "Anarcho-Syndicalist Deviation" resolutions adopted in the final hours of the Tenth Congress. Many Workers' Opposition members were quite prepared to observe the decision and were in fact in the process of disbanding as a faction. Yet they were still purged.

Their victimization was a deliberate decision. In addition to these "oppositionists," almost all other unionists who favored the resolution on union democracy passed by the Congress were likewise attacked. As Shlyapnikov later reported: "The struggle took place not along ideological lines but by means . . . of edging [these people] out from appointments, of systematic transfers from one district to another, and even of expulsion from the Party. . . . Every single member of the Party who took the floor in defense of the resolution on workers' democracy passed at the Tenth Congress was declared a supporter of the Workers' Opposition and guilty of disintegrating the Party."[4]

As Leonard Schapiro points out in his concise treatment of these incidents, "comparison of the lists of delegates to the Tenth and Eleventh Congresses shows that of the 37 oppositionists who attended the private meeting with Lenin during the Tenth Congress, with the objective of persuading Shlyapnikov to serve on the Central Committee, only four reappeared as delegates with a vote at the Eleventh Congress the following year."

The Workers' Opposition appealed their case to the Central Committee, which investigated but rejected their complaints as untrue.[5] Yielding a bit, instructions were sent down the chain of command that the sympathizers of the Workers' Opposition were not to be expelled in the extensive purge then in progress under the direction of the control commission. Schapiro points out that an oppositionist, Chelyshev, was a member of the control commission during 1921, and in all likelihood victimization of the membership was curtailed somewhat by his presence.

The Rebellion of May 17

But the Central Committee continued to encounter resistance with the unions in spite of the purge. One of the first rebellions to occur within the Party ranks over Party-union policy took place on May 17, just several hours before the gavel hammered open the Fourth Trade Union Congress. The formal business of this Congress, which met May 17–25, 1921, was the revival of private enterprises, shortly to be put into effect, and the tasks of the trade unions.

Tomsky (chairman of the A.R.C.C.T.U.) and Tsyperovich were assigned the responsibility of preparing the Party position for the Central Committee, and then were charged with ensuring the acceptance of the Central Committee's final version by the Communist fraction and by the full Congress. Meeting at a pre-Congress fraction session, the delegates, after listening to Tomsky's advance reading of the Politbureau's report "On the Role and Tasks of the Trade Unions," discovered that the section on electing trade union officers did not contain the term "normal methods of proletarian democracy" which the resolution of the Tenth Party Congress, had included two months earlier. The fraction, which had been expected to abide by Party discipline and accept the statement *in toto,* voted to amend the resolution. Under Ryazanov's leadership, and against a strong formal objection by Tomsky, they voted by more than 150 to 30 to include in the Politbureau's statement a section providing for elections by democratic procedures.

Although in essence the revision repeated the Party position on trade union democracy, the passing of Ryazanov's revision marked a breach in discipline. The Politbureau, after the fight at the Tenth

Party Congress, was not prepared to tolerate any infractions of Party rules. On May 18, the very next day, the Central Committee suspended Tomsky as the Central Committee representative and delegated Lenin, Stalin, and Bukharin as the new fraction representatives, and ordered them to see that the fraction changed its ways.

Meanwhile, as Schmidt reported to the delegates on the progress of the Central Committee of Trade Unions since the Third Congress, a hastily called fraction meeting convened. Lenin himself guided through the deletion of the revision. The Party members, constituting a majority of the delegates, then returned to the Congress and the orthodox version was presented for acceptance.

Tomsky, who had voted against Ryazanov's revision, was ordered to stand for investigation by a special committee headed by Stalin. After examining the evidence the commission acquitted Tomsky of violating Party discipline, but it officially reprimanded him for "criminal indifference" and for not showing sufficient zeal. On orders of the Central Committee he was removed from its membership and relieved of all work in the A.R.C.C.T.U. The lone wolf, Ryazanov, on the other hand, was banned from all trade union affairs.

As for the fraction, it behaved much like the reluctant dragon which fumed, snorted, and made terrifying noises—but refused to fight. It attempted to have the decision on Tomsky reversed and trade union democracy affirmed, but it did not force the issue. At the second session of the Congress, Tomsky was not elected to the presidium of the Congress. In the final elections for officers of the Central Committee of Trade Unions, Andreev, not Tomsky, was elected president. Tomsky was demoted to the level of candidate and within several weeks was assigned to work in Tashkent. His demotion and exile, however, did not last for long. For Ryazanov the effects were different, though he did "bite" the Party again at the Fifth Trade Union Congress.

There were other bumpy spots at the Congress. Andreev, who delivered a report on organizational defects, proposed further centralization of the administrative machinery. He favored extending the authority of the inter-executive organs over the lower units in order to: (1) improve relations between the inter-union offices and the different branches; (2) obviate the excessive amount of leeway which existed on the local levels; and (3) combat the corruption of relations that had set in between the members and the trade union officials.

Andreev's proposal aroused a great deal of criticism. The delegates argued that the changes would lead to the destruction of industrial unionism and to the creation of a single "trade union commissariat with local sections." They put up a staunch, rather effective fight. They even attempted to amend Andreev's resolution, but lacked the necessary support. Their amendment was defeated by a vote of 593 to 453.[6] As Carr notes, for a Party-controlled Congress, this was a very close vote. It was terribly revealing of the depths of the discontent at this Congress.

The Revolt of the Metal Workers

The heavy hand of the Central Committee also swatted other unions, and in May 1921 the Metal Workers' Union rebelled. The Metal Workers' Union was a symbol of the November victory. It was one of the few unions the Bolsheviks had had on their side in the pre-November period. It was one that had fought the hardest and endured some of the severest sacrifices during the civil war—all to sustain the Bolsheviks. During the course of the trade union debates, however, it revealed strong sympathies for its former leader, Shlyapnikov, and in large part supported the syndicalist arguments advanced by the Workers' Opposition.

In May, the month of the Fourth Trade Union Congress, the Central Committee prepared to clean up the unions. It submitted to the Communist fraction of the Metal Workers' Union a list of candidates to be elected to the key positions in the union. The list contained new and "loyal" substitutes for those who had supported the Workers' Opposition. By an overwhelming vote of 120 to 40 the fraction rejected the Central Committee list. Incensed by this infringement of discipline, the Central Committee ignored the vote and appointed people of its own choice to the key positions. It then proceeded to reorganize the union. In protest, Shlyapnikov once again submitted his resignation to the Central Committee. Once again his resignation was refused.[7]

Loyalty of Trade Union Leaders

In July, two months after the Fourth Congress, the first steps were taken to ensure loyalty and enforce discipline. On July 30, 1921, Molotov, the Party Secretary concerned with trade union questions, and Andreev, the president of the Central Committee of Trade Unions, jointly issued instructions on Party discipline in fractions. Their order stated that complete fraction obedience to Party directives was required of all members of the fraction on the pain of expulsion, and furthermore that all members were denied the right to speak at any meeting without the permission of the fraction.[8]

Then in December, at the Eleventh Party Conference, a resolution imposing a tighter system of Party control over appointments and trade union personnel was passed. "Only old experienced members," whose membership dated back to the pre-1917 period, could be assigned to the key trade union posts. The resolution passed at this Conference stated that, because of the "enormous significance of the trade union movement and the danger of opportunist deviations therein, without the constant and firm leadership of the Party," only long-term "experienced" Party members who had not belonged to any other political party should hold responsible union positions. This transfer was to be effected gradually and cautiously. Pre-November Party membership would be the requirement for chairmen and secretaries of union central committees, and three years' membership for secretaries of provisional trade union councils.[9]

Finally, at the Eleventh Congress, Andreev presented the incomplete results of the loyalty study ordered by the Central Committee on January 20, 1922. Speaking on behalf of the commission, he urged a reorganization of the trade union leadership posts. This was necessary, he said, because many Communist trade union leaders were recent converts to the Party and were unable to distinguish between the interests of the various groups of workers and the interests of the working class as a whole; more reliable leaders were required because the unions, deprived of their usual role, thought only of wresting more and more privileges from the state. "At present," he said, "we want to create from the trade unions stable organizations for our Party, which would, to a greater degree, strengthen the link between the Party and the non-Party masses." [10] But, significantly, he did not feel that the changes in the trade union cadre had to be consistent with the methods of formal democracy. "It is obvious that for the present it is unnecessary to have recourse to official nominations," he said. It would be sufficient to rely solely upon co-option if "the militant Communists whom the Party will choose to manage the union first of all spend a certain time in the [lower] organizations in order to make themselves known and to acquire the necessary experience." Once these chosen Party members are known, then democratic procedures can be adopted, and then "they must be elected to the trade union executive organs by either a departmental congress or by the next All-Russian Congress.[11] All of this was a reaction to the trade union debates of the previous year. Little could reveal more about the uneasiness of the Party.

The delegates of the Eleventh Congress, acting on this advice and rejecting an appeal voiced by remnants of the Workers' Opposition, voted to fill, gradually, all offices with loyal Communists.

Loyalty was to be established by the date each man joined the Party, using as a guide the resolution passed by the Eleventh Conference.[12] To confirm the absolute control of the Party over the unions, the Congress voted that all the conflicts and frictions on union questions—which would inevitably occur as a result of the contradictions of N.E.P.—would be solved not by the unions themselves, but by the Party and the Comintern. Thus they wrote "finish" to trade union independence.[13] The Party had affirmed not only its absolute control over trade union appointments, but also over the right to settle all trade union questions.

But if the Party leaders succeeded in narrowing the range of trade union freedom of action, at least the Politbureau was unable to realize two of its principal objectives: the development of a relationship between the Party and the unions which was free from friction, and the development of strong trade unions which could maintain order in the economic marketplace and serve as a "transmission belt" for building up a mass base for the Party. This is not to say that the Party did not have control over the trade unions. Rather, it is to say that even if the Party did have control, it was only able to prevent the unions from becoming a threat to the one-Party dictatorship. It was not able to realize its objectives in regard to the development of economic order, political stability, and support for the system. To this extent the technique of quashing the unions was one of marginal utility to the Party.

Dissidence at the Eleventh Congress

This Eleventh Party Congress was hardly free from internal fighting either, and once again one of the primary issues was the fractional activities of some of the former members of the Workers' Opposition. In February 1922, on the eve of the Congress, twenty-two of the most prominent members of the Workers' Opposition had made a desperate, though ineffectual, bid for the support of the Communist International. They had submitted a list of grievances to an enlarged Plenum of the Executive Committee, but they had done so without the consent of the Russian Communist Party. The Communist International had then set up a commission to investigate the case, but being more favorably disposed toward the Party had passed a vote of censure against the oppositionists.

The Russian Communist Party took up the question at the Eleventh Congress. The Central Committee reported the complaint of the Workers' Opposition and the verdict of the International. The Central Committee proposed that the Congress create a special commission composed of Dzerzhinsky, Zinoviev, and Stalin to examine the case and report back their recommendations. The delegates, however, reflecting the deep unrest in the Party and country, refused to vote the official recommendation. Resistance from the floor was strong and the chair had difficulty in maintaining order. In the process of trying to establish the special commission the chairman was unable to prevent debate on the question. Fearing he would not have a majority on the question, he was able to force two votes on it by means of parliamentary rulings, thus having to yield only after the second vote—once it was obvious the majority wanted a floor debate on setting up the question. Before Kollontai and Shlyapnikov presented their case the chair tried to shut off debate. Again the delegates voted down the chair's ruling. The chairman tried to reduce the time allowed to each speaker; again he was defeated.[14] Nonetheless, when the final vote was taken the chair had the majority he had feared he lacked, and the Congress voted to establish the commission. In the course of the debates, however, the Party had been embarrassed by the public expression of serious complaints about attempts to silence criticism from within. Ryazanov, ever the opponent of Party dictatorship, summed up the bureaucratic tendencies and heavy-handed methods which led to actions such as this. A comment about the Central Committee hit the mark in this case as well: "They say that in England Parliament can do everything except change a man into a woman. Our Central Committee is far more powerful. It has already changed more than one not so strong revolutionary man into an old woman, and the number of these old women is increasing daily."[15]

The commission delivered its report at the final session of the Congress. It found the Workers' Opposition leadership guilty of violating the ban on factionalism and Party discipline. It accused Shlyapnikov, Kollontai, and Medvedev of having created a secret organization, and cited a letter describing efforts of Shlyapnikov and Medvedev to elect workers sympathetic to the Workers' Opposition to factory committees in the Donetz basin.[16] The commission recommended the expulsion of Shlyapnikov, Kollontai, Kuznetsov, Mitin, and Medvedev. Medvedev, Shlyapnikov, and Kollantai were promised reinstatement within one year on the basis of good behavior. The Congress, then entering into secret sessions, defied the Central Committee by refusing to expel Kollontai, Shlyapnikov and Medvedev, though it did expel Mitin and Kuznetzov. It also condemned the opposition for its continued existence as a separate group and issued a warning to the others to cease their anti-Party activities.

Lenin Demands Shlyapnikov's Ouster

By August 1921 the longstanding friendship between Shlyapnikov and Lenin was over, once and for all time. Utterly dejected by Lenin's ruthless policy and arbitrary reprisals toward the unions and the workers, and unable to make his peace with N.E.P. and its concessions to capitalism, Shlyapnikov bitterly and cynically criticized the Party. At a private Party cell meeting in August, he sarcastically criticized a VSNKh decree on private enterprise prerogatives. An official report of Shlyapnikov's criticisms was submitted to the Central Committee.[17] Years later, Rykov told the story of the incident. According to Rykov, Shlyapnikov "presented a report, or rather did not so much present a report, as launch into a criticism of government decrees. . . . As the basis of his criticism he took the resolution of the Presidium of VSNKh on the granting of concessions to . . . private capitalists." Rykov adds that Shlyapnikov began with a paragraph stating in effect that the national economy had been managed without any organization. "Comrade Shlyapnikov burst out laughing. . . . 'What *does* this mean? Four years of management, and no organization? It doesn't make any sense!'" Rykov further reported that Shlyapnikov reacted emotionally to another part of the report which stated: "In spite of the fact that the workers were supplied with clothes and provisions, productivity dropped to a minimum." Shlyapnikov is reported to have stated bitingly that "productivity at some factories was even higher than the prewar period." Rykov states: "the third point to which he objected was the passage about pilfering at work. Comrade Shlyapnikov said it was not the fault of the workers, but of the economic departments. They have reduced the workers to thieving." To clench matters, "at the end of his criticism he announced that the whole resolution stank of prejudice against the workers and that the workers should be on their guard."

Lenin was infuriated. At a plenary session of the Central Committee on August 9, Lenin personally demanded that his old comrade, Alexander Shlyapnikov, be expelled from the Central Committee. Undoubtedly Lenin had sanctioned the earlier Committee action to expel Shlyapnikov, but this time it was startling news, for he had never before publicly identified himself with the idea. Earlier, in March and May, Lenin had fought to prevent Shlyapnikov's attempted resignations. Probably his reason was primarily a desire to effect a united Party. Now, in August, after his first efforts to secure control of the unions and to initiate N.E.P., this final criticism by Shlyapnikov angered him so that he felt compelled to oust Shlyapnikov openly and formally. It is interesting, as Schapiro has noted, that it was this sort of act, this kind of criticism, that "in Lenin's view justified the expulsion of an old Bolshevik, his principal lieutenant between 1915 and 1917." [18] And this occurred at the very time Lenin was making concessions to critics of N.E.P. by saying the time had come to end the retreat.

Lenin's demand troubled the Plenum, and he was unable to muster the necessary two-thirds vote to expel a member of the Central Committee. The Plenum did, however, take steps to censure Shlyapnikov. In a secret resolution made available only to higher Party echelons, Shlyapnikov was told that his attitude was "quite inadmissible" and was warned that continued behavior and critical outbursts of this sort would lead to his expulsion. Further, he was relieved of his duties in connection with the purging of the Party of former oppositionists. In effect, Shlyapnikov was isolated, shunted into political limbo. He would only appear on the scene again for a fleeting moment—to help settle the succession crisis. But his career was over. Thus came the climax of an old friendship and a bitter fight. Thus marked the end of a principled old Bolshevik, sadly disillusioned with the bitter fruit of the Revolution to which he had dedicated his whole life; he went down fighting for the people he loved.

THE UNIONS OVERSHADOWED

1922: "New Course" Policy for Unions

It was not until 1922, when the character of N.E.P., free trade, cost accounting, and reconstruction were sufficiently structured, that the Bolsheviks were able to delineate trade union policy. The new policy, issued by the Politbureau after a series of hearings on the trade union question, built the contrary tendencies of N.E.P. right into trade union policy. The major premise was that contradictory forces would operate throughout the entire economic system. The unions unavoidably would have to perform contradictory roles which would create problems for them. The specific argument on the role of trade unions was that in the context of free trade, the unions, as defenders of the workers, would have to strike to protect the worker from the abuses and encroachments of the capitalists.

In the context of economic reconstruction, however, the unions, as defenders of the Soviet system, should not be so militant—in their attack on private enterprise, in the defense of their membership, and in collective bargaining—that they forced wages up and held productivity down. Nor should they strike, if the strikes could be avoided. By no means were they to jeopardize economic expansion. In addition, as defenders of the Soviet system, the unions not only were to do their utmost to raise productivity, but were not to interfere with production or management.

All these points were reiterated by Tomsky at the Fifth Trade Union Congress, which met in March 1922. He enthusiastically endorsed the new policy on contradictions, which he called "The New Course" and "our trade union revolution." He urged, in essence, that for the good of the workers and the workers' dictatorship, the unions should think in terms of the national interest rather than the defense of their membership. The net effect of the policy was that the unions were not able to operate with any degree of clarity of purpose, were fragmented institutions, and were placed in a very weak bargaining position.

The 1922 Labor Code

If Tomsky's and the Politbureau's policy statement did not sufficiently indicate that the Party was running roughshod over the unions, discussion of a new labor code tailored for N.E.P. did. It was announced by Commissar of Labor Shmidt at the Fifth Trade Union Congress. In the course of delivering his report, he informed the delegates that a new labor code had already been drafted and approved.

Shmidt's announcement was startling. It became apparent during the course of the discussion that many of the delegates, knew little or nothing about the code; the local trade union organizations were unaware of it, and *Trud,* the organ of the Central Committee of Trade Unions, had barely mentioned it; furthermore the Congress had not even established a special committee to deal with the preparation of a new code. Tempers flared and complaints were acrimonius. To mollify his critics Shmidt assured them that the drafting of the new code had been a joint effort of the A.R.C.C.T.U. and the Commissariat of Labor—that labor had in fact not been ignored.[19]

How successful Shmidt was in appeasing the delegates remains a matter of conjecture, though the congress did pass a vote of endorsement of the new code. But this outrage to union pride was soon compounded. After this incident, changes of which the A.R.C.C.T.U. was not aware were introduced into the final version.[20] The significance of both events could have been missed only by the most innocent. The unions had been deliberately by-passed. The denial of a role in drafting the new code and in introducing changes was a sign that the unions were going to lose even more power once the new code was promulgated. On the other hand it revealed that the Party was still too afraid of the trade unions to submit the question to them; the Party feared rebellion.

Larin and Ryazanov took up the cudgel for the unions at the meeting of the fourth session of the Executive Committee of the Soviets. Arguing that the substantial changes in the amended version of the new labor code were not to the advantage of the Soviet workers and unions, they protested that the new provisions appeared to favor management over labor. They objected to the fact that collective agreements were not mandatory; that management was not required by law to sign one (which was just the reverse of an earlier draft provision); that although all hiring had to be done through the labor exchanges, the employer had the right to refuse or accept men sent to him; that in instances where a worker sought permission to quit his job over the nonpayment of wages, the burden of proof was on him rather than on management; that an obligation of the factory committee was "collaboration" with management.

They also raised objections to an elastic provision which, if enforced, could have led to holiday work and inadequate compensation for lost leisure time. Further, they objected to the change in the length of the workday in dangerous fields from a first-proposed six hours to an unstipulated number of hours to be decided upon by the Commissariat of Labor. They also objected to a reduction in unemployment insurance, and last but not least, to a long list of grounds upon which management might dismiss a worker without compensation, saying that it placed a "trump card" and veto power in the hands of management. In essence, this long list of provisions marked a sharp reduction in benefits and powers the workers had won and enjoyed since 1917.

Their protest was impotent. The provisions to which Ryazanov and Larin had objected were included in the code which was promulgated on November 9, 1922. Perhaps most significant of all was that Tomsky, who was active once again in union politics, defended the changes and was unreserved in his endorsement of the new code. Once again the A.R.C.C.T.U. was instrumental in writing the unions out of politics.

The Twelfth Party Congress

The Twelfth Party Congress met in April 1923, the year of the "Scissors" crisis, the year when the peasants struck for more consumer goods and the workers for higher wages and more food, the year when it appeared that the policies of N.E.P. were not working well at all. At this Congress the Party had another taste of opposition over the worker question. In one form it sprang from underground Menshevik activity; in another, from the formation of two new Communist opposition groups: the "Workers' Truth" and the "Workers' Group." Each reflected the deep dismay of the worker; they also reflected the other proletarian-oriented groups that were still pressing for major concessions to the worker.

The Workers' Truth group, led by Lenin's former colleague Alexander Bogdanov, published an appeal in January 1923 [21] in which Marx was quoted as having said that "the liberation of the workers can only be the deed of the working class itself." The appeal accused the Communist Party of having become a party of the "organizer intelligentsia," of having lost touch with the working class, and of having introduced policies of "state capitalism" which contradicted the interests of the working class. It called on all "revolutionary workers and active class-minded elements" to organize propaganda circles within the Party, the mills and factories, the trade unions, the soviets, and every other organization that would lend itself to the purpose of liberating the workers.

The Workers' Group was founded by the arch-heretic Miasnikov, one of the few members of the Party ever to demand freedom of discussion for all socialist political parties, not just Communists. Miasnikov was one of the Party members expelled for the petition of the Twenty-Two to the Comintern. His group appears to have been solely proletarian in social composition. It too hammered away at bureaucracy, privileged Communists, and a loss of contact with the working class.[22] His demands were very close to those of the Mensheviks, so similar in fact that, as with the earlier Menshevik plea, his position extended freedom of speech and election to all socialist parties but excluded liberals, professors, lawyers, and doctors from any enjoyment of these rights.

For the short while that these opposition groups were on the scene they were effective in organizing worker discontent. Apparently both played active roles in a wave of strikes which broke out in the summer and fall. These opposition groups were effectively liquidated by the Cheka, which also suppressed the strikes. Ironically, Tomsky—the trade union leader whom Lenin said was closest to the masses and most interested in defending their interests—not only did not protest, but as a member of the Politbureau participated in the decision to call out the Cheka to crush the strikes.

9 ✿ The Social Problem

Conditions improved during N.E.P., but life was incredibly hard, the standard of living extremely depressed. People were swallowed up by poverty. Food rations were so short that in the early twenties the daily norm of nutrition of a worker performing eight hours of work was one pound of bread and one and one-half pounds of vegetables. For overtime he would receive one and one-quarter pounds of bread for each additional two hours' work. But Rykov, who reported these figures, stated that there were 1,200,000 workers for whom they could not provide at all.[1] This chapter presents a picture of why people turned against the regime and why workers turned against their unions.

Walter Duranty, whose grasp of the party politics of the time leaves something to be desired, but whose reportage is unsurpassed of life in Russia in 1921:

> Moscow in 1921 was a strange hybrid between a modern city and a village. . . . For two and half years at least there was no running water in Moscow. . . . And no steam heat, in a climate where thirty below zero occurs almost every winter. Somehow they kept the street-cars running and I don't think there was anything I saw which affected me so horribly. They were free of course . . . and they looked like long, dingy boxes on both ends of which bees had swarmed; but the bees were human beings hanging on to each other . . . at a corner the tail of a truck just flicked the edge of a similar swarm and knocked them off like insects. Some got up limping and one, a woman, lay where she had fallen. And no one seemed

to care. . . . When the Muscovites called 1919–1920 the hard years they knew what hardship meant. I myself saw a Persian prayer rug, which Fifth Avenue would sell for $500 any time, depression or not, cut into a sort of kilt for a little girl with its fringe hanging down in front and behind.

When a window got broken they nailed a board across because there was no more glass. Later they took the board for fuel and sealed up the window with clay and bricks. There were plenty of bricks in Moscow for anyone to take from the houses there smashed in the revolutionary fighting, and from the larger number that were gutted by fire when there was no water to quench the flames, and from others which had fallen down through age and lack of repair.[2]

For the villagers the situation was worse, particularly in the Volga region where two years of drought and famine raged. C. E. Bechhofer tells this story:

"What did he die of?" I ask. ". . . of hunger?"

"He died of eating too much," replies the old man. . . ." [He] had not eaten . . . for a long time; and then his wheat ripened, and he was so hungry that he ate it as he plucked it, husks and all. . . . He ate so much that his stomach swelled up . . ."—he describes a huge arc in front of him—"and then he got very ill and died. . . ."

I ask why . . . his neighbors [hadn't helped him. Could they not] have given him a little food . . . until his harvest was ripe?

"Ah, in the old days everybody helped his neighbor. . . . But nowadays . . . [?] Just look at the bread I am eating."

He takes [a piece] out of his pocket. . . . It is a loathly greenish-purply mess. . . . Traces of flour embedded in patches of clay, and held together by . . . fibres of grass and weeds. . . . I try to eat a little . . . but I cannot swallow it. My gorge revolts. . . .[3]

[A little later Bechhofer adds]: I notice a woman and her [fourteen year old pregnant] daughter. . . . They are so thin as almost to be transparent. . . . Reduced by want, [they are] the slaves of the village, doing whatever work [there is for] a little of that "bread." In the towns it would mean prostitution and the filthier . . . domestic work. Here in the village it means, in addition to this, the incessant carrying of water and heavy burdens. . . . Mother and daughter have become like animals. . . . [Clearly] they are marked out to be the next victims of the famine. One could foretell almost to a day . . . when they must crawl away to die.

Duranty tells of a refugee camp of about 15,000 peasants at Samara:

"The adults were wan and haggard but far less dreadful than the children . . . with . . . bloated bellies and . . . shriveled limbs. . . . That came from eating [indigestible] clay and bark and refuse. . . .

Like cattle in a drought they waited . . . for death. . . . Right across [the road] from this herd of moribund humanity there was a food market [guarded by] one policeman. . . . It was only a little market, the first fruits of N.E.P.'s new private enterprise, but there was fish . . . for those who had money . . . even roasted meat, whose savory smell . . . carried . . . to the starving peasants, who neither moved nor seemed to care. . . . They lacked strength . . . to cross that narrow road or face the sentry's rifle and seize [some food]. The local authorities gave them . . . black bread, two ounces daily, and hot water in which bones . . . of animals had boiled. No medical attendance . . . and for each one that died there came five more trudging slowly . . . from the countryside. . . .[4]

(Duranty's description of the attitudes of the people very much fits the Nazi concentration camps of World War II, and also makes one wonder even more about the charge that only the Jews permitted themselves to be led to death without resistance.) He also tells of a visit he made to a "children's home" in Samara, which "was more like a 'pound' for homeless dogs."

They picked up the wretched children, lost or abandoned by their parents, by hundreds off the streets. . . . At the place I visited an attempt had been made to segregate those who were obviously sick or dying from their "healthier" fellows. The latter sat listlessly, 300 or 400 of them . . . too weak and lost and sad to move or care. Most of them were past hunger; one child of seven with fingers no thicker than matches refused the chocolate and biscuits I offered him and just turned his head away without a sound. The inside of the house was dreadful, children in all stages of a dozen different diseases huddled together anyhow in the most noxious atmosphere I have ever known. A matron and three girls were "in charge" of this pest-house. There was nothing they could do, they said wearily; they had no food or money or soap or medicine. . . .

"At least you could make fires and heat some water and attempt to wash them, even without soap," I said indignantly, "and surely you can get some rations from the city Soviet to make soup or porridge for some of them."

The matron shrugged her shoulders, "What is the use?" she said. "They would die anyway."

At first she had tried to do something, she said, and the city had tried, but now there were too many. . . . She slumped into a chair and buried her face in her hands.

I went away feeling sick, and hating myself for being healthy and well fed. There was nothing I could do either, except write the story in its naked ugliness and hope that it would move people in America and hurry their promised aid.[5]

And Anna Louise Strong tells the story of an American Relief Administration man who "had seen men arrested for cannibalism; they had killed and eaten a young boy. Other cannibals did not kill, but stole corpses. Someone asked the prisoners how human flesh tastes, and they said: 'Quite well; you don't need much salt.' " Miss Strong remarked: "They were half-witted people." [6]

Yet, N.E.P., in its early stages, was also characterized by "boom town" growth. While the peasants and children starved to death, in Moscow and Petrograd lively gambling halls, night clubs, and fleshpots thrived. It was *La Dolce Vita* for many. Champagne and vintage wines from France and Germany, 50-year-old cognac, real fragrant coffee, meat and chicken, and everything from fresh caviar to sugar and peaches was available. People gorged themselves with the sweets of pleasure, trying to "tear from life the joys they had been denied so long." [7]

As Duranty states: "the authorities . . . for a time . . . deliberately 'took the lid off.' " The condition they demanded was that part of the receipts of these "hot spots" be reserved for the state. The opportunities of N.E.P. indeed gave stimulus to quick and easy profits, to opportunities of all kinds, but also to "a growing contempt for the rules and restrictions . . . previously enforced by the Bolsheviks." [8]

In describing the biggest gambling house, the Praga, Duranty captures the mood of the "gay" Moscow.

> It was a strange sight, this *Praga*, in the center of the world's first Proletarian Republic. Most of the men looked like . . . the low-class jackals and hangers-on of any boom, . . . but there were [also] former nobles in faded broadcloth and Red Army soldiers in uniform, back from fighting Moslem rebels in Central Asia or from "liquidating" Makhno's anarchist movement in the Ukraine, eager for Moscow's fleshpots and flutter at the tables. A smattering, too, of foreigners, fixers, agents and the commercial vanguard of a dozen big firms attracted by Lenin's new policy of Concessions, hurrying to see if [it] was true that Russia might again become a honey-pot for alien wasps. And women of all sorts . . . mostly daughters of

joy whom N.E.P. had hatched in flocks, noisy . . . as sparrows.
Later in increasing numbers the wives and families of N.E.P.-men,
the new profiteers, with jewels on their stumpy fingers. . . .[9]

He describes another place, "a restaurant called 'Bar' not far
from the Savoy Hotel."

By the fall of 1922, "Bar" was doing a roaring trade as a snappy
restaurant, night club and brothel all in one. The sale of wine
and beer became legal that year, but at "Bar" there were vodka and
liquors as well. In the winter of 1922–1923 they went further and
cocaine and heroin were to be had, for a price, by clients in the
know. A merry little hell it was in the spring of 1923. . . . In the
end the game was spoilt, not by police interference, but by a tax
collector who somehow nosed out the fact that "Bar's" profits were
much greater than reported.

No better than "Bar," if less flagrant and luxurious, less "pro-
tected" and profitable, was the Red Light district . . . near the
Trubny Square. . . . In the . . . big tenement houses . . . were
corridors . . . where . . . beside the name and number of the
small . . . rooms was tacked a photograph of its fair occupant in
the scantiest of costume. . . .[10]

1922 was a good year for most Russians.

As spring passed into summer, the mortality from typhus, which
had been terrific during the past three years, dwindled almost to
nothing, and other diseases of malnutrition rapidly decreased. In
the regions afflicted by famine some 25,000,000 souls were being fed
daily by the combined efforts of the A.R.A., the Nansen and Quaker
Relief organizations, and the Soviet Government itself. In addition
they were given ample supply of seed grain with animals to work
the land. On the Volga, which had suffered most from the famine, river traffic, which had been enormously reduced during the
Civil War and Militant Communism period, began suddenly to
flourish.[11]

So successful a year was 1922 that some Communists believed
(and hoped) it marked the end of N.E.P.[12] They were particularly
heartened by Lenin's speech to the Eleventh Congress. Attacking
the pessimists and the critics within the Party, he said that it was
nonsense to talk of wholesale surrender to capitalism, that there was
no reason for them to retreat or to talk of retreating further. His
wife and others close to Lenin indicated that he was very uncom-

fortable with the success of N.E.P. and was itching to start once again on the road to socialism.

But 1923 and 1924 saw somewhat of a reversal. In the autumn of 1923 the peasants went on strike and the government faced what has become known as the famous "Scissors" crisis. Two relatively good harvests had taken place and there was an abundant food supply, but the peasants were screaming for more consumer goods. They were refusing to market their produce and threatening to reduce their output. The workers, on the other hand, had to have low food prices. It did not appear that the problem could be solved by satisfying both the peasants and the workers at the same time. Compounding the Party's anguish was the fact that the "N.E.P.-men," who allegedly had been in control of all but the commanding heights of the economy, were making enormous profits and living a reckless life. And every time the government made an effort to place goods on the market at lower prices, they merely bought up the goods (usually paying graft to catch it before it hit the market) and made bigger profits than ever. The workers, in turn, were deeply resentful of all the splendor, luxury, and carefree living while they lived in poverty and filth. Their hate swelled in their hearts as their wives, daughters, and sweethearts supplied the human flesh for the gambling dens, the night cafes, and the bordellos; but it was a hate directed as well against the Party which allowed this degradation to take place. The Party was aware of the deep resentment among the workers and many Party rank and filers, and this was one factor which led it to begin to clamp down on the N.E.P.-men.

The year 1923 marked the opening of a period of mass terror. W. Reswick, an eyewitness, says that its victims were the "Lishentsi," the name coined for the N.E.P.-men, "who were torn from their homes, shorn of all human rights"; they came to be known as "the deprived ones." At the October Terminal, Reswick stood for hours and watched the "Chekists load victims on a freight train." But "as the . . . terror mounted," he observed, "Muscovites became aware of a new breed of sadists, worse even than the professional Chekists." These were the Communist Youth Shock Brigadiers, the Russian equivalent of the Chinese "Red Guards." "On instructions from Stalin's headquarters" these young men and women "went through Moscow's homes in search of suspects. . . ." [13]

Walter Duranty also refers to the activities of the Soviet "Red Guard." He tells how "one morning four youngsters about twenty, dressed in black leather jackets and breeches, the favored unofficial uniform of the Communist Youth organization, rang my doorbell. The leader said curtly, 'We have come from the financial depart-

ment of the Moscow Soviet to estimate the value of your apart-
ment. . . .'" After a bit of an argument, a departure, they returned
ten minutes later to use Duranty's phone to call for police help to
investigate the N.E.P.-men who owned the building. The conversation ended, Duranty reports, in the following way: "The boy
grinned. 'N.E.P.-men—fin-ish,'" he said slowly in English, then drew
his hand quickly across his throat, with the Russian gesture equivalent to "thumbs down" in the Roman arena." [14]

In 1924 inflation followed on the heels of the "Scissors" crisis,
and the economy took another tumble. The Russians had to accept
the bitter pill of devaluation. With it came additional unemployment and hard times, but the problem in Russia was that there was
no cushion, no reserves. People were already living too "close to
the bone." Indeed, the upset of 1924 made it look as if N.E.P., with
all its concessions, was not working very well at all.

This is exactly the point that was being made by men like
Trotsky in the halls of the Party Congresses and Central Committee
Plenums. Toward the end of 1923 he had delivered a furious at-
tack upon Party policy and organizational methods. Alarmed at the
"Scissors" crisis, and all its implications for a socialist system,
Trotsky had opened the debate on industrialization. He and other
prominent Party figures had issued the "Declaration of the Forty-
Six," and had called for the end of both the dictatorship of the
Secretariat and an economic policy which was leading to disaster.
More will be said about this in the next chapter, but the point here
is that his attack, as well as the Cheka raids, were at once indica-
tive of both the success and failure of N.E.P.

Meanwhile, life for the worker went on and the situation did
improve. But at the end of 1928, although more food was available,
the standard of living for most Russians was still very depressed.
Articles appearing in *Trud* and *Pravda* between February and
August 1928 graphically describe just how desperate the housing
and living conditions were:

> Textile workers (Naro-Fominsk, Moscow Government) are liv-
> ing in overcrowded conditions. Rooms have only one window and
> are so narrow they are more like prison cells than decent dwellings.
> . . . Kitchens are crowded. There is no room on the stoves for
> kettles and pans for all the housewives. Hence the women con-
> stantly quarrel, and not infrequently engage in a free-for-all fight.
> The children roam the corridors. In the winter-time these corridors
> are the only place where the children can [play] and exercise. Pests,
> of different kinds, are abundant in these barracks. Sleep is possible

only when one is absolutely exhausted. The little bodies of the children are covered by red spots, the results of bug and lice bites.[15]

The long narrow room has only one window, which cannot be opened. Some of the panes are broken and the holes plugged with dirty rags. Near the doorway is an oven which serves not only for heating but for cooking as well. The chimney spans the entire length of the room from the doorway to the window. The smell of fumes, of socks hung to dry, fills the room. It is impossible to breathe in the closeness of the air. Along the walls are crude beds covered with dirty straw ticks and rags, alive with lice and bugs. The beds have almost no space between them. The floor is strewn with cigarette ends and rubbish. About two hundred workers are housed here, men and women, married and single, old and young—all herded together. There are no partitions, and the most intimate acts are performed under the very eyes of other inhabitants. Each family has one bed. On one bed a man, a wife and three children live, a baby occupies the "second floor"—a cot hanging over the bed. The same toilet is used by men and women.[16]

The erection of new workers' settlements in Stalino (Don Basin) was completed only last year, but already the barracks look shabby and dilapidated. There are no tables, benches, or chairs in the barracks, and workers are eating on their beds. There are no mattresses on the beds; the workers sleep on the hard boards. The lavatories in the barracks are in a dreadful state; they have never been cleaned. Dirt is everywhere, even in the kitchens, which are more like stables. Everywhere are greasy pans and heaps of rubbish. The barracks are overcrowded. Married and single are herded together. Some of the workers sleep in the lavatories.[17]

Throughout N.E.P. the situation was mixed, but most people were just preoccupied with the business of keeping alive. They tried to avoid being consciously miserable, but most people were unable to find living space adequate for either maintaining sanitary conditions or realizing any personal privacy; nor was it always possible to find enough to eat. Under the conditions of terror and hardship one could neither trust nor depend upon one's friends. Political loyalty was also not very high, reflecting the high levels of dissatisfaction; but as is the case with dissatisfaction and loyalty, no necessary one-to-one relationship exists. Some workers and peasants who were dissatisfied were loyal, and some privileged individuals, such as the N.E.P. men, who were satisfied, were not politically loyal.

Paradoxically, this was a period of high social and upward mobility. Workers and peasants, formerly oppressed by rigidly drawn class lines, now had an opportunity to rise depending upon their abilities or willingness to join the Party. Many, like Khrushchev, did. But random figures from a couple of years show that the total number of those who joined was insignificant. In a wave of enthusiasm following Lenin's death, 250,000 adherents rushed to join the Party between January and June 1924. On the eve of the Thirteenth Party Conference in 1925, 100,000 were admitted to membership, but this was due to a concerted effort on Stalin's part to develop a consolidated base of Party *apparatchiki*. Most of course did not join, and so for the vast majority of the people the prevailing condition was misery. Some comfort, some element of additional material security—these were the objectives of the Russian people, a people whom many commentators write about as a populace who were supposed to have missed the disintegrating experience of the 1929 depression and the earlier political and economic chaos which in Germany gave rise to Hitler.

Under such circumstances it is not surprising that the people turned against the regime, to say nothing of the unions, which were supposed to help and protect them. On the other hand, conditions like these made it difficult for the unions to fulfill their tasks, and contributed to their internal malaise.

In the final analysis, it is the minority dictatorship to which the problems of poverty, corruption, alienation, and miserable living conditions must be attributed. Some aspects of the problems were due to exogenous factors that had a logic of their own and developed willy-nilly, but most of the problems can be attributed to the Party's insistence on doing things its own way. The poverty, misery, and brutality were a direct result of the minority dictatorship, of the Party's effort to build a world in its image of reality.

10 ✿ Unions, Leaders, and Members: Bureaucracy and Membership Rift

> In our larger undertakings the factory committees are submerged under a mass of documents and are consequently unable to pay sufficient attention to what is going on in the workshops. Many presidents and secretaries are so absorbed in their office work that they never find time to put in even a brief appearance in the workshops or to speak to workers. . . . Many of our organizations are entirely lacking in initiative and the officials are content to allow things to slide. Their chief occupation seems to be to ponder and reponder over instructions and regulations.[1]

> We know cases where workers were expelled only because they criticized trade union policy, or because they demanded wage increases. If any one criticizes a member of a factory committee or the activities of a District Trade Union Council, in a month or in a fortnight he is expelled . . . for discrediting the trade union movement. Expulsion for these "offenses" is very frequent.[2]

Government by dictatorship had an adverse effect on internal union politics. It gave rise to a bureaucracy which was characterized by the usual problems of petty tyranny, nepotism, buck-passing, and indifference to the needs and wishes of the membership. In its wake came mass disenchantment. The leadership either could not or would not deliver the needed and desired package of benefits. Union officialdom also revealed a strong tendency to accept unquestioningly the lead of management, subordinating worker interests to managerial interests.

By the end of the twenties, criticism by Party leaders revealed that the problem of alienation and bureaucracy had reached a crucial level. Workers were violating labor discipline, selling their membership cards, not paying their dues; they scoffed at their leaders and did not attend meetings. Occasionally they went out on wildcat strikes and sometimes, in desperation, they had been known to maul, even murder, their labor officials.

The objective of this chapter is to probe the problem of bureaucracy, the breakdown of the unions, and the effort in the late twenties to re-establish ties with the workers. It seems best to start with a picture of the formal institutional arrangements, with an eye to the political controls and general political make-up of the unions.

THE STRUCTURE

For several years after the Revolution, the development of union structure and organization was accompanied by a variety of prevalent ideologies, as well as trial-and-error experiments with craft, industrial, local, and national unionism, workers' control, democratic centralism, and collective bargaining. These early attempts at organizing unions were quite haphazard, frustrating and self-defeating. Only after 1919, after the victory of the Party over the unions was established, was the organizational pattern standardized. The result was that over 967 unions, organized on a craft, shop, city, and industry basis, were gradually united into 23 All-Russian unions, standardized on the principles of industrial unionism and centralism.[8] Superimposed on the industrial union structure, and seriously qualifying it, was a horizontal web of inter-executive agencies.

The All-Union Congress and Central Council

At the pinnacle of the union institutional hierarchy was the national Congress, composed of representatives from all affiliated unions and administrative trade union units. At biennial Congresses it determined policy on political, economic, and social questions, and elected officers to administer the entire movement. It also established the All-Russian Central Council of Trade Unions (A.R.C.C.T.U.), so known until 1924 when it became the All-Union Central Council of Trade Unions (A.U.C.C.T.U.). This was the "supreme authority" on trade union questions between national Congresses; its decisions were binding on all union organs.

The Council, consisting in the early years of 89 members and 40 alternates, elected its own presidium, or managerial board, which in turn consisted of 14 members and 6 alternates. The Presidium, for purposes of administrative efficiency, appointed its own secretariat, consisting of 5 members and 2 alternates. According to its rules, the full membership of the A.R.C.C.T.U. was required to meet at least every three months, or as frequently as circumstances dictated, though the Presidium and secretariat sat in continuous session. In special cases the Presidium had the authority to convene the entire Council, and in cases of urgency it had the right to convene a meeting with just those Council members who were present and available in Moscow; in other words, no quorum of the entire Council was necessary for binding decisions to be made. The Presidium, the secretariat, or any portion of either, could convene as the entire A.R.C.C.T.U. and make decisions for the entire movement if it was felt that political or economic circumstances warranted such a move. Acting through its delegated and discretionary authority, the A.R.C.C.T.U. was a self-contained body responsible only to itself and the Politbureau.

The A.R.C.C.T.U. dominated the movement. The Council had exclusive authority to represent the organzied proletariat "in all state and public organizations."[4] It was responsible for drafting labor legislation and had control over the purse strings of the movement. It had authority "to direct the activity of the All-Russian Trade Unions and inter-trade union federations,"[5] to charter unions, withdraw recognition, supervise and administer the bureaucracy, and appoint and transfer personnel. The Council in addition enjoyed the prerogatives of determining the principles of union membership and good standing, of issuing orders to all members, and of resolving conflicts. It was also responsible for convoking new congresses and conferences, as well as supervising the issuance of all written and oral propaganda. Throughout its history the Council did not hesitate to use its authority to charter unions; transfer and purge officers; set up rival power centers; deny accreditation to hostile unions; use its power over the purse strings, which it derived from a system of state subsidies and a centralized trade union fund common to the entire movement; or use a check-off system to manipulate the movement and subordinate the local units to itself— in short, to do all it could to entrench itself and destroy any opposition. The men who were elected or co-opted to the A.R.C.C.T.U. were the real holders of power in the Soviet trade union movement, thus constituting a genuine power elite.

The Inter-Union Executive
Directly subordinate to the A.R.C.C.T.U. were the interexecutive bodies, the crucial administrative hands of the Council. These

administrative units were organized on horizontal lines to intermesh union units on every level from top to bottom throughout the country. Crosscutting industries and spanning the administrative divisions of the country, they contributed to the cohesiveness and single purpose of the movement.

On the level of each Republic the inter-executive bodies were united in a council which operated through a presidium and a secretariat. Their significance lay in their function of counterchecking any tendencies on the part of the unions to develop into autonomous power centers. The council was meant to effect a system of dual responsibility, but this did not work very well, for the overlapping resulted in conflicts of allegiance between the council and individual central committees of the industrial unions.

In 1926, on the eve of the Seventh Trade Union Congress, the inter-trade union structure, with their number of bureaus, ran—from top to bottom—as follows: [6]

A.R.C.C.T.U.	1
Inter-Union Councils within Republics	16
Provincial Bureaus	4
Department or Regional Inter-Union Councils	59
Inter-Union District Bureaus	312
Inter-Union Regional Bureaus	115
Delegates substituting for Inter-Union Bureaus	47
Local Secretariats	1,000

Industrial Unions

On the other side of the organization structure was the industrial union, which, organized along vertical lines, rested on the principle of uniting all workers—skilled or unskilled—in an industry into one union.

The principal right of an industrial union was "to participate in the organization and economic regulation of the country"—in the registration and distribution of labor, in the improvement of labor output, and so forth. The principal duties were: improvement of the workers' conditions by establishing uniform wage rates and hours, promoting measures for the improvement of labor protection and social insurance, and making studies of these questions. Further, it was to educate its members by "raising the level of education and class consciousness." It also had the duty to "represent and protect" the interests of its members in state and public organizations.[7]

Labor Code Definition of Unions

As defined by Article 151 of the Labor Code of 1922, a union was an association for the representation of citizens working for gain in public and private undertakings, establishments, and enterprises. Its purpose was to act for them in all negotiations with the various state institutions, in the conclusion of agreements and contracts, and in all discussions on questions relating to labor and social welfare.

Vertical Organization

The industrial union was structured on the principle of vertical organization on an industry-wide and nation-wide basis, and was highly centralized. For example, in the metal trades union, all industrial units in the different areas of the country were subordinate to its All-Union organization, which had its central offices with the Central Council of Trade Unions in Moscow. The highest organ of each industrial union was its All-Union Congress, which met annually in the early years and biennially in the late 1920s. The delegates were elected at Republic congresses of the union. In some unions, such as the leather workers', elections were direct; in others, including the textile workers', elections were indirect. The ratio of deputies to members in the 1920s was one to one thousand. Each congress elected its own central committee. Politically, the relationship between the central committee and the congress reflected that of the A.U.C.C.T.U. and the All-Union Congress. Formally, the congress made policy, and formally the central committee was its steering committee. In reality, the latter was usually the policymaker as well as the administrator of the union. Of course, in its relation with the A.U.C.C.T.U. the industrial union had to act within the framework of the instructions and policy determined nationally for the entire movement by the A.U.C.C.T.U. and the All-Russian Congress.

The Organization Department

Various departments were organized under the central committees. The organization department had the primary function of looking after the health of the union and the morale of the members. It acted as a troubleshooter for the entire union and performed those jobs which the other departments either could not or did not do. In most instances the primary nerve center of this department was on the provincial or district level, though the departments at these levels were directly subordinate to the central committee organization department.

The Factory Committee

Factory committees were organized at the shop and work-bench level, though the size and structure of the committee varied with the size of the shop. The factory committees can be said to have been the most important of all union organizations, for it was on this level that the crucial link between the union leaders and the rank-and-file workers was established. In the factory committee meetings the members saw grievances handled, took part in elections, appraised union affairs, and either became directly involved or did not. In other words, it was on this level that the workers directly felt and judged their unions. It was here that a union's ties with its members were tested. To fulfill its duties, the factory committee had several permanent committees, heads of which were appointed to preside over each committee. Such subordinate committees existed for questions of wages and conflicts, labor protection, auditing, education and culture, production and mutual aid. They met during both working and nonworking hours.

Membership Rights and Obligations

During War Communism, no freedom of association, no choice was open to the worker. Membership in the unions was automatic and compulsory for all workers. It was not, however, without its benefits: It brought the right of citizenship and enfranchisement, which in reality meant the very real blessing of an element of protection from the Cheka; second, a membership card entitled a person to a ration card, priority for food, clothing, housing, medical care, and recreation—at a time when many were homeless and starving.

Membership requirements and benefits changed with the introduction of the New Economic Policy. Membership was put on a voluntary basis and the worker was given a choice of remaining with the union or cutting his ties with it. The closed shop did not exist and membership was not held to be a condition of employment, though preference was to be given to union members over nonunion members. The benefits of union membership and the idea of trade unionism were to be the incentives making the workers want to remain or become members of the unions.

Membership was available to all persons engaged in productive work. To join, the worker had to apply in person to the local trade union unit in the shop where he was employed. Admission was decided upon by the plant shop committee and was usually a formality. If a problem arose, however, either political or personal, the case was sent to the next higher district or provincial committee, where all membership questions were ultimately decided. All workers who became members of unions, and were at least seventeen years of age and in good standing, were entitled to vote in union elections and run for office. Good standing meant, formally, that he paid his dues, attended meetings, maintained union discipline, and lived up to the terms of the constitution.

During N.E.P. the benefits of membership in a union were not inconsequential. Union members were entitled to free dental and medical care. They were assigned better appointment hours and given preference in lines at clinics. X-rays and examinations were free to anyone holding a union card. The union member also had a better chance than the nonunion member for admission to a sanitarium or a rest home, for the unions were not only entitled to a number of free places, but decided who was to have the right to use these "union beds." Housing accommodations were provided for the union member before the nonunion member. Rent and electricity were reduced in price. Since housing was extremely scarce and poor, this was indeed a major attraction, even if the accommodations meant living in a barracks.

Dunn, one student on the question, reports that union members were entitled to 25–60 per cent reductions for public baths, ferry boat crossings, movies, railroad excursions, botanical gardens, bathing beaches, museums, and so on.[8] The union member enjoyed the privileges of using the available athletic facilities, for the gyms, pools, and sports fields were controlled by the unions. In addition, the union member could: send his children to nurseries and summer camps before others could; seek up to one month's credit every three months at the city's consumer cooperative; obtain free legal advice; expect better treatment within the plant, such as a chance to go to school and be promoted to more demanding and highly skilled work ahead of the nonunion member; and gain the cherished privacy which the man who is no longer a primary target of a union organizer has over the nonmember.

It must be noted, however, that the worker's rights were seriously curtailed. Although the principles of voluntary membership and freedom of association were introduced, they were not extended to the point where the worker could organize unions independent of the national movement and the A.R.C.C.T.U. Thus the choice was between joining a Bolshevik-controlled union or no union at all. Membership meant enjoyment of substantial benefits without any ability to influence the union; not joining a union meant not only doing without real benefits and abandoning the principle of worker combination, but registering a protest against the Party-controlled unions.

Infractions or violations of union discipline were punishable by expulsion from the union. No provisions were made in the constitution for the right to organize an opposition slate, or to publish or distribute campaign literature. In this regard it must be noted that all elections in many unions were by show of hands, making it impossible for members to oppose and escape recrimination should one venture to cast a negative or opposition vote. Thus, without the right to dissent, to enjoy minority rights, or to organize an opposition and accede to power by the democratic process, the dictatorship of the leadership over the membership was guaranteed. The rights of the member to vote and run for office were hardly more than a device used by the Party to engineer consent, to legitimatize its rule.

Political Composition

The Bolsheviks organized Party units in 1919 to control the unions. Although a minority within the unions, the Bolsheviks had little difficulty in dominating all the Trade Union Congresses and the administrative positions of the union organization itself. Except for the Third Trade Union Conference in July 1917, at which they had only 36.4 per cent of the votes, the Bolsheviks enjoyed a majority at each Congress. From that low level in 1917 they rose to 65 per cent at the First Trade Union Congress, dropped to 60 per cent at the Second Congress, climbed to 78 per cent at the Third Congress, and went to the Fourth Congress in 1921 with 82 per cent of the 2,357 voting delegates.[9]

Appointments and Leadership Control

Control of appointments and administrative posts was also a key to Bolshevik success. In the first available set of statistics on executive bodies, issued in 1921 and 1922, a survey of inter-trade union executive branches revealed that in 1921, of approximately 2,126 functionaries, 67 per cent were Bolsheviks; in June 1922, of 2,232 functionaries, 71 per cent were Bolsheviks. In 1922 the Bolsheviks revealed that 51 per cent of the men holding executive posts on the provisional and district level were Bolsheviks. From the above figures it is clear that, although the Bolsheviks' majority had declined by 1921-1922, leaving them less secure on the provisional and district levels than on the higher ones, their position was still secure enough that they could run matters with a relatively free hand.

Loyalty and Per Cent of Communists as Union Leaders

Of great importance was the Party's criteria for judging the loyalty (and hence eligibility) of persons in principal administrative posts. Following the loyalty probe which had been instigated by the trade union debates of 1920–1921 (see chapter 8), the Central Committee of the Party appointed a committee to study and report to the Eleventh Party Congress on the number and reliability of Communists holding executive positions in the trade unions. The committee, in an incomplete report, informed the Congress that on the level of trade union central committees, of 39 presidents and secretaries only 19 possessed the qualification of extended Party membership. Of the remaining 20, 18 were Party members but unqualified because they had formerly been members of other parties (Menshevik, Socialist Revolutionary, and so on).

Of 140 Party members who sat on the presidiums of the central committees, 34 were alleged to have been members of the Party during the pre-1917 period, 74 had joined the Party between 1917 and 1920, 27 after 1920, and 60 had converted at unspecified times. The term "alleged" is used advisedly, for in the committee's report the total number of those investigated did not always balance with a total breakdown of each of the group classifications. Yet the committee's report was accepted and acted upon by the Congress—in this rests its significance.

Of the 330 members of the central committees, it was alleged that 72 had records of membership dating back to the pre-1917 period while 211 joined between 1917 and 1920, 47 after 1920; 100 had the taint of former membership in other parties. The report also indicated that some central committees of the various unions were stronger than others in that they had more old-time members than others; some, like Tsektran (railway and inland water workers), which had only six Party members, had very few and were therefore weak. On the provincial level, the committee breakdown of Party members, ranked in terms of the hierarchy of loyalty with top priority to old-timers, revealed that not more than half had an adequate background.

The Eleventh Congress, acting on the advice of the committee and of the A.R.C.C.T.U., ordered a revamping of the trade union administrative apparatus. It translated into reality the Eleventh Conference recommendations and held that length of Party affiliation would be the determining factor for appointments to executive positions. Presidents and secretaries of the central committees were required to have joined the Party before 1917. Members of the executive bodies of central committees and presidents and secretaries of provincial inter-union councils were required to have had at least three years' preliminary training as Party members; members of the provincial level inter-union councils' executive bodies were to have had a preliminary membership period of at least two years.[10]

Apparently the Central Committee had no difficulty in removing and transferring officers elected to trade union posts by trade union members. A report on the changes ordered by the Eleventh Congress was presented at the Sixth Congress of Trade Unions in 1924. This report was summarized by the International Labor Organization, and it revealed that the shuffling and reshuffling of personnel necessitated by these changes had taken place. The number of "loyalty suspects" had diminished, while the number of loyal old-timers holding crucial positions had risen.

The results revealed that the changes which had occurred between the Fifth and Sixth Congresses were significant, particularly on the level of the central committees.

CHANGES IN POLITICAL COMPOSITION OF
LEADING TRADE UNION POSTS BETWEEN
FIFTH AND SIXTH TRADE UNION CONGRESSES [11]

Central Committee		Pre-1917 Members	Post-Nov. 1917	Inde-pendents	Other Parties
Presidium of the Central Committee	V Cong. (1922)	28.4	63.6	8.0	—
	VI Cong. (1924)	31.4	65.8	2.8	—
Complete Committee	V Cong.	18.8	65.5	12.8	2.9
	VI Cong.	27.9	65.2	6.9	—
Paid Staff	V Cong.	6.2	42.0	43.3	8.5
	VI Cong.	9.3	49.6	41.1	—

In terms of other changes, the report indicated that on the departmental level and in the inter-administrative units, the number of Communists had increased, while the number of nonmembers had dropped by approximately 25 per cent.

	Communists	Independents	Other
V Congress	78.9	18.5	2.6
VI Congress	91.9	8.1	—

Furthermore, the Report stated that the majority of presidents and secretaries of these committees were Party members, with membership records dating back to the pre-November period.

On the district level, the inter-administrative office, it was reported that the vast majority, 83.5 per cent, were Communists, but that of the officials of these bodies a minority of only 41 per cent were Communists. Of the trade union sections a majority of the officials, 65 per cent, were Communists.

At the Seventh Trade Union Congress in 1926, Tomsky revealed that of the 1,295 delegates attending the Congress, 85 per cent were Party members; that of those attending the individual Republic congresses, 60–70 per cent were Communists; on the regional and provincial levels, 30–40 per cent. He stated that the number of members varied from union to union, particularly on the level of the local committees. Party membership was highest in the mine, paper, water transport, textile, and chemical workers' unions, and lowest in the medical workers and art workers' union, where it dropped to the level of 13–14 per cent. Tomsky further reported that on the shop level the number of Communists making up the committees had decreased and the number of non-Party members had increased. In 1925 approximately 30 per cent of the members of the factory committees had been Communists, whereas in 1926, only 25 per cent were. The same held true, he said, for the subcommittees, where in 1925, 24.3 per cent of the members were Communists and in 1926, only 14.4 per cent were.[12] The decrease of Communists on these lower levels can be taken as a sign of the Party's effort to secure more non-Party worker support and activity, but it may also be taken as a sign of the Party's failure to recruit workers into its own ranks; probably both suppositions hold some truth.

Per Cent of Worker Communists

The high percentage of Communists holding trade union posts stood in sharp contrast to the total number of workers who were Communists. From an evaluation of official, though conflicting, reports, it is clear that of the number of Communists who were workers between 1921 and 1928 did not exceed 57 per cent of the Party membership, and that the number of workers who were Party members between 1921 and 1928 was not even 10 per cent of the total trade union membership.

In regard to the number of Party members who were workers, the following official figures list the workers as hovering just around the 50 per cent mark for the years 1922 to 1928. In 1922 the total Party membership was, according to one set of figures, 386,313.[18] The number of workers in the Party was listed as 171,625, or 44.4 per cent of the total Party membership. In 1923 the total membership was 345,034, of which 44.9 per cent were workers; in 1924, the total membership was 446,089, of which 196,339 or 44.0 per cent were workers. In 1925, of a total membership of 798,802, 453,-141 or 56.7 per cent were workers; in 1926, of 1,076,814, 612,202 or 56.8 per cent were workers; in 1927, of 1,144,053, 637,768 or 55.7 per cent were workers; in 1928, of 1,304,471, 740,731 or 56.8 per cent were workers. It is difficult to say whether these figures are accurate, for a discrepancy exists between the total membership figures cited above and those cited in other sources, though the correlation is relatively close. For example, against the above figure of 386,313 for 1922, Fainsod [14] reports 528,354; for 1923, 354,034 against 499,100; for 1924, 446,089 against 472,000; for 1925, 798,801 against 801,804; for 1926, 1,076,814 against 1,079,814; for 1927, 1,114,053 against 1,212,505; and for 1928, 1,304,471 against 1,305,854.

On the other hand, other reports dealing with the membership problem during N.E.P. indicate a much lower percentage of Party members who were workers. For example, two reports in *Pravda* disclose that in July 1927 the number of workers in the Party was less than 36.7 per cent of total Party membership and in January 1928, 40.8 per cent; [15] these percentages are 55.7 and 56.8 respectively in the previously cited report. The best one can do here is to agree with Lenin that the Party faced a constant problem: Most Party members were not members of the proletariat, and from the framework of Leninism, the makeup of the Party was not sufficiently proletarian.[16]

Communists in Trade Unions

In regard to the number of Communists in the unions, the following estimates can be made: In July 1922 the total trade union membership was 5,846,000, while 171,625, a mere 3 per cent, were in the Party. In July 1924 union membership was reported to be 5,822,700, of which 196,339 or 4.3 per cent can be said to have been Party members. In January 1926 total union membership was reported as 8,768,200 with 612,202 Party members, indicating that only 6.9 per cent were Communist. In 1928 total union membership was 11,060,000, of which 740,731 were Party members, giving the Communists 6.7 per cent. Since the Party was to be a small elite, there is little that is striking about this small percentage. Yet it is revealing about Party control and the deterioration of support within the unions. The Party did not want to be isolated from the workers, yet it very clearly was.

The All-Union Central Committee: Power to
Charter and Recognize

A better grasp of the dynamics of Party controls can be gained if we look closer at several techniques and one further incident which occurred during the period under study. An excellent example of the power and scope of the A.R.C.C.T.U. was its authority to charter trade unions. Under the terms of Article 151 of the 1922 Labor Code, trade unions did not have to register with state agencies to be licensed, but "the trade unions shall be registered with the inter-union bodies to which they are affiliated in accordance with the conditions prescribed by the All-Russian Congress of Trade Unions."[17] The conditions of registration were made even tighter with the severe penalty of dissolution and nonrecognition prescribed for every union which did not register. Article 153 stipulated:

> Other associations not registered with the central inter-trade union federations under Section 152 shall not be entitled to style themselves trade unions nor to claim the rights of such unions: a) acquire and manage property, and b) to conclude contracts, agreements, etc., of all kinds under the legislation in force.[18]

Clearly the need to register was imperative; clearly the right to be registered implied meeting the conditions set forth by the A.R.C.C.T.U. and conforming to its orders and rules, which covered general structure of union and staff, union budgets, and delineation of the immediate tasks for the unions.

Many instances of the A.R.C.C.TU. (before it became the A.U.C.C.T.U.) using its powers to destroy opposition unions can be cited, particularly the power of chartering. One such case involved the Printers' Union (described in Chapter 3), and another, the Moscow Chemical Workers' Union, both Menshevik unions.

The A.R.C.C.T.U. and the Moscow Chemical
Workers' Union

In the case of the Moscow Chemical Workers' Union, the situation was somewhat different from the case of the Printers' Union, but the results were the same. The *casus belli* occurred on March 26, 1921, the day of elections for the post of honorary chairman of the union. The Bolsheviks had nominated Lenin for the position, as they did in most unions. The membership, however, were not inclined to see things this way, and to the chagrin of the Bolsheviks, elected Martov rather than Lenin. As a consequence, several weeks later, in April, the first steps were taken to crush the Moscow Chemical Workers. The A.R.C.C.T.U. sent orders to the central committee of the Chemical Worker's Union, the parent organization of the Moscow union, to reorganize the Moscow unit. At the same time the Bolshevik minority in the Moscow unit began to maneuver toward the goal of taking over the organization.

Until their congress in the fall, the Menshevik leaders showed they were in complete control of their union, for all attempts to oust them proved to be in vain. At the congress a motion was introduced condemning union neutrality and calling for support of the Revolution, a euphemism for the support of the Communist Party. The delegates defeated the resolution and passed an alternate one which called for the independence of trade unions from political parties. At that point the Bolshevik minority arose as one and walked out, marking the complete and final rupture between the Bolsheviks and the Mensheviks. Shortly thereafter the Bolsheviks, with A.R.C.C.T.U. approval, seized the Menshevik headquarters by force and issued a call for a new congress. The new congress proved to be Bolshevik-dominated and a series of resolutions endorsing the Party position were passed. The A.R.C.C.T.U. recognized it as the official congress of the Moscow union, thus legitimatizing the Bolshevik seizure of the union's reigns of power.[19] From the fall of 1921 the Bolsheviks had no trouble maintaining complete control of the union apparatus, without which the Menshevik members were impotent. Thus the case of the Chemical Workers' Union followed the pattern of the other Menshevik unions.

Centralized Purse Strings

State subsidies and centralized control of union funds also contributed substantially to A.U.C.C.T.U. domination of the entire movement. Through centralized control of the purse strings, the A.U.C.C.T.U. actually placed the unions in a position of dependency for the monies necessary for maintaining their operations.

The system of state subsidies was originally introduced in 1918 to resolve a very real problem: financing membership and organizational growth at a time when the unions were transformed literally overnight from a handful of small, fragmented units into a nationwide institution embracing a membership of two and one-half million workers. This transformation was too rapid and the unions, possessing no real organization or reserves, were unable to meet the costs of their growth out of their own pocketbooks. Since many of the worker-members could not and did not pay their dues, the unions had a first-class problem on their hands: They could not afford their own growth. It was only after the system had been effectively set up, however, that it was used as a device for maintaining political control over the industrial unions.

In addition to subsidies, the centralization of trade union funds also contributed to the A.U.C.C.T.U. political hegemony. As stated in the Model Trade Union Constitution of 1919,[20] all monies were to belong to the central units. The amount to which the local units were entitled was rigidly fixed, though they were allowed up to 40 per cent, or enough for normal administrative purposes. The funds transferred to the higher units cut sharply into local independence. Furthermore, the local units were not permitted to use the funds retained to create strike funds, and so forth, but only for operational costs. The significance of this system was that a union could not undertake activities, such as a strike, that the A.U.C.C.T.U. did not approve.

An integral part of this system of centralized funds was the creation of a "central fund" common to all unions and executive agencies. It was derived from contributions from the local units and was placed under the jurisdiction of the A.U.C.C.T.U. This fund was used to finance the activities of some of the poorer unions, but its primary purpose was to provide funds for underwriting the Profintern, political education, newspapers, and so on.

INTERNAL UNION PROBLEMS

If the Party succeeded in maintaining control over the unions, it also faced a major internal union crisis. This question of internal difficulties was first broached openly at the Fifth Trade Union Congress, when Andreev took a hard look at the membership figures and the number of strikes. Over 50 per cent of the workers had quit the unions during the period from July 1921 to August 1922. In September, at the time of the Fifth Congress, the unions could report a membership of only five million.[21]

Quixotically, this radical decline was attributed to economic contraction, the problem of a previously inflated membership, the dismissal of temporary workers, and the exclusion of artisans, members of artels, administrators, and other nonproletarian elements from union membership. Only to a minor extent was it interpreted as a vote of no confidence in the unions. It was observed that now that the unions had resolved the problem of an inflated membership and hence were in a position to determine how many truly valued their trade union membership, the unions were in a position to make progress.

They did not make much headway, however, and it was not until 1925 that major attention was focused on internal structural problems. In March of that year Andreev, as chairman of the Railwaymen's Union and secretary of the A.U.C.C.T.U., delivered two major addresses on the question of internal union conditions and initiated the famous "closer to the masses" drive,[22] which was launched in the hope of rebuilding the unions.

Andreev quite forcefully contended that the moral condition of the trade union movement was distinctly unhealthy. He said that workers who paid dues should receive, in return, the right to state their views on questions which directly concerned their welfare; that the union, permeated with discontent, should be "housecleaned," and the old remnants of War Communism swept out and replaced by N.E.P. In July he pointed a finger at the chief defect in the trade union situation, calling it a "bureaucratic spirit." Referring to bureaucratic distortions, he stated that the trade union officials had lost all contact with the working masses and had ceased to feel any responsibility toward them. The officials confined themselves to carrying out orders from the higher trade union or Communist Party organization and acknowledged no responsibility except to such organizations. These bureaucratic attitudes, the inertia and irresponsibility of the trade union officials and their lack of comprehension of the workers' needs, were the main causes for trade union ills: embezzlement of funds, corrupt officials, curtailment of worker criticism, worker apathy, failure to pay dues, strikes, and so on.[23]

Worker Apathy

On July 18 the A.U.C.C.T.U. picked up the argument and published a circular in which it listed the evils crippling the unions and the remedies necessary for restoring health. The A.U.C.C.T.U. pointed out that general membership meetings were attended by no more than 15 per cent of the total membership and that dues were paid by no more than 50 per cent of the members. Andreev, speaking on this circular, resolved that "there is no intention this time of talking merely to impress foreigners"; and further that "it is the intention of the trade unions' leaders and of the Communist Party to conduct to a satisfactory conclusion the campaign of trade union reconstruction. Those officials who do not conform will be dismissed." [24]

Andreev went on to explain some of the reasons for the apathy among the membership. General meetings, he said, were usually flat and uninteresting. The proceedings usually amounted to little more than a formal reading of reports and the adoption, without opposition, of all the submitted resolutions. On the question of trade union democracy, he frankly reported that the vast majority of elections, particularly on the factory committee level, were little more than a hoax. No opportunity was given for a discussion of the candidates at the general meetings. Rarely were the individual candidates presented. The workers usually had to accept the official list, which was passed in bloc. The outgoing committee did not always submit a report on its administration; when it did, all awkward questions were glossed over. If members criticized the proceedings, retaliations frequently occurred, sometimes going as far as expulsion of the worker from the union. This in turn, he said, usually meant that the worker lost his job.

To help alleviate the problem of alienation, the A.U.C.C.T.U. proposed that the factory committees use "education and persuasion" as their watchword, rather than "arbitrary authoritarianism," as had been the case. While recognizing that the work of factory committees was particularly difficult because wage increases had to correspond with what the national economy allowed, the A.U.C.C.T.U. believed that the committees could, if they used sufficient finesse, win the confidence of their members.

On the question of elections and the right to criticize, the A.U.C.C.T.U. urged the unions to adopt democratic procedures. The factory committees were told to submit detailed reports to plenary meetings of the workers and to encourage criticism. Candidates were to be discussed and voted on individually. Then the A.U.C.C.T.U. stated that the higher trade union organizations should not, on their own authority, alter the composition of the factory committee during the course of the year unless it was absolutely necessary.

Collusion

Another problem which was raised was that of collusion between the factory committees and management—or, as it was officially termed, trade union "deviationism"—on piece rates, wages, and the dismissal and blacklisting of those whom management labeled "undesirable." It was even noted that there were cases on record in which the factory committees, with management's consent, had threatened workers on strike with a lockout. This abusive policy was to be terminated. (On the other hand, what was not condemned was union leadership consent to the use of the G.P.U. to crush wildcat strikes.[25]) As in the case of other problems, the unions were to correct these abuses by activating their membership and by strengthening the factory committees. Only then, it was avowed, would the problem be solved. In October the Communist Party Central Committee picked up the question of managerial deviations and criticized the trade unions for neglecting their "chief task," the defense of their members.[26]

Party Interference in Trade Unions

At the same time the Communist Party Central Committee focused attention on Party interference in union matters. It criticized the local Party units for "petty meddling and the usurpation of normal trade union functions," a practice which was undermining the unions. The "petty meddling" in "normal" trade union affairs amounted to the Party organizations' choosing (often too lightly) the managers of the unions, their replacing or transferring officials too frequently in defiance of the established rules, and their interference with trade union funds and the repeal of trade union instructions. In regard to trade union activities, the Party units were criticized for taking almost all questions relating to the conditions of labor, wages, and collective agreements out of the hands of the trade unions. In both instances, the C.P.C.C. contended, the local units had violated the normal methods of trade union democracy and had damaged the authority of the unions in the eyes of the rank and file.

The C.P.C.C. went on to remind the local Party organizations that through the trade unions the Party possessed a powerful weapon for bringing non-Communists under the influence of the Communist Party. It stated further that the trade unions could not serve their purpose unless the great mass of workers could see the unions as organizations that were able to defend their interests. The Party and its local units should act in such a way that every non-Communist worker would feel that the trade unions represented him, and that he controlled them, elected the officers, and held the unions accountable to him. Only then, the C.P.C.C. stated, would the unions be able to realize their true objective—to be schools of Communism.

With this end in view the C.P.C.C. called on all local Party organizations to abandon direct domination. It called on them to exercise their controlling power by means of the Communist fractions and groups within the unions.

Tomsky's Criticisms—Fourteenth Party Congress

At the Fourteenth Party Congress in December 1925, Tomsky dwelled on the same theme. In a report entitled "The New Conditions for Unions," [27] he dealt with the internal ailments of the unions. Significantly, however, he emphasized the crisis as a product of the structural conditions of N.E.P. rather than the Party-union relationship. In attributing the weaknesses to the New Economic Policy, he argued that the Party and union leaders were still unwilling to admit or recognize, and probably not just publicly, that the dictatorship was the principal source of the alienation.

Tomsky was much more candid and realistic in other parts of his address. On the relation of unions to Party and state, he said that during the transition period the unions should collaborate with the Communist Party and the Soviet Government to abolish the bureaucratic weaknesses in the administration of the trade unions —weaknesses which could prove to be fatal.

In discussing the duties of unions, he said one problem was that, for some time, the trade unions had been bewildered by the multiplicity of the economic and political duties that fell upon them. Since they were unable to do everything expected of them, they had had to choose between duties; and they had not always chosen to perform their essential duty, namely the advancement of the interests of their membership, materially and intellectually.

As for membership, Tomsky indicated that, along with Soviet industry, the unions were regaining lost ground; that membership was growing, as was the proletariat. But mere numbers were no longer enough. Now the question of the composition and loyalty of the workers was the vital factor. Tomsky stated that the industrial proletariat was then composed of new workers who had not yet been "through the mill." They were "the children of the revolution," who knew nothing of the conditions of labor or of life in pre-Revolutionary industry; or they were young peasants who came straight from the country and had no conception of the factory system, the class war, or the work methods of organized labor. Unfortunately, these persons—in many cases totally illiterate—retained a peasant mentality. In many cases they tended to hold themselves apart from the proletarian man, considering themselves to be no more than "birds of passage" in the factories and towns. These new elements inflating the ranks of the trade unions, he said, created a problem. They led to the development of a new type of trade unionist, one who took more interest in the possession of the trade union membership card and the advantages afforded by it than in a general knowledge of trade union matters and the objectives of the movement. These elements, he said, had to be "educated."

Finally, on the question of trade union democracy and closer links with the people, Tomsky said that from every point of view the watchword of trade unionism in Russia should be "keep in touch with the people." The importance of realizing this close relationship, he emphasized, rested not in itself but in its preparation of the workers for the part they should play, namely the support and defense of the state against all elements hostile to the dictatorship of the proletariat.

Seventh Trade Union Congress

The recognition of these problems and the initiation of the "closer to the masses" drive did not, however, lead to any major improvements. At the Seventh Trade Union Congress, December 6–18, 1926, the union leaders revealed that they were still groping with the problems of bureaucracy. Tomsky turned once again to the problem of the social composition of the unions. At the Fifteenth Party Conference (October–November 1926) he had denied Trotsky's charge that a large number of nonindustrial workers with an essentially nonproletarian psychology and political outlook were joining the unions and diluting their proletarian character.

Tomsky had also argued that the industrial elements comprised 53.1 per cent of the total, the transport workers another 14 per cent, and salaried employees not more than 32 per cent. He had argued bitterly that it was fatuous to consider as "middle class" those salaried employees who earned less than 80 rubles a month— a condition which was true for 73 per cent of the total salaried employees in the towns and 99 per cent of those in the provinces.[28]

Now, at the Seventh Trade Union Congress, Tomsky warned the delegates that the cleavage between the membership and the unions—originally due to bureaucratic practices—was sharpened because of the influx of a new type of worker, a peasant worker who was joining the labor force at the rate of 14 per cent of the total annually. His denial of the Trotsky charge reflected the intensity of the succession question, which now dominated Party attention. Tomsky said that these newcomers were very different from the old workers.

> [They] are persons who have no conception of what the Soviet state really is, whose only desire is to earn as much as they can in order to satisfy the needs of their families which have been left in the country, and who make no distinction between a Soviet undertaking and a private concern.[29]

The trade unions for them, he said, were merely a means of remuneration, and they were opposed to all efforts which did not lead to the immediate improvement of their material situation.

On organizational questions, the delegates heard Dogadov report that the trade unions were endeavoring to draw their members into various plant committees on labor protection, education, propaganda, and so forth, and that there were about 642,000 members in these committees; that efforts were being made to attract more workers to the general meetings, with good results; and that since the last factory committee elections there had been a change, or a shake-up, of 50 to 60 per cent of the staffs of these committees. In general, Dogadov gave a very promising report on union committee work.

A less encouraging picture was drawn by Melnichansky,[30] who reported that the great mass of members did not attend shop meetings, and that relations between the members and their unions were still far from healthy. He attributed their lack of interest to two factors: bureaucratic union procedures and exhausted workers. He indicated that many workers lived as far as ten to fifteen *versts* from their work. At the end of the day the workers, who were tired and lived great distances from their homes, were ill-disposed to remain at their plants and spend their free time at meetings. He emphasized also that meetings were too frequent, agendas often badly drawn up and loaded with irrelevant questions, and that meeting rooms were much too small and not at all appropriate for meetings. He also indicated that the workers were showing a growing impatience with their leaders.

A report published in *Communist* on December 4, 1926, on the eve of the Congress, painted essentially the same picture. It related instances where members were forced to attend meetings, where doors were locked and members not allowed to leave. The report pointed out that in one case, where the workers had shown no inclination to attend a meeting called on payday by the factory committee secretary, the secretary had ordered the payment of wages delayed until the meeting was over. The workers therefore attended, but sat silent throughout the entire meeting, which lasted into the late hours of the night. At this Congress Tomsky also complained that the general factory meetings were poorly attended and that critics were dismissed as "grumblers" and "windbags."[31]

Eighth Trade Union Congress

By the time of the Eighth Trade Union Congress, December 10–24, 1928, the picture within the unions had not changed radically. Some gains could be noted, but the dominant feature was its conflicting trends. The major gains were in the realm of increased trade union membership, which had climbed consistently from a low of six million in 1924 to the all-time high of 11 million in 1928, though growth had declined slightly between 1926 and 1928 as a result of the tighter admission rules introduced at the Seventh Trade Union Congress.[32]

In 1924, out of the total membership of six million, 3.7 million members were industrial workers and 2.3 million were "employees" —white collar workers, doctors, teachers, foremen, salaried workers, and so on; 80 per cent of the total had joined unions individually.[33] In 1926 the total membership figure had jumped to nine million. Of these, 5.5 million were industrial workmen. In 1928, agriculture, food, and building had grown by 46.1 per cent, 51.8 per cent, and 36.3 per cent respectively. By 1928 the percentage of organized workers had climbed from the low percentages of the early twenties to a new peak. Now Russians could boast one of the largest trade union movements in the world, with a claimed enrollment of 91 per cent of all wage earners. The growth is directly attributable to economic expansion and a larger labor force; to a relatively improved standard of living which accompanied the industrial recovery in the mid-twenties; to a lesser extent, as can be inferred from Tomsky's report, to the concerted and relentless drive the unions waged to organize the workers; and finally, to the advantages attached to trade union membership which made it worthwhile for the average worker to join a union.

On the other side of the picture, little headway had been made with the problem of bureaucracy and alienation, which offset the gains in membership growth. Tomsky, in his progress report on organization and membership at the Eighth Trade Union Congress, emphasized the gains in membership over the preceding year; he used this fact as evidence of a healing of the rift between membership and leaders.[34] But actually, as he outlined the sore spots, he revealed that the rift was as serious as ever, if not more so.

Some improvements could be noted in trade union democracy, but the success, he stated, was entirely inadequate. The democratic spirit could not be called remarkable, rank-and-file criticism was halting, the principle of election lame, and discipline ailing. Criticisms still came mainly from above, revealing that the bureaucrats were guilty of impatience and neglect. It was still a common occurrence that, when a worker criticized a trade union chairman, the latter used his authority to crush the worker immediately. Usually just calling the worker a factional person or a Menshevik was sufficient. Once destroyed and "hung like a rabbit skin in a shop window," the worker was cured of any further urge to criticize a leader.

Embezzlement was still a problem. Tomsky estimated that as much as 12 per cent of the union membership were guilty of thievery. He stated that thefts took place on every level; not even Communists or chairmen of unions were wholly innocent. Union membership cards, he reported, were still being sold on the black market. Like shares on the stock market, you could estimate the relative value of a union from the quotes for the cards. Strikes, Tomsky indicated, happened without the union's knowledge; the work of the unions in preventing strikes was "hardly commendable." Obviously, if strikes were occurring it could hardly be said that the workers had been sufficiently disciplined. While legal, strikes were inadmissible unless the workers had exhausted all other possible avenues of peaceful settlement open to them.

Discipline had been undeniably relaxed. It needed to be tightened, but in a "civilized" manner and largely by means of public opinion and collective agreements. He declared that a repeat of the experience of War Communism—when the unionists sat with management, inflicted disciplinary penalties and turned the unions into a kind of prison—had to be avoided. "Civilized discipline" meant raising the awareness of the workers by educating them. Only by creating an attitude, a form of public spirit—which would lead the workers to consider every act of negligence, every misuse of machinery and material to be an intolerable, antisocial act hostile to the interests of the working class—could a civilized form of discipline be accomplished.

What Tomsky found particularly disturbing was that acts of violence against the unemployment officers and foremen, especially by those workers who were "backward," "coarse," or "members of the new strata," were increasing. The violence, he felt, revealed the extent of the alienation from the leaders. He cited a case in Leningrad where, at the Skorokhold factory, a worker killed a foreman. Tomsky asked, "What strange relations must have existed between the foreman and the worker to culminate in murder?" Reflecting on the murder, which obviously deeply troubled him, he remarked on how little confidence the worker had had in his union. "Why had he not appealed to the factory committee? If the foreman was malicious . . . why had not the worker asked for help from the union organizations?" [35] That Tomsky, a hard, disciplined Communist, still retained an element of innocence and idealism is evident. Tomsky and others like him were becoming embittered men. It is not unreasonable to assume that incidents like this led him to resist the program of intensive industrialization which the Party was then debating.

Throughout the year, reports in *Trud* indicated that the situation had not altered very much. A case in the Urals was cited, describing how eleven workers were dismissed from an undertaking for criticizing its administration. In another case in Sverdlovsk, workers who began to criticize management at a general meeting were told to "shut up." [36] In Smolensk, *Trud* reported that a serious situation had developed in the Communal Workers Union, where "every speech made by a rank-and-file member was considered as a counterrevolutionary utterance." [37] In Taganrog, *Trud* reported that "two workers were dismissed for criticizing the factory administration." [38]

Elections, particularly on the shop level, were also criticized by *Trud*. In September it reported that the discovery of irregularities in 91 trade union elections in the Ukraine led to the dissolution of 58 of these organizations and to 33 re-election orders. But most significantly, it stated that in no case was the discovery due to a rank-and-file complaint. [39]

In August a letter from Odessa, published in *Trud*, revealed the following story. "At a clothing factory [a] member of the district trade union council was elected chairman of the election committee." The chairman, the article stated, juggled the ballot, but quite crudely, for "candidates who received a majority of the votes were not included in the list of those elected to the new worker committee." Also, candidates who had lost were declared to have won, and were elected as the new members of the committee. It further reported that "out of seven new committee members only two received over 50 per cent of the vote." The chairman, the report continued, had erased the results and ordered the returns filed without being published. The report went on to state that "factory committees do not enjoy any authority among workers. The workers are discontented. They do not trust the committees and the trade union officials." [40]

Thus, by the time of the Eighth Trade Union Congress, the problem of internal disorder had not been solved. The breakdown of the unions and the growth of these cancerous elements had a drastic effect on the unions' position *vis à vis* the Party. Union strength was contingent upon internal cohesion. Any loss of union strength due to a lack of support of the membership necessarily meant a weaker bargaining position against that of the Party. And further, it meant the union leadership had to rely upon the Party to maintain its control over the union command posts and the workers. Of necessity the unions had to maintain internal unity and stability if they were to influence or determine the relationship between themselves and the Party. Anything less than unity was bound to mean a weakened position, a poorer bargaining position with the Party on any and all questions which the unions sponsored independently of Party wishes. Unfortunately for the unions, their internal condition was distinctly weak.

11 ✪ Union Performance, Economic Backwardness

To the extent that the unions failed to gain control over the labor force or to show even reasonable ability to control the labor market until 1928, they contributed to their own undoing. In part, they were responsible for their own failure. In part, the larger economic problem of backwardness and disruption was beyond their reach and just swallowed them up.

By the mid- and late twenties, marked gains had been won, but the over-all picture remained mixed. The national trend was one of persistent growth, but the economy continued to be vexed by problems of underdevelopment, exhaustion, and stagnation in many areas. By 1926–1927, gross industrial output reached the 1913 level. The prewar standard of living had almost been realized and, although the prewar level of agricultural production had not yet been attained, the recovery was substantial. According to one estimate,[1] real national income grew at a rate of better than 5 per cent, if not close to 7 per cent, which was substantial compared to earlier gains. And, as we shall see in Chapter 12 (p. 241), the level of investment in 1927, about one-third of the national income, was extraordinarily strong. This is the positive side of the picture.

Militating against these impressive gains was the serious problem of an underdeveloped economy. To have attained the 1913 level of industrial production was encouraging, but in 1913 only 5 per cent of the labor force was industrial, and Russia still had a long way to go to complete her modernization. In addition, the attainment of the prewar level of living accomplished during N.E.P.

meant mere subsistence—a typically East European diet, low in meat, milk, eggs, and fat, and high in cabbage, cereals, potatoes, and bread. It also meant crude living facilities. No one had been happy with 1913, and there was little to be thrilled about in 1927, with 80 per cent of the national income being spent on consumption.

Third, there was the depressing factor of widespread and uncontrolled industrial unemployment and a serious problem of rural overpopulation. The *rate* of growth, impressive as it was in the middle and late twenties, was not high enough to absorb the unemployed. Fourth, the state was operating in the context of a peasant economy. Most people lived off the land, and the agricultural system was antiquated. Most peasant holdings were too small and primitive to be efficient. Old-fashioned methods were employed; fertilizer and mechanized equipment were not generally available. In addition, rent and taxes were almost completely eliminated and what savings the peasants had were hoarded. The peasants either could not or did not care to produce more than they could consume, or refused to market additional output because of the "goods famine" and an unstable currency. Thus the government lacked the grain surpluses it needed to feed an expanding industrial base; it lacked the surpluses the Tsar had relied upon for foreign trade and expansion capital.

There was also the question of help from abroad. This proved to be a very sticky problem, for some, like Bukharin, wanted foreign aid; some did not believe capitalists would come to the aid of the Soviet Union. Some, like Stalin, did not want it even if it was available. Others, including Preobrazhensky, wanted it in large amounts, and still others only on a limited basis. Not surprisingly, for ideological reasons, all apparently underestimated the amount they could have borrowed from abroad. These were the problems of backwardness. The situation was mixed, and the picture was not pretty. Stalin was right. Russia was roughly a half-century behind all the other major powers.

UNION PERFORMANCE

Against this picture of backwardness the question was how to effect a major change in the structure of the economy. But given a situation where the crucial factors were the development of industrial capacity and investment capital, the unions could do little, particularly in the early period of N.E.P. when the problem was felt acutely. These questions were beyond the more limited range of union jurisdiction and union capability. They could not tax the peasant, provide the capital resources required for expansion, or control investments. Furthermore, against a background of severe economic stresses and strains—stagnation, rural overpopulation, industrial unemployment, low real wages, inflation, and so forth— what the unions could do was of necessity limited to relative improvements within the framework of severe structural problems. Marginal changes were possible, but the range of reform was sharply limited by the structural weaknesses.

Nevertheless, the unions were not without recourse to some measures bearing on the investment-growth problem. Within the domain of wages and prices the unions could contribute to the accumulation of investment funds by freezing union wage demands; by holding wages to a minimum; by maintaining tight reins on all wage movements to prevent wage drifts, particularly inflationary ones; and by actively enforcing a worker-sacrifice policy. This was very much their declared intention, for, as Tomsky stated at the Seventh Trade Union Congress, in the interests of socialist accumulation no Russian worker would advance the same argument for higher wages that he would under capitalism. He said: "The interests of today must be subordinated to the general class interests of tomorrow and the immediate future." [2]

The unions enjoyed little success in achieving this goal. They quickly bogged down in a problem of low real wages and a runaway wage drift, and were able to make little or no contribution to the investment policy with their attempt to retain tight control over wage movements.

WAGES

The problem of low real wages was a product of backwardness, of devastation from the civil war, and of inflation. During the civil war real wages had fallen sharply; Zagorsky estimated they were about one-third of the prewar level.[3] With the economic growth of N.E.P., wages climbed, slipped with the currency reform of 1924, and climbed again, until they reached the prewar level in 1927. Finally in 1928–1929 wages exceeded the prewar level. Once again, however, the 1913 level was a low basis for comparison. In 1925, Ryazanov, deeply depressed about the low standard of living, caustically commented that even if a workman earned 110 per cent of his prewar wages, he still existed at "100 per cent below the level of a human being." [4]

The wage drift problem was twofold: a steadily widening wage spread between the skilled and the unskilled, and runaway wage increases with strong inflationary pressures in the upper brackets. For the most part the problem was structural. While unskilled labor was plentiful, it was skilled labor that was in great demand; thus a job shortage developed. Managers were willing to pay high prices to attract specialists, engineers, and so on, and salaries in these upper brackets jumped rapidly—leading to sharp inequities and uncontrolled purchasing power. The wage drift also resulted from the introduction of an unlimited piece rate and bonus system, both of which led to very uneven earnings within each wage scale. The inequity of the wage situation was called by one commentator an "orgy of salaries" for state employees and the "anarchy of wages" for the industrial workmen.[5] Among industrial workers, however, the inequality was less than in 1914.[6]

The unions tried to tackle the problem by fixing wage scales, by bringing pressure to bear on employers to refrain from paying optimum salaries to attract specialists, and by not pressuring for wage increases above cost of living increases. Their wage scales, however, proved to be highly complicated and unrealistic. Until 1924 a 17-grade scale system operated, having a ratio of 1:2.7 for the first nine grades (manual workers), and a ratio of 1:5 for the tenth to seventeenth grades (higher qualified workers). Oddly enough, the unions agreed to the introduction of other scales paralleling this one, but with different ratios between the skilled and unskilled. It is not easy to understand why they did this, for it made enforcement difficult if not impossible. Highly sought-after workers had no qualms about changing jobs if a new position paid better. Managers, under great pressure and operating in a fluid market, could not and did not abide by the 17-grade scale system. In no time the situation was completely out of control.

In 1924, at the Sixth Trade Union Congress, the need for reform was recognized and a new system was introduced. It rested on a 1:8 ratio, but it did not cover technicians or specialists, who were in great demand. The new system was a scale for manual workers only, thus quite as unrealistic as the earlier scale. It was ineffective in checking the wage drift, in narrowing the gap between the skilled and unskilled, and in controlling the upward inflationary drift.

By 1926 the wage drift and wage gap had spread so far that Tomsky, at the Seventh Trade Union Congress, urged that an attack be made to gain control over the situation. He recommended the introduction of a system based on state regulation (*gosreguliro-vanie*) of wages.[7] This approach was basically unappealing to the trade unionists, who opposed state control of wages on the grounds that acceptance of such a system would reduce the unions to cultural-educational organizations. Therefore Tomsky had to defend the proposal by arguing that this system meant state guidance, not state determination (*gosnormirovanie*), of wages. It was nonetheless a major step in the direction of state control. This reform meant in effect that union controls had not worked and that the state would determine wage movements by setting the upper limits of the wage fund.

Second, it was also recommended that supplementary payments and piece rates be limited and cut down so that a more normal relationship between the skilled and the unskilled, between time and piece workers, might be established. These reforms were adopted and helped somewhat. In 1928 a further step was taken with the introduction of a new wage scale consisting of 16 grades with a ratio of 1:8. The new scale was devised to push up the bottom and to narrow the gap between categories, a long sought-after socialist objective. By 1928 the effects of the reforms were beginning to take hold: 83 per cent of the workers were covered by the new wage scales and the proportion of piece work to total industrial work fell from 57.3 per cent to 34.3 per cent. Furthermore, increases leveled off and real wages began to climb.

Thus, only in 1928—on the eve of planning—were the unions able to effect control over the wage drift, to close the wage gap, and to contain runaway wage increases. Only then were they in a position to hold wages steady and to contribute to the investment program.

One might ask whether the unions could have done more if they had not bungled the early reform efforts. Clearly, the unions could have been more successful had they been more zealous and efficient in their implementation of the wage reforms introduced prior to 1928. Clearly, a more rigorous policy of union control over wage and labor allocation would have contributed to the wage freezes and the control of inflationary drifts that the unions were supposed to fight in their effort to contribute to the investment program.

LABOR PRODUCTIVITY AND DISCIPLINE

A related problem was labor productivity and discipline. Economic success depended in theory upon increased labor output as well as on higher capital outlays. Increased labor output, however, was not a simple matter. On the one hand, the level of productivity was approximately 50 per cent [8] below the prewar level; on the other, the general scarcity of capital meant that outlays for new and improved equipment had low priority. At the same time the predominant characteristics of the labor market were: high turnover, a breakdown of labor discipline, low worker morale, and friction between labor and management. The prospects for increasing labor productivity were not very encouraging.

Against this background, the question was: What could the unions do to maintain labor discipline and increase productivity? Starting in 1924, after a fight at the Sixth Trade Union Congress, the unions consented to a program stressing labor intensity methods. They agreed to increased output norms, piece rates, efficiency drives, and increases in the number of working days; they stressed a no-strike policy and stringent disciplinary measures, tried to control the flow of labor, and so forth. All in all, as Tolstopiatov, the Deputy Commissar for Labor, said, the emphasis was on increased human effort. "The standards of individual output were increased by 15 per cent without any corresponding improvement in technique." [9]

The results were mixed. Output increased steadily, but so did costs. Zagorsky's analysis indicates that in 1923–1924 productivity increased over the 1922–1923 level by 16 per cent, but was offset by a 32 per cent increase in nominal wages. In 1924–1926 labor productivity increased by 11 per cent, but nominal wages rose by 20 per cent. In 1926–1927 a breakthrough was finally realized; wages and output were balanced for the first time. Individual output rose by 12 per cent and nominal monthly wages by 12.3 per cent. The proportion of wages to production fell from 19.4 per cent to 19.2 per cent. In 1927–1928 the increase in output was 13.7 per cent over the preceding year, while the increase in average monthly wages was 10 per cent. The cost of production had fallen by 5.5 per cent, though the target had been 6 per cent. Thus progress had been made, but only quite late in N.E.P., and it had been made by stressing labor intensity over capital output methods. For unions opposed to "speedups" in principle, this was a bitter pill to swallow.

Labor Discipline

One of the principal factors that slowed up headway between 1924 and 1928 was the breakdown in labor discipline. It was in this area that the unions had been expected to bring order out of disorder. The breakdown of discipline assumed the typical forms of any industrial system in its early stages: absenteeism, drunkenness on the job, late arrivals, sleeping during working hours, assaults, thefts, destruction of tools and machinery, poor workmanship, slowdowns, and in desperate cases, murder.

The total number of manpower days lost per worker between 1922 and 1927 was estimated at between 34 and 40 days a year; the turnover of personnel in many large plants was reported to be as high as 100 per cent. The rate of disobedience was so high that it bordered, in the regime's eyes, on sabotage, and a warning was issued that this would not be tolerated. To contain turnover and absenteeism, new regulations were instituted. Three unjustifiable absences in a month, three departures in a month from the factory without permission, two refusals to perform obligations or to work overtime if necessary, and serious infringements of the technical safety regulations resulting in accidents were all punishable by dismissal. Three offenses involving the theft of tools, a high percentage of waste, alcoholism, and playing games in the plant were also punishable by dismissal.[10] To add a carrot to the whip, efforts were made to force management to clean up the factories and abandon the use of policies—such as blacklists, arbitrary dismissals, and so on—that contributed to worker disobedience.

With all these measures a degree of success was achieved. Lost manpower days dropped from a high of 41 in 1922–1923 to 34 in 1928. Unjustifiable absences fell from 9.60 to 4.54, but remained nearly three times higher (4.54 to 1.60) than justifiable absences. These changes in all probability were due to the efforts of the unions. Of course they may also have been due to the fact that the breakdown of discipline had peaked and leveled off.

But if some headway was won, the progress was not very great. Although the level of lost manpower days due to poor discipline, turnover, and absences declined, the number of lost days was relatively high for unions that were making a major drive to raise productivity by cutting down on lost time and inefficient workmanship. This was particularly the case with labor turnover, which apparently continued to be as high as 100 per cent in many factories until the late thirties and early forties, when labor mobilization decrees, freezing, and assigning workers to jobs were introduced. Also on the negative side was the fact that steady gains were offset by a rise in lost days in 1925–1926, and that major headway was not made until 1928, the year of the First Five Year Plan. If we are to think in terms of union political power as in part a derivative of union ability to effect controls in the labor market, the unions were not in a very good bargaining position.

Strikes

Strikes remained a persistent problem adversely affecting productivity throughout the 1920s, even though the unions pursued a
no-strike policy and were able to effect some control over the situation. There were fewer strikes in the late 1920s than formerly, but
there were still far more than the union and government officials
wished to see.

In 1921–1922, 102 strikes involving 43,000 workers were reported.[11] In 1924, 267 strikes involving 42,000 workers were reported; most of these occurred in state-administered industries. In
1925, 186 strikes involving 43,000 workers from state industries
occurred, none of which were union sanctioned. In 1926, 327 strikes
by 32,900 workers from state industries occurred.[12] In 1927 there
were 396 strikes involving 20,100 state employees; in the first half
of 1928, 90 strikes involving 8,900 state employees. It was further
reported that in 1926 and 1927 the workers had won approximately
one-third of the strikes and lost two-thirds of them, hardly a record
of great success.[18]

The issues over which the workers went on strike were quite
typical: unfair dismissals, controversial output norms, overtime pay
and bonuses, holiday work, inadequate labor protection, bad housing, and so on. By far the greater number of grievances were settled
by arbitration, indicating a better than fair degree of control on
the part of the unions.[14] The number of disputes reported in the
first six months of 1926, however, was between 2,456 and 3,155,
depending upon the reporter.[15] This number is high, but apparently
fairly representative of the mid- and late 1920s.[16] It indicates that
the unions were failing seriously in the negotiation and enforcement
stages.

COLLECTIVE AGREEMENTS

The collective agreements system, another side of the productivity-
discipline problem, did not bring about the improved labor harmony
necessary for making the most effective headway with output. Reintroduced in 1922, they were the principal device used for fixing
authority and responsibility, for regulating wage levels and work
conditions, and for defining the jurisdiction of management and
labor. By 1928, collective agreements, which were not compulsory,
were used extensively and covered 90 per cent of the workers.[17]

The main problem was that the contracts were too complex and the unions did not know how to draw them up, or how to enforce the implementation of the provisions. Furthermore, both sides were prone to disregard those provisions distasteful to them. In good measure the failure may be attributed to a lack of understanding and experience, the results of a late beginning and a limited tradition of bargaining.

Tomsky, at both the Sixth and Seventh Trade Union Congresses, revealed just how serious a breakdown in collective bargaining agreements had occurred. Hoping to induce reforms by focusing on failures and weaknesses, he stated that the 1922–1923 contracts had as many as 185 clauses and were signed for one to three months only. The result was complete and utter confusion. He urged the delegates to sign one-year contracts to help stabilize the situation.[18] At the Seventh Congress Tomsky focused on another aspect of the breakdown: the endless disagreements and delays in concluding contracts, which often lasted months rather than weeks. He warned again that if the meaning of the contracts were not to be seriously impaired, they had to be drawn up quickly and without excessive conflict.[19]

Along these lines, some other factors that made progress difficult were nonrecognition of union rights, forcing overtime work, ignoring agreement provisions, hedging on wages, dismissing at random, and so forth. Perhaps the classic tactic to which the state administrators resorted, however, was the blacklist. An article appearing in *Trud* as late as 1928 revealed that managers kept lists of undesirables and marked the personnel papers of dismissed workers "never to be employed again."[20] What makes the above fact particularly interesting is that a January 1928 census revealed that 71 per cent of the directors of industrial trusts and 89.3 per cent of the factory managers were members of the Communist Party.[21]

At the Fourteenth Party Congress Tomsky played on a related theme—the bureaucratic disregard of the workers and its subsequent impact on the meaningfulness of the contracts. He said that the workers, for whom the collective agreement was drawn, did not know what it contained. No one, he added, knew the workers' demands. At the Seventh Trade Union Congress he said that it was indeed quite common for the workers to be entirely ignorant of the fact that negotiations were taking place; that they only became aware of the fact after an agreement had already been concluded and signed.[22] In all cases, he warned, the danger was to the union, for collective bargaining carried on in this way could only result in the alienation of the rank and file.[23]

Dogadov also criticized the practice of infrequent contacts with the members and of concluding agreements without their knowledge. The result was an excessive number of disputes and a tendency for the workers and management not to take the contracts seriously—an attitude particularly true of management. He urged that the union leaders not sign contracts without consulting with the members, and that they check constantly on the fulfillment of the terms.[24]

In 1929 there were as many complaints as formerly about the bad organization and lack of preparation for the discussion of collective agreements.[25] But now a new problem was emerging. The union leaders were beginning to find that where the workers were consulted, where democratic methods were applied, the workers frequently adopted resolutions contrary to the policy of the union.[26] Thus, just as N.E.P. was coming to a close, the union leaders were discovering that collective bargaining was a complicated matter and one not responsive to crude manipulation.

But in regard to the over-all picture of collective bargaining, no general improvement took place, regardless of the extent and frequency of the union leaders' criticisms. The union record in restoring discipline, raising productivity, and maintaining labor peace was less than remarkable. Perhaps one of the major reasons why the unions did not perform better was that the problem stemmed from conditions beyond their control.

FACTORY CONDITIONS

Life was hell in the early twenties, and so were the unsanitary factories. Factories were old, dimly lit, and unsafe; a high level of industrial accidents and over-all worker dissatisfaction were major sources of the problem with which the unions were trying to cope. Two complaints, typical of the period, reveal just how bad the conditions were. In 1928, reporters in *Trud* wrote:

> The majority of the industrial enterprises in Moscow are overcrowded, resulting in stuffiness, poor lighting and high temperature. Ventilation appliances are not installed in all factories; where installed, supervision is either bad or absent. Very often ventilation supplies cold air, and workers turn it off, for they prefer the dust to the danger of catching cold.[27]

> [Another report in *Trud* stated]: The great majority of the factories (in the Kiev district) are kept outrageously dirty and in an unsanitary state. Windows are covered with thick layers of grime

and soot, and do not allow sunlight to penetrate into the workrooms. . . . Heaps of various odds and ends block the passages. In the majority of cases the factories are not provided with artificial ventilation, and machinery is not supplied with protective covering, rails and other safety devices.[28]

A corollary of these poor conditions was a constant increase in the rate of accidents right up to and including the period of the introduction of the First Five Year Plan. Reports delivered at the Fourteenth Party Congress and the Seventh and Eighth Trade Union Congresses stated that up to 80 per cent of the accidents could be attributed to technical problems, poor working conditions, and managerial negligence; the other 20 per cent could be attributed to the workers themselves, to fatigue, sickness, neglect, and ignorance.[29] Given factory conditions such as these, an acute housing shortage, and over-all privation, it is hardly surprising that the unions were not able to do better; the heart of the problem was beyond their control.

UNEMPLOYMENT

Another aspect of union ability to gain control over the labor scene and to effect changes was the position of the unions on unemployment. It is incredible to see how poorly the unions performed on this level. Soviet Russia suffered from a severe unemployment problem throughout N.E.P. It was a structural problem, typical of an underdeveloped country undergoing modernization. It was a problem of a simultaneous rise in the level of employment and unemployment, a problem of rural overpopulation, a large labor reserve of unskilled workers, and a severe shortage of skilled workers. Unemployment first developed in 1920 with the demobilization of the troops, and continued to rise without abatement throughout the twenties. Although estimates of the magnitude of the unemployment depended much on who was doing the reporting, a conservative appraisal would place it as hovering between one and two million out of a labor force of approximately six to eight million.

At the Sixth Trade Union Congress in 1924, the number of unemployed registered with the exchanges was reported to be 1,400,-000.[30] On November 1, 1927, the total number of those unemployed and registered was 1,178,000; on May 1, 1928, 1,598,000; and on April 1, 1929, 1,755,000.[31] The difficulty in determining the extent of unemployment arises from several facts: First, only those who were unemployed and registered with the labor exchanges were counted; the rest were not. Second, workers did not have to register to seek employment after 1923,[32] thus only those who qualified for unemployment benefits registered; the rest, who could gain no benefits, did not. Thus the actual number of unemployed might very well have approached three million. If the under-employed, those with only part-time work, had been counted, the number might have been above three million. Third, different agencies and analysts reported different levels of unemployment. For example, on January 1, 1928, official statistics put the number at 1,352,800, and of these some 900,000 were listed as members of trade unions. On the same date, trade union statistics listed 2,036,-800 as unemployed, over one million of whom were said to be trade unionists.[33]

Although the level of unemployment climbed throughout the twenties, so did the level of the industrial labor force. In 1913 the industrial labor force was reported to be approximately 2,600,000. In 1921 it was below 1,250,000. From then on it climbed, reaching 1,620,000 in 1923–1924 and approximately 2,300,000 in 1926, almost the 1913 level. Attempts were made by the unions and other public authorities to arrest unemployment, to cut into its severity with relief projects, registration of the unemployed, collection of statistics, vocational training, and educational programs. Needless to say, all the measures undertaken helped. Relief triumphed over misery, men were better off, and progress was made. More could have been done, however, to curtail the drift and to alleviate the suffering; some of what was done could have been done more effectively.

Two points strike home: First, the high level of union inefficiency; second, a tough line and a sense of despair. Little effort was made to control the flow and allocation of manpower in a rational and efficient manner. In 1925 the use of the labor exchanges was abandoned. Instead, workers were instructed to find their own jobs and management was given the right to hire freely.[34]

Unemployment benefits, fixed in accordance with a cost-of-living index relative to the different wage rates in the country, were supposed to cover between 13 and 45 per cent of the worker's normal wage. Reports, however, indicate that only a fraction of those unemployed received any benefit at all, and that many who did received only between seven and 27 rubles a month—not even adequate for a subsistence level of existence.[35]

According to a report of the Commissariat of Labor, the average monthly number of unemployed who received benefits in 1928 was 725,000,[36] while the total number of unemployed was reported to have been above one million. Union unemployment funds, existing in every union for the relief of unemployed members, were either inadequate to meet the needs of the members or were not utilized. In the case of the Metal Workers' Union, it was reported that 60 per cent of the members who were unemployed received no benefits at all.[37] One observer stated:

> We know of many cases where the funds are either not utilized at all, or are spent most irregularly; in some cases they are kept in the safes of the trade union to show how strictly the officials adhere to the policy of "economizing." Subsidies to union clubs are paid out of the unemployment fund, general expenses or deficits in the union budget are also covered, and so are loans and subsidies to the workers.[38]

It is difficult to understand why the unions did not make better use of their funds and provide more relief, for it is clear that they could have.

Public works projects undertaken to alleviate hardships and insecurity were also not extensive enough. According to the Soviet press, only 5 to 10 per cent of the registered unemployed were expected to be employed at these works during 1927 and 1928.[39] In all probability more projects could have been initiated so that more of the unemployed could have been absorbed. Clearly, what was done was negligible and hardly corresponded to the needs of the country. One cannot but wonder why the unions did not do more to extend and rationalize the approach to public works projects, which posed a partial solution to the alleviation of hardships.

Most sobering about the Russian unemployment situation, however, was that the union leaders saw the question as one beyond their reach; they had no solution. To deal with it, they assumed a tough line. In 1925 *Trud*, editorializing on the question, had this to say:

> The unions have never made it their business to defend the interests of persons not earning wages. The mere intention to get a job and join a union is not enough. The unions fight for organized labor, for the organized securing of jobs, and, as a matter of course, for the employment of those already organized. If the unions acted otherwise, they would lose their class character and deny their essence—the defence of the members' interests. . . .
>
> Unemployed who are not union members will not agree with us, because they want to get jobs. . . . Yet it must be stressed once again that the unions will not and cannot protect all those who are not wage workers.[40]

As a matter of policy, the unions—in the main—rationalized the industrial machine and agreed to the dismissal of redundant labor at a time when employment was at a critical level.[41] Finally, at the Seventh Trade Union Congress of 1927 the union leaders revealed that they were reconciled to the continuation of the unemployment problem for at least the next five years.[42]

Thus, in the realm of unemployment policy, as in the realm of productivity and discipline, the unions failed to effect any major changes. They did not adopt a well-defined policy; they did not establish control over unemployment; they did not provide protection on an adequate scale; and, more often than not, they failed to realize their own potential or to do what was in the realm of the credible. They did not realize their Party-assigned tasks. They were unable to do the one thing that would have won them respect and authority once they had been squeezed out of the realm of managerial and economic decision-making. The net effect of their failure was political weakness.

To the extent that the unions failed to gain control of labor or make a reasonable showing until 1928, they contributed to economic failure and to opening the question of the need for rapid growth by means of forced draft methods. In a way, they were the source of their own undoing.

12 ✪ Unions and the Succession Question

The Opposition, headed by Trotsky, came forth with the slogan of smashing the party apparatus. . . . Such wholesale criticism and attempts at directly discrediting the party apparatus cannot objectively lead to anything else than . . . to divorce the governmental organs from the party. . . .

Trotsky not only tried to counterpose himself to all the rest of the Central Committee, but also permitted accusations which could not but evoke unrest in broad circles of the working class and a stormy protest in the ranks of our party.[1]

Bukharin's and Tomsky's declaration is completely without substance in saying that they are being "worked over" in the party, that an "organizational encirclement" has been created, in view of which they are compelled to insist on resigning. . . . Of what does intraparty democracy consist?[2]

THE SUCCESSION PROBLEM

By 1923 all questions—including those of the trade unions—dropped to a position of secondary importance. The succession fight became the prime issue. The hope of reforming the unions and of winning a place for them as a major force in the Soviet system was side-tracked until the larger issue of the Party fight was resolved. The high drama of the succession struggle has been recounted with great expertise and subtlety by numerous commentators. It would be out of place to attempt to tell the whole story of the Machiavellian struggle and Stalin's final victory, but since the labor issue was settled within the context of the succession question, some aspects of it are relevant.

Its context is significant. It arose at a time when the C.P. was extremely isolated and close to its low ebb of popularity. Workers were hostile to the regime; over 50 per cent had quit the unions when given an opportunity to do so in 1921. Some, including Trotsky, thought it was essential to consolidate the Party's dictatorship by means of rapid economic growth and to forget about the unions if they cried that the price was too high. It was also a time when the Communist Party was faced with the crisis of a peasant buyer strike; when Lenin appeared to be excessively optimistic, declaring at the Eleventh Congress that the end of the retreat had come. At the same time, bureaucratization within the Communist Party was occurring rapidly.

The succession question also came at a time when no one party leader had a mass base large enough to settle the question quickly. Tomsky did not have one, even though he controlled the trade unions. Trotsky no longer controlled the Red Army. Stalin actually was the strongest person within the Party but had yet to complete building his apparat. It was within this context that the succession question was fought.

What also impresses the outside observer is the interplay of personalities and former political positions in effecting the coalitions formed, stands taken, and defeats suffered. Stalin's ultimate victory was effected in no small part by the almost unbridgeable gulfs between Trotsky and Zinoviev, and Trotsky, Tomsky, and Shlyapnikov. Trotsky, looking back on his defeat ten years later, quixotically remarked that the fact that his Left Opposition position "offered a more correct analysis" was irrelevant to the outcome of the struggle; his judgment was that "a political struggle is in its essence a struggle of interest and forces, not of arguments." Personalities, although not "a matter of indifference, in the last analysis [are] not decisive." The determining factor was "a triumph of the bureaucracy over the masses," a bureaucracy that had grown since the Revolution, and was "raising itself above society" and devouring it.[3]

One might agree with Trotsky on several points, but it appears that he was incredibly dense. By April 1923, the time of the Twelfth Party Congress, Lenin lay dying. The scramble for power was on. The Troika had been formed and Trotsky was the target. Trotsky, however, was caught up in policy questions, which were soon to be the arena within which the power fight was waged.

Trotsky chose not to do battle with Stalin at the Congress, though he could have delivered a telling blow on the nationality question, over which Lenin and Stalin had just feuded. Instead, Trotsky concentrated on economic policy, which he saw as the vital question. He recommended that N.E.P. be modified or abandoned if socialism was to be attained. This was the first open declaration of the left wing position on radical industrialization.

The core of the problem, in Trotsky's eyes, lay in the fact that while N.E.P. was producing gradual "prosperity" in agriculture, industry was stagnating and the over-all economy was facing a grave crisis. The capital necessary for investment and replacement in industry was simply not available. Yet only industry could "create an unshakable foundation for the proletarian dictatorship." [4] Though adopting a pro-industrialization stance, Trotsky, in characteristic disregard of the unionists, called for the adoption of one-man management from "top to bottom" and made no concessions to either the unions or the workers.

Thus Trotsky closed the door to a coalition with Tomsky and the unionists, though he was arguing a pro-industrialization position. Conceivably he could have set the stage for one at this juncture. It would have been difficult because of the longstanding animosity between Trotsky and Tomsky, and because Tomsky was committed to a respite for the workers. Nonetheless, an alliance was conceivable. If Trotsky had introduced sufficient concessions to the workers at a time when workers were complaining of unfair peasant advantages, Tomsky would undoubtedly have been attracted to it. This could have meant the gradual advance of the unions to a position of power once again. Trotsky could have couched his proposal in these terms; it would not have been too difficult. What he did, however, was to cut himself off from a political machine which could have been useful to him, and which later he was to try to win.

At the same time, by raising the issue of abandoning N.E.P., Trotsky added tension to his relations with Bukharin, who was closest to him as a result of earlier stands. Bukharin was firmly committed to a gradualist position and to concessions to the peasantry; he was becoming the chief exponent of this point of view. He could not endorse Trotsky's rapid industrialization proposal.

On the other hand, Trotsky's position on economic policy was very close to that of Zinoviev, who was beginning to attack Bukharin's "creeping socialism" and was grumbling about Stalin's Socialism in One Country. Animosity was so great between Zinoviev and Trotsky as a result of their earlier feuding that, although they were in basic agreement on economic policy, the two could not get together, at least not until it was too late.

At the same time, Zinoviev's position on economic policy and his own personal ambition contributed to his split with Stalin. They schemed and clashed. So great, however, was their desire to destroy Trotsky that they covered up their personal and policy disagreements and adopted a stand of Socialism in One Country that was sufficiently ambiguous to satisfy both and to perpetuate their alliance. They merely reminded the Party that Lenin had agreed to this proposal in 1915. For approximately five months they succeeded in keeping their disagreement within confined quarters. During the course of those months they succeeded in dismounting Trotsky.

But while the fight against Trotsky was going on, Zinoviev and Kamenev openly campaigned against Bukharin and the Right Wing's economic policy. Stalin, at the same time, initiated steps to effect a coalition with the Right Wingers—Bukharin, Tomsky, and Rykov. But by the summer and fall of 1925, Zinoviev was openly attacking Bukharin's policy of concessions to the peasantry, a policy that Bukharin had cautiously committed himself to that year.[5] There was now very little difference on economic policy between Zinoviev-Kamenev and Trotsky, but neither they nor he were willing to form an alliance.

Highlighting the personality-intransigence syndrome was the fact that Zinoviev had hard evidence of moves by Stalin to isolate him as they had isolated Trotsky. By that time Zinoviev had published a book in which he openly criticized the idea of Socialism in One Country. In it he argued that a backward Russia could not hope to realize full socialism. But still he made no move to effect an alliance with Trotsky!

Sharp infighting followed and the Central Committee several times had to postpone convening the Fourteenth Party Congress. By the fall of 1925, long overdue, the date was fixed for December 18. The details of the Congress need not detain us. Excellent accounts are available. Of particular interest is the fact that Tomsky played an incredible role.

Krupskaya, on the eve of this congress, joined forces with Zinoviev and Kamenev. From the rostrum Krupskaya told the Congress: "there were congresses in which the majority were wrong," [6] referring to the 1906 Congress when the Mensheviks had been in a majority. Whether she was trying to conciliate the delegates or was pointedly telling them they were wrong on economic policy and Stalin even if they had the votes, her remark produced such an uproar that she backed down and withdrew it. Kamenev did not.

Realizing the courage of his convictions, he led a one-man, head-on charge: ". . . Stalin cannot fulfill the role of unifier. . . . We are against creating a doctrine of one-man rule, we are against the emergence of a leader (*vozhd*)." [7] If Krupskaya had caused an uproar, Kamenev produced pandemonium. First stunned, then furious, demonstrations broke out on the floor amid shouts of indignation and insults. Unlike Krupskaya, Kamenev refused to withdraw his remarks!

Stalin's lieutenants and supporters, of whom Khrushchev was one, performed their expected role. But it fell to Bukharin and Tomsky to play the most incriminating roles. Bukharin, rebutting Krupskaya, whipped back: "what about the party?" Bukharin used the same argument that Trotsky had when he said: "My party, right or wrong." Tomsky followed Kamenev. He tried to dismiss Kamenev's warning. Tomsky said:

> It is ridiculous to speak as some comrades have spoken here, attempting to protest someone as having concentrated power in his hands, while the rest of the majority of the Central Committee back him up.
>
> How could this happen? No, comrade Kamenev, if you put the question that a system of individual leaders must not exist, we say: "We have all the time struggled against it; a system of individual leaders cannot exist, and will not, no, will not!" [8]

Tomsky not only defended Stalin, but continued his attack on Zinoviev and Kamenev. He reminded the Congress it was these two men who, one year earlier, had called for the most ruthless reprisals against Trotsky:

> Some thought that if somebody had erred—well, that's uncouth, beat him and kick him. Others thought that our party is not so rich in resources that it can afford, in the case of everyone who errs— and many of us have erred on various questions—instead of letting him enter the channel of normal work, to put forward the proposition: Finish him off. Such a proceeding was thought incorrect. [9]

Tomsky, the man who, alongside of Shlyapnikov, had the greatest antipathy for Trotsky, now cynically baited them by contrasting Trotsky's "crystal clear lucidity" of views and integrity with their muddleheadedness and evasions. He could not have shown greater contempt for these men. Tomsky closed his speech urging Kamenev and Zinoviev to "apply to yourselves the lesson which you taught comrade Trotsky" and "bow your heads before the will of the party." [10] Before yielding the floor he commented on Krupskaya's complaints. "Comrade Krupskaya," observed Tomsky, "said that the concept of what is true and untrue is a subjective concept. We have one measure. For the working class, led by its party, there can be only one measure—*the will of the Leninist party!*" [11]

To have used this argument against Krupskaya is surprising, given their high esteem and personal affection for the wife of Lenin. But what is even more surprising is Tomsky's denial of Kamenev's charge. Could he not have believed it? It is difficult to tell what was going on in Tomsky's mind, but he was either one of the densest or most Machiavellian men to walk the floor of the Congress.

Following the Fourteenth Congress, Zinoviev, Kamenev, and Trotsky finally formed their United Opposition. Their platform was rapid industrialization and the rejection of Socialism in One Country. But they united too late. Zinoviev's jealousy and ambition had precluded an alliance when there was still a chance to win.

Isaac Deutscher adds that thirteen years after the Fourteenth Congress, Trotsky stood before the Dewey Commission in Mexico and confessed he had been astonished to see Zinoviev, Kamenev, and Stalin clashing as enemies. [12] He explained that, although he was a member of the Politbureau, his opponents had carefully concealed their disagreements from him and fought out their battles in private. Deutscher states: "The explanation, although true, is astonishing. For the controversies over socialism in a single country had already been conducted in public," and, Deutscher adds, "Trotsky could not have missed its significance if he had followed it." He could not have missed the significance of items like the demand for an open debate in October. "[Trotsky's] surprise," Deutscher states, "resulted from a failure of observation, intuition, and analysis. . . . Evidently his mind remained closed. He lived as if in another world, wrapped up in himself and his ideas." [13]

THE CASE OF SHLYAPNIKOV AND TROTSKY

Personality factors entered in another way to affect adversely a united left wing alliance. Apart from Trotsky's followers, the other leftist groups were the remnants of Shlyapnikov's Workers' Opposition and Sapronov's Democratic Centrists, each inactive since the Tenth Congress. Though victimization of individual sympathizers of these groups continued, they were still in existence; theoretically an alliance of the Left would have included them. At the Fourteenth Party Congress, Zinoviev dropped the first hint that he would attempt to unite these groups. He suggested that all members of all former leftist groups should be brought back for active work in the Party.

Stalin apparently realized the danger of a left wing alliance, but he also sensed the simmering hostilities and was too clever a politician not to see his opportunity and grasp it. In a shrewd move at the Fourteenth Congress, Stalin maneuvered the opposition into a position where it declared it would not form an alliance with either of these two former opposition groups, thus piling insult upon old injury. Next Stalin turned to Shlyapnikov, exploiting old personal wounds and the anger of the new one, and convinced him that an attack on Trotsky was in order. In *Pravda* on January 18, 1924, in an article he was allowed to write, Shlyapnikov criticized Trotsky and the Left Opposition. Shlyapnikov pointed out that Trotsky and these "leftists" had all supported the disciplinary measures applied against the oppositionists at the Tenth Congress; that the "Oppositions'" activities were power-directed, geared only at capturing the Party apparatus; that under the circumstances there was no reason to suppose that the "left opposition" would behave any differently. Shlyapnikov ended ringing true to his old beliefs. Lasting improvement, he said, could be obtained only if the worker element in the Party were increased and if freedom of activity were allowed to the rank and file.

Shlyapnikov later explained that the relative safety of his group during 1925 was due to the power struggle; he hinted that his group was useful to a "certain" group in the Central Committee which made persistent efforts to secure their support against Zinoviev and the Left Opposition.[14] To Shlyapnikov, Stalin did not appear to be half the monster that Trotsky was.

THE LEFT OPPOSITION GOES TO THE WORKERS

The Left Opposition decided it could win only by openly campaigning and by winning mass support. It now turned to the workers, the very group Trotsky had spurned at the Twelfth Congress. (Like so many others in the Party, they were victims of their own propaganda and believed that the worker basically supported the regime.)

By 1926 the wages situation was particularly bad. In order to win worker support, the Left Opposition demanded a review of real wages. Their hope was to identify themselves with the reform effort and an increase in real wages. It was a clever move. Their petition hit on a very sensitive issue and one within the limits of Party law, but without hesitation the Central Committee rejected the demand. Its grounds were that goods were scarce, and that wage increases unrelated to productivity would cause further inflation—worsening, rather than improving, the workers' lot.

In reply, Trotsky and Zinoviev instructed their supporters to carry the issue to their comrades, to speak up in the cells, and to go to the factories themselves. This was, in fact, a declaration of war. Stalin rose to the occasion. He challenged them to lay their case before an open "proletarian tribunal," and he urged Trotsky to address the workers himself. At the same time, Stalin instructed his supporters to make sure the Left was properly received in the factories.

Trotsky, against the advice of many of his friends, accepted the challenge. The workers, utterly dejected and disillusioned, and goaded on by Stalin's henchmen, received Trotsky and his supporters with either apathy or open hostility and contempt. Reswick, an eye witness to the events, states that within a week "all of Moscow knew that the Trotskyists were near the end of their rope. Nowhere had any of them got a chance to speak his mind." He further states: "Everywhere they had been yelled at, yanked and pushed off the platforms. Everywhere flying wedges from the Apparat had been busy breaking up the meetings." At a factory meeting, he had personally seen "Trotsky hissed, spat at, and all but kicked off the . . . platform." [15]

Tomsky played a major role in the Right Wing counterattack. He used all his union resources to fight the Left, and he himself spoke at factory meetings. He must have been secretly surprised, though, that Stalin had so many members of the Apparat working alongside and within his union organization.

But if harassment was not enough, the Right moved to offset any appeal the Left Opposition might have had on the wages question. In September the Central Committee voted a wages increase for workers in the lowest categories. Thus it did what it had refused to do in July. This act signified at once the victory and the failure of the Left. No longer did they have an issue upon which to build a base.

Deutscher [16] writes that two years later Karl Radek, already in exile and pondering the failure of the campaign, wrote to Trotsky suggesting that they had failed because they approached the campaign as propagandists dealing in abstract theories, rather than as political agitators seeking to arouse a popular response. As Deutscher points out, there "was some truth to Radek's remarks." [17] But the leftists lost because the rank and file were weary and disillusioned. They craved, as he and Varga put it, peace and stability. And they saw more hope in Stalin's Socialism in One Country than in Trotsky's grandiose scheme of economic revolution. There are several additional lessons Trotsky might have learned. First, he lost because he had little direct contact with the workers, whereas Stalin had Tomsky's machine. Trotsky had made a mistake at the Twelfth Congress—he should have pressed for worker reforms then as he later did in 1926. Second, the personality factor proved to be deadly. Assuming he maintained his tough line, his willingness to form an alliance with Zinoviev and Kamenev came much too late to do any good. So too, Shlyapnikov's enmity hurt him as he tried to effect a left wing, pro-worker alliance. But of all the lessons that Trotsky should have learned there is one that is most important. The indifference and hostility with which the workers greeted him was the telling point. He lost not merely because Stalin had built or captured a bureaucracy, but because neither he nor the Party had any real popular support.

THE DEFEAT OF TOMSKY AND THE RIGHT

As the fight was nearing its close in 1927, Stalin began to turn against his Right Wing allies. It began in the summer. In the wake of the English war scare and massive GPU arrests, a rumor circulated that there was a desire to expel the United Opposition leaders from the Party, but that a "right wing" group of the Politbureau consisting of Bukharin, Tomsky, Rykov, and Kalinin were opposed to doing so. Rumor was fact. After a stormy July-August Plenum, Stalin won. A resolution was passed expelling Trotsky and Zinoviev from the Central Committee.

At the Fifteenth Congress, long delayed because of protracted infighting, Stalin enjoyed the full fruit of his victory. The Congress wrote its approval of their ouster and that of over 75 others of their group; also expelled were some members of the Democratic Centrist opposition. Stalin was not in any way dependent upon the support of the Right at this Congress. Though the rightists did not aid him, they were under the impression that they had won a mandate for a grandualist approach to industrialization. It was not long before they realized how wrong they had been.

Following the ouster of the Left Stalin shifted his position on economic tempo, though it would appear that he was beginning to do so as early as 1926. At that time, he was forced to develop his theory of Socialism in One Country to meet Trotsky's attack, and he began to warn of "capitalist encirclement" and to suggest strongly that it was necessary to strive for a socialist victory as completely as possible.[18]

In early January 1928 rumors began to circulate that a policy shift amounting to the abandonment of N.E.P. was imminent. The April Joint Plenary Session of the Central Committee and the Central Control Commission passed a resolution unanimously denouncing rumors that N.E.P. was to be reversed. If there was any doubt as to where Stalin stood at this Plenum, there was none after his performance at the Central Executive Committee of the All-Union Congress of Soviets which soon followed. At this Congress, he supported a proposal to deprive peasants of their right to the use of land in perpetuity. The Right objected and the proposal was tabled.

Then, in May, Stalin indicated he was in favor of a rapid tempo industrialization program. Kuibyshev, his lieutenant in charge of the Supreme Economic Council, declared that the economists of Gosplan should expand their proposals into a comprehensive plan to increase the development of industry by 130 per cent for the next five years. This was, in effect, the position of the "super-industrializers." It challenged the entire premise of N.E.P., on which the economic planners had based their targets.

The conflicting proposals came up for discussion at the July Politbureau meetings and the Central Committee Plenum, which lasted from the 4th to the 12th. At both meetings Stalin clashed with Bukharin, Tomsky, and Rykov. And at both sessions Stalin lost, or yielded—just which is not quite clear. N.E.P. was reaffirmed as the only meaningful basis upon which the construction of socialism could occur. All talk of its repeal was repudiated.[19]

Stalin's speeches at this meeting (published years later) reveal that he urged collectivization and a rapid tempo industrialization program. Stalin declared that, for the country to industrialize, the peasants were going to have to "foot the bill." To provide the capital for speeding up industrialization, a "tribute" was going to have to be exacted from the peasants. It was going to be an "unpleasant business," but Bolsheviks could not shirk their duty because things were unpleasant. There was no alternative. The Soviet Union had no colonies or other countries it could exploit. The capital had to come from within the economy. It appeared that people had forgotten, but N.E.P. had been meant to be an attack on capitalism as well as a retreat. To realize socialism, it was unavoidable that the class struggle within the land would be sharpened. The capitalist elements were too strong. Collectivization would be necessary, but Stalin temporized at this point by urging that it be "gradual."[20] But as Leonard Schapiro remarks: Stalin said nothing about the process being voluntary.

So sharp and strained were relations at this Plenum, and so

worried was Bukharin, that toward the very end of it he paid a visit to his old comrade and opponent Kamenev, who had just been readmitted to Party membership. Filling him in with an excited account, Bukharin expressed his fear that Stalin was an "unprincipled intriguer," a "Genghis Khan" who was only interested in consolidating his own power. It was clear to Bukharin that Stalin was now shifting positions, as he had in the past, to ruin his opponents. Bukharin was convinced that Stalin had refrained from pressing for victory at this Plenum only to trap Rykov, Tomsky, and himself. Stalin's policies, he said, were dangerous to the revolution, and could only lead to civil war, bloodshed and terror.[21] Desperate, Bukharin now proposed an alliance with Kamenev, hoping Kamenev would be astute enough, after his Fourteenth Party Congress warnings about a *vozhd*, not to allow himself or Zinoviev to be coaxed into a reconstructed alliance with Stalin.

Bukharin indicated he did not consider the position of the Right to be very strong, though they had won at the Central Committee meeting. Bukharin claimed the support of Yagoda, the deputy chief of the OGPU. But he also indicated that Kalinin and Voroshilov had, at the last minute, changed sides and were now supporting Stalin. Ordzhonikidze also shifted, though he had criticized Stalin's policy at the very beginning at the Plenum. Their strength, Bukharin confided, lay in the Moscow organization with Uglanov, who was in full agreement with them. Significantly, he did not suggest Tomsky or the trade unions. He did state, however, that Stalin was already taking steps to oust Uglanov and replace him with Kaganovich. Bukharin further indicated that the plan of the opposition was to play possum, publish articles, and try to expose Stalin. Bukharin believed that the Party would turn against Stalin once they realized the kind of man he was. (One wonders how naive men can be.)

At first Kamenev was not prepared to commit himself unequivocally, even if he knew what Stalin was up to. He decided to wait for feelers from the Stalinist camp. Undoubtedly, the rapid tempo industrialization position Stalin was adopting appealed to him. Certainly he was not impressed with Bukharin's chances; nor could he forget the old feelings of animosity still smoldering beneath the surface. In spite of his reservations, he ultimately did form an alliance with Bukharin, for the Stalin issue remained in his mind the paramount danger to the Party. One thing was clear. Bukharin had been incautious. In his desperate appeal to Kamenev, he had given Stalin ammunition for a counterattack. The interview, and all its details, quickly fell into the hands of the secret police. Kamenev, however, does not appear to have been the informer.

After much vacillation, on September 30, 1928, Bukharin assumed the offensive. In an article entitled "Notes of an Economist (The Problem of Planning)," published in *Pravda*, of which he was the editor, Bukharin set forth a complete statement of the views of the Right Wing.[22] Bukharin focused on the coming year and the achievements of N.E.P. The share of investment in new industrial construction had risen from 12 per cent in the first three years of N.E.P. to 23 per cent. The investment increase amply demonstrated how rapid the pace of industrialization had been. Just as important was a technological revolution in agriculture. Three times more agricultural machinery was available than in prewar years. Also contributing to this transformation was the marked socialization of agriculture. Capital investment in the state-operated sector had risen by 14 per cent.

Bukharin stressed the point that the strength of industry depended on the vigor of the peasant market. He warned that the Left's position would, in effect, trigger recession, for they would deprive the peasants of their capital. Tackling the grain crisis, Bukharin denied that the peasants had willfully withheld produce; thus he challenged the major premise of Stalin's argument. The increase in peasant income from nonagricultural work, a poor pricing policy, an inadequate supply of goods to the villages, and an inadequately taxed kulak group mirrored the real problem.

Planning for industrialization, he agreed, was essential, but he warned that it was necessary to avoid destroying "spontaneity" as well as to maintain a "balance" between the various sectors of the economy. Industrialization should not impoverish the village. Any other policy would lead not to rapid development of the economy but to real setbacks.

The fight continued, with Stalin holding the stronger position. At the end of 1928 and into 1929, Bukharin and Tomsky caught the wily Stalin off guard by threatening to resign, but they did not hold their advantage for long. At a Plenum of November 16–24, 1928, Stalin managed to placate Bukharin and Tomsky, yet he ran circles around them. Bukharin's "Notes of an Economist" was justified as being an acceptable alternate point of view. Rykov was placated with a resolution endorsing more consumer goods and the development of the individual households of the poor and middle peasants. Simultaneously, Stalin delivered the famous speech in which he said that the victory of socialism could only be ensured by "catching up with and overtaking" the capitalist countries. This was a high tempo position; Bukharin did not attack.

Stalin also publicly denied there was any dissension within the Politbureau. Inexplicably, Stalin also convinced Bukharin to endorse an unsigned denunciation of the right wing deviation within the Party. When Bukharin later related this to Kamenev, Kamenev was dumbfounded. Whether Bukharin realized it or not, he had undermined the rank-and-file supporters of the right wing position within the Party. Stalin now hunted them down with vengeance. Tomsky was the first to suffer defeat. Stalin neutralized the one man who potentially could have posed the greatest political threat.

THE EIGHTH TRADE UNION CONGRESS

It was at the Party fraction meeting, held to prepare for the Eighth Trade Union Congress in December 1928, that Tomsky and his supporters were defeated. With a majority of the delegates Party members bound and instructed by the Central Committee, and with the co-option of Stalinists to the A.U.C.C.T.U., Tomsky did not stand a chance of winning. He was denied the use of his trade union machine to outflank Stalin.

On the floor of the Eighth Trade Union Congress, Valerian Kuibyshev, the Chairman of the Supreme Economic Council, acted as Stalin's chief spokesman. He argued for a maximum program of economic development at the cost of imbalanced growth for the purpose of economic survival. He contended that those who talked about "overindustrialization" and an excessive rate of development of heavy industry did not understand how inadequate was the present output capacity of heavy industry and how urgent it was to increase it as rapidly as possible. There was no choice in the matter; it was absolutely necessary to accelerate the pace of industrial development because the alternative was to perish. History would not permit a slower development.[23]

Tomsky fought back with animation. He resisted the "rapid growth or perish" argument. He warned that the program would be resisted by the workers, who were interested in immediate improvements in consumer commodities. The inevitable result of their opposition would be the further alienation of the worker; an extension of the union-membership problem; and the unlimited transformation of the unions into institutions which would have to stand behind the state, regardless of how much conflict existed between the two.[24] In short, the unions would have to force the workers to obey; to do this they would, of necessity, have to fall back upon repressive measures; and once coercion was resorted to, the unions would become the prisons they had been during the civil war.

Another result which could be expected was the extension of the powers of the economic organs and the introduction of direct state controls in order to bring wages, manpower, and disputes under control. The result would be that the unions would have no real function in Soviet society, and would amount to little more than "propaganda agencies."

Tomsky, as Deutscher points out, never directly countered Kuibyshev's argument that if growth were not extensive, if all priority were not assigned to heavy industry, the result would be economic catastrophe. Why he did not deal with this is difficult to say, since Tomsky knew the importance of the question. It appears he was primarily concerned with warning the Party of the political resistance that he was convinced would follow. He believed that a margin existed, and that perhaps he could convince a majority of the delegates he was right. He thought he might be able to produce a grass roots rebellion on the floor of the Congress. If so, he failed. He failed in spite of the fact that a majority of the union delegates knew an about-face on economic growth would hurt their drive to rebuild the unions, that it was coming just at the time they were beginning to make some headway with their reform drive. To take a stand in favor of rapid growth meant that they would have to face, once again, the basic dilemma of a choice between growth-and-production and wages-and-membership. They would have to deny the transfer of monies to wages, better housing, and more consumer goods. The net result would once again be extensive worker alienation and a rift within the unions between membership and leadership. Clearly this was a program which could hardly preserve the integrity of the unions, much less a role for the unions in the industrialization of the economy.

Still the Congress, in dutiful fashion, voted approval of the intensive industrialization targets proposed by Kuibyshev. Then, as if to accent their own demise, the delegates voted a resolution stressing the need for democracy within the unions. Opposition to democracy, the stifling of criticism, and the bureaucratic spirit were to be ferreted out "wherever it was to be found." [25]

It mattered little whether Tomsky fought for the unions on the floor of the Congress or the right wing engaged the Stalinists in an animated floor debate over Kuibyshev's proposal. The real fight had already taken place and the real decisions had been made behind locked doors. At the earlier Party fraction meeting, Tomsky and the opponents of Stalin's industrialization program were defeated. Shmidt, the Commissar of Labor, who supported Tomsky and the right wing, resigned from his post. Shvernik and Kaganovich—both Stalinists—were elected to the A.U.C.C.T.U. It was not until the Spring of 1929, however, that Tomsky was ousted. On June 1, at a plenary session of the A.U.C.C.T.U., the Executive Committee of the A.U.C.C.T.U. was reorganized by its Communist fraction on the orders of the Sixteenth Party Conference. Tomsky was relieved of all his duties. Five others—Mikhailov, Ugarov, Perfileff, Udanov, and Yaglom, the editor of *Trud*—were also dismissed. Ginsberg was permitted to resign. The reorganized Executive Committee maintained its size of twenty-one members. The position of President was replaced by a Secretariat of five members. Shvernik was elected to the Secretariat. Dogadov, formerly Secretary of the Council, became First Secretary. The other members were Akulov, the representative of the trade unions of the Ukraine, who became Second Secretary; Weinberg, the representative of the Food and Drink Workers' Union; and Evreinov, head of the Educational Service. Three others—Alekseev, Strievsky, and Semogin—were co-opted to the Executive Committee.[26]

Earlier, in April, the Sixteenth Conference had passed a resolution indicating the ugly frame of mind that prevailed.

> Tomsky, Bukharin and Rykov are prepared in a most dangerous fashion to oppose the Party on trade union problems; actually they are doing this by aiming at the weakening of the Party leadership in the unions, by blurring the defects in the work of the unions, by defending craft trends and the manifestation of bureaucratic ossification in parts of the trade union machinery, and by presenting the Party's struggle against these defects as a Trotskyist "shake-up" of the trade unions.[27]

Finally it was made quite clear that the entire question was closed.

> The Party [the resolution further states] . . . rejects with determination such freedom of criticism which the right elements demand in order to defend their anti-Leninist political line.[28]

Thus ended the union question. Bukharin's defeat followed Tomsky's. It took place in the early part of 1929. Bukharin, however, was formally removed from all of his posts before Tomsky was. Tomsky was not expelled from the Politbureau until July 1930.

In conclusion, several observations stand out. First, the policy debates set the context within which the game of succession was played. Power was fought for within the arena of policy questions; yet the policy questions did not determine the outcome of either the power issue or the policy adopted. Rather the power question determined both. Stalin's personal victory settled the succession question and the policy line to be followed.

What further points up the importance of the power question is the fact that, almost throughout N.E.P., the Left and Right had split over economic policy. Their disagreement was fundamental, involving a question of value: whether a "hard" or "soft" policy was the freeway to socialism. It is extremely significant that in 1928, when all realized Stalin's true motives, Bukharin sought an alliance with Kamenev; and although there was some initial hesitation, they were able to breach the fundamental issue dividing them—economic policy—and agree to attempt to block Stalin. They still disagreed with each other, but clearly the power factor, not the economic aspect, was the decisive question.

Second, with Tomsky's defeat and the adoption of a high tempo growth program, the curtain was drawn—once and for all—for the unions. If there had been any doubt about the negation of the unions as managers and policy makers, the issue was now a closed one. Not only did the unions lose any powerful voice and prounion sentiment they had had in the Politbureau when they lost Tomsky, but the introduction of a centrally planned and administered economy and a rapid development program definitely meant that their position as bargaining agents and determiners of wages was over. The tragedy is that under the Bukharin approach the unions would have had meaningful functions to fulfill, and there is reason to believe that the Bukharin alternative could have worked.

Soviet statistics for the period may be rough, and they do not tell all, but if the statistics for 1928—which the Soviets themselves used as a frame of reference for projection of the First Five Year Plan—are accepted, we have the following investment picture: for 1927–1928, 7.99 billion rubles, or one-third of the national income, of 24.7 billion rubles, went to "gross investment"; 15.1 per cent went to "growth of fixed capital"; and 18.9 per cent went to accumulation in both fixed and working capital. At the same time, 80.1 per cent of the national income went to nonproductive consumption.[29]

An investment rate of one-third of the national income is high— incredibly high. If this 1927 rate, or something close to it, had been maintained, steady marginal headway under the Bukharin approach could have been made. A rapid development program was not necessary and could hardly have done better. Indeed, under Stalin, the 25 per cent investment level was not better.

Everything in the Bukharin scheme hinged on marginal increments. The diseconomies experienced during N.E.P. as a result of poor performance, opposition, and unpredictable circumstances were not costly enough to undermine the steady gains. Alexander Erlich, in his careful examination of the problem, also concludes that there was a possibility the Bukharin approach could have succeeded.[30]

There is an additional factor which adds weight to the Bukharin gradualist approach. According to official Soviet reports, the socialist sector of industry was growing rapidly and at the expense of the private sector. Its output is reputed to have risen from 81 per cent of the total system in 1924–1925 to 86 per cent in 1926–1927; conversely, the total output of the private sectors declined from 19 per cent to 14 per cent. Large-scale socialist industry grew by 18 per cent in 1927 over 1926. Industrial output had risen to 42 per cent of the total output of the country, which was the prewar ratio. This was scarcely a decisive share, but it does indicate that the over-all trend of industrialization and socialization was well under way in the late twenties. Though it is possible that the elimination of the private sectors might have resulted in a drag on the economy, the development of the socialist sector in the twenties adds further weight to Bukharin's belief that the socialization of the economy was taking place, and could continue under the gradualist policy of N.E.P.

Thus, I am inclined to believe the Russians were on the verge of solving the problem of backwardness. Drastic measures were not necessary. Indeed, against the rapid progress made and the possibility of additional marginal increments, the misery of the First Five Year Plan and collectivization was not necessary for further growth. But alas this did not happen. Stalin had his way in 1928. It was a sad ending for the unions, but it was an ending. Stalin had, with his Third Revolution, solved the union question. He had brought to an end a problem which had plagued the Party from the days of the November coup.

It would not be until the end of the Khrushchev era that some discretionary authority would be given to plant managers to fix the size of the plant labor force and the wages bill; even now, the role that labor will play in the determination of plant decisions remains unclear. Labor may, of course, influence the over-all policy and wage decisions on the Politbureau level, but this possibility appears as remote now as it actually was in 1928–1929.

And last, Tomsky's career came to a close. He was not merely a victim of Stalin's intrigue, he was also a victim of his own policies, and of the Party dictatorship which he had helped to build. So effective was the system of Party Controls which he had constructed within the unions that he was not able to control the union-Party fraction at the Eighth Congress; so isolated had the Party unionist leaders become that they could not run the unions except by loading all Congresses with a majority of Party members or supporters. This meant the Congress was Stalin's, not Tomsky's. Tomsky, the man who fought for worker concessions and for a place for the unions in Party politics, now could do nothing for his workers but voice a final protest.

Thus Tomsky was a victim of his own doing. Tomsky was the man who was responsible for ensuring the Party's monopoly of power within the unions, for denying the unions any modicum of autonomy, and for isolating the leaders from the members and rendering the membership politically impotent. His defeat by Stalin at the Eighth Congress goes back to the First and Second Trade Union Congresses, when he had fought the Mensheviks and Lozovsky and all who demanded trade union independence. His defeat marked the culmination of his efforts to convert the unions into agencies of the Party. He was a victim of his own policies.

Tomsky was now a lost and beaten man. He had no present and no future. All he could do was stand by and suffer in silence as Stalin ran roughshod over the nation, the unions, and the Party. This was the last of the man. There was only one way left for him to assert his dignity, and that was to die. On the eve of the purge trials Tomsky took his own life.

13 ✹ Conclusion

It is to the Bolsheviks and their act of 1917 that one must look for an assessment of the success and failure, the nobility and ignobility, of the Revolution. With the fall of Nicholas II in 1917, Russia was at the crossroads of history. She may have had a despotic past, but a fledgling democratic movement took root and helped to shape the political environment of the late nineteenth century. Russia could have gone either way in 1917. Democracy would have been difficult to secure, but it is not at all obvious that dictatorship was inevitable. The tragedy of the Russian Revolution is not one of obdurate fact or inescapable past, but one of human will operating on a broad spectrum of open options.

The Bolsheviks had high hopes of realizing what Kerensky had not: a Russia ruled by the people and free of divisive and brutal conflict over class and wealth. They wanted what men had dreamed of for ages—a land united and free of injustice. The Bolsheviks had a choice even after their *coup d'état*. Had they agreed to a coalition government with the moderate socialists and built a government on the will of the overwhelming majority of the workers, soldiers, and peasants who had voted socialist in the Constituent Assembly elections, there is a good chance that Russia could have secured a democratic, socialist system, though not a highly industrialized one. Yet the Bolsheviks preferred to try to rule alone with the 25 per cent urban vote they had received. Their decision against a socialist coalition made worker and soldier support more critical than ever. The problem was that the 25 per cent was not unequivocal. A sufficient element of opposition developed, particularly in the critical area of urban labor, to undermine any prospect of Bolshevik success. Time and again labor support appeared as a critical factor delimiting Bolshevik options. Cognizant of reluctant support, but committed, they turned a blind eye to the dissension in labor's ranks. If labor was in fact a force giving rise to a democratic alternative in the pre-1917 period, it was a decisive power contributing to Bolshevik failure in the post-1917 period. The Bolsheviks failed in part because of labor opposition. It was an opposition of many dimensions, not least of which was a demand for a nondictatorial process.

Contrary to a longstanding myth, labor was not united behind the Bolsheviks. The unions were fragmented and a majority of them opposed the Bolsheviks. At first Lenin could take heart in the fact that he had strong rank-and-file support on the local level in many unions. But a number of white- and blue-collar unions, including the teachers, printers, and railwaymen, were opposed to a minority dictatorship. The problem of a majority of unions opposing him was a serious one. He needed not only rank-and-file support to help secure the Bolshevik coup but, since the Party did not have the machinery essential for ruling alone in late 1917, he needed the apparatus of these mass member organizations to help him administer the economy and rule the country. Also, he could not afford to have strong mass labor organizations opposing him or standing politically neutral. If they were strong and against him, either they or he would have to be crushed. This was his dilemma. He had to declare war on the very institutions upon which he depended for realizing the goals of the November Revolution.

Lenin's difficulty with the unions was compounded by the fact that worker support fell away rapidly after November. So sharp and steady was the decline that Lenin remarked in 1918 that the workers "were tired." The fall-off continued steadily, and if Bolshevik control of the unions contributed to the Party's ability to secure power, it contributed little to the abatement of worker alienation or control of the urban labor force. Immediately after union membership was declared voluntary in 1921, over 50 per cent of the workers quit the Party-dominated unions. In the middle and late twenties the unions recouped their losses, but during this same period the number of workers who held Party cards fell to the startling low of 4 to 6 per cent of the urban labor force. What makes worker alienation even more startling is the fact that it occurred in a period of rapid upward mobility for many workers and peasants. Not all workers and peasants, however, were Khrushchevs, willing to join the Communist Party, though enough were to keep the Party ranks growing. But most remained by choice outside the Party. The point is that the Bolsheviks did not want to be isolated from the workers, yet this is exactly what they accomplished. Little testifies more to the failure of their Revolution than their isolation from the very class they had counted upon as a mass base for a socialist Russia.

Another aftereffect of the labor battle was the emergence of dictatorship within the Communist Party. The whole issue of labor's role spilled over into the Party to divide it badly. Factional fights developed on a host of policy questions, but the trade union debate almost wrecked the Party. So severe was the internal battle on this question at the end of the civil war that Lenin and Trotsky split on it and the Central Committee was completely paralyzed in the spring of 1921. The issue, which took its most extreme form in the "workers' control" debate, went to the heart of the dictatorship and opened the question of viable alternatives to the system forged in the crucible of civil war. Coming at a time when nine-tenths of the workers were against the Party, or were non-Party members, Lenin felt he was in no position to afford strong unions or division within the Party. He could not afford a democratic process either in the Party or in the system while he was hanging onto power by a sheer thread. In response to a two-pronged threat, Lenin outlawed factions and thus so curtailed all remaining democratic procedures within the Party as to render them meaningless symbols. Dictatorship within the Communist Party was one of the unavoidable costs of the labor fight, but again it was one that Lenin was prepared to pay.

Looking at the problem from the view of the worker and the unions, several impressions stand out. Labor played a role in post-1917 Russia very similar to the one it had played in pre-1917 Russia. It was again in opposition to dictatorship among other things, and although labor's positions ranged over a wide spectrum, there was a greater collective commitment to a democratic alternative than to any other single goal.

The Russian worker was hardly a democratic personality. For the most part he was a product of an autocratic social and political system, a paternalistic family structure, and a messianic apocalyptic church; he tended to hold views which were black and white. Yet he played a democratic role. He did so not only because of his discontent with a repressive regime but also because a socialist and trade union intelligentsia committed to democracy had reached him earlier. Ideologically as well as morally, he saw democracy and socialism as his one great hope. Psychological authoritarianism and the lack of a democratic tradition cut into his efforts, and certainly left him too confused and weak in his opposition to the Bolsheviks to oust them. But at critical moments like Kronstadt it was no accident that strikes broke out and posters appeared in the working-class districts calling for democratic elections and Soviets without Bolsheviks. It was no accident that the Bolsheviks had to create the Cheka. It was no accident that Trotsky and Zinoviev admitted that in 1920 and 1921 the workers were once again rallying to the ranks of the Mensheviks. The message is that Durkheim's and Wallace's observation that there is no one-to-one correlation between personality and a social system can be amended to read: There is no one-to-one correlation between social aculturality and personality on the one hand, and political role and commitment on the other. People without a democratic personality or tradition may still opt for democracy and play a democratic role.

What makes the workers' opposition even more significant is the fact that although they emerged as major beneficiaries of the Bolshevik social revolution (indeed they enjoyed a much more privileged position than the peasants and middle class), the workers still turned against the Bolsheviks. By no means can their hostility be explained merely as a result of disappointment, though this indeed triggered some. Theirs was opposition over motive and intent as well. The point is that a revolution in expectations had swept the lower ranks of society. Not all workers (and certainly not all peasants) understood or were committed to democracy, but enough were to warrant the generalization that as a class and a movement they were democratically committed. The overthrow of Nicholas II was certainly more than a protest against the war. On the whole, the people were ready for and wanted democracy. Though Russia faced severe problems, the option was there. The failure and the ensuing despotism is difficult to attribute to the masses, particularly since the fifty years of Soviet rule have been largely the history of a war between the people and a despotic Party. The prime factor for the failure, it would appear, is Bolshevik millenarianism.

REVOLUTION AND MILLENARIANISM

Lenin and his fellow Bolsheviks are best viewed as millenarians acting in a period of transition. One could argue a "radicals of transition" explanation that would describe the role they played in terms of the profound social change and political polarization that accompanied the industrial revolution. But this does not quite satisfy, for it does not identify sufficiently the characteristics that mark them off from other radicals and make their behavior so uniquely Bolshevik. The Bolsheviks were the prophets of Communism in a society torn by problems of backwardness, social fragmentation, and modernization. Add a politics and a psychology of millenarianism and a more adequate explanation is obtained.

The Bolsheviks came to power as a small band of radicals isolated from the rest of society by their sectarian "style of life," their *Weltanschauung*. They were the prophets of doom for the old, apostles of hope for the new. They combined politics and ethics in their concern for man's salvation. Unwilling to compromise and intolerant of opposition, they saw themselves as the only party which could serve as the legitimate moral fountainhead of the Russian people. So convinced were they of the righteousness of their mission that they were prepared to sacrifice all material comforts and even their lives. So convinced were they of the justness of their cause that without hesitation they were prepared to divide men and the world into two kinds—one to be consecrated in blood, the other in Communism.

By no means can their policies be explained in terms of "welfare" politics, of all parties seeking the general interest or common good. If a general welfare were ascertainable, the Bolsheviks' own goals were more important to them. The lesson of their rule is not one of societal forces impelling parties to move toward integration and cohesion, but one of messianism and civil war. The Bolsheviks were clearly prepared to impose their own views upon the people, even if the price were civil war, starvation, and the fragmentation of society.

Like many other millenarians they had a very distorted view of reality. They were hard-headed and critical, and their analysis was profoundly penetrating at times. Yet they had a flawed sense of reality. They lived in a world of false consciousness. They saw only what they wanted to see and rejected what they did not like. Many of their political decisions were based upon a logic that was deadly wrong. The Bolsheviks deluded themselves when they thought they could build a communist society in a Russia still breaking away from feudalism and autocracy. They deceived themselves when they believed that they spoke for the workers and the lower stratum of the entire society. It never occurred to them, or they refused to believe, that the workers would turn against them or that their seizure of power would end in the Party's political isolation. Finally, they refused to believe that their Revolution would not succeed in the face of substantial labor opposition.

Lenin and Tomsky, two men central to the story told above, tell the whole story in their personal lives. Lenin most certainly was the great revolutionary of the first half of the twentieth century. He was something of an enigma in the sense that very few people, if any, got a chance to see the real Lenin or know of his innermost fears and doubts. Lenin kept his own counsel. But judging from the role that he played and the public positions he held, one thing is clear: Lenin was a millenarian. He changed the fate of the world on the basis of a dream and a mission. Armed with apocalyptic visions of the future society and infuriated with the inequities he witnessed in his own, he united ethics and politics. He ate, slept, and dreamed revolution until the opportunity arrived when he could take the tools of power and begin to fashion his new society. It was more than power he sought; he wanted the hearts and loyalty of men. Armed with a deep moral passion for the people and convinced of the justness of his mission, neither a superego nor societal disapproval inhibited him.

Yet he was blind, and while at times his blindness was a source of great strength that enabled him to succeed where others failed, his blunders led to a sense of false consciousness and logic which were ultimately deadly. By not anticipating the opposition of the workers and refusing to accept the fact that labor was opposed to him, he plunged Russia into a civil war which wracked the country and cost him the very principles and dreams to which he had dedicated his life. But there is more to it than that. When Lenin died, the system for which he sacrificed all crumbled around him. What he produced was a Stalin and a police state. Such was the price of his millenarianism, his unwillingness to compromise or tolerate opposition. It is a prophetic lesson, and it would seem to point up the wisdom not only of clarity and hard-headed realism regardless of one's prejudices but of the inestimable value of tolerance and compromise in politics as well.

Tomsky points up a slightly different message, yet there were few who played so crucial a role in the development of the Soviet labor movement, or in the consolidation of Party power. As a person he appears to have been a mediocrity, a good organizer and administrator, and unquestionably loyal, but a man who was not of the caliber of most of his associates and opponents. Yet his impact was crucial. It was Tomsky who fought and won the battle of the trade unions for Lenin. It was Tomsky who, with all his weaknesses and limitations, ensured Lenin of continuous control and support, even when many other Party union leaders balked.

In the West, Tomsky has often been treated as a "tragic hero." He has been seen as a "reasonable man" who was quite close to the rank-and-file workers and was considerate of their interests; a man who was not afraid to fight Trostky and Lenin at times, and finally Stalin, when he felt Party policies would have had an adverse effect on the workers. It has also been suggested that he was the one who remained faithful and true to the principles of the Bolshevik Revolution. The irony is that it was Tomsky more than any other Bolshevik, perhaps with the exception of Lenin, who was responsible for the destruction of strong, independent, and democratic trade unions in Russia. It was Tomsky who did Lenin's hatchet work in the union movement, who chartered and rechartered unions to serve the Party's purposes, who destroyed the independent and anti-Party unions, who fought for the denial of an autonomous and neutral role for the unions. It was Tomsky who helped Lenin push through one-man management and curtail union participation in decision-making on the shop management level. It was Tomsky who ensured full and loyal Party control over the unions. Yet at the same time he was so deeply committed to the Russian workers that he resolutely fought Trotsky on labor discipline issues at the end of the War Communism period, and even opposed Lenin at some crucial times in an attempt to force some concessions from the Politbureau.

Thus we have a man who played a dual role. He remade the union movement in the image of the Party, destroying the unions as an independent force well before Stalin. Like so many, he was caught in a squeeze between his devotion to the unions and his loyalty to the Party. He supported Stalin loyally against Trotsky and the Left Opposition for the good of the worker and Party unity, only to break with Stalin in the late twenties to defend the union movement against the decisions of the Party. Finally, he was the man who committed suicide in the thirties to escape what Stalin was doing to the unions and the Old Bolsheviks. But one wonders whether his desperate act was not also an effort to escape an awareness of what he himself had done to the Russian trade union movement and to Russian socialism. His emasculation of the trade union movement in the early period helped pave the way for Stalin and a one-man dictatorship. His destruction of a democratic labor movement, an idea for which he had fought with such great love and devotion, helped render the Revolution stillborn. What irony in a man's deeds! And if we were to look closely, we could generalize many times on Tomsky's role and outcome in the Revolution. His was not an isolated case.

MILLENARIANISM AND WORK

In the field of industrial relations we can see the same process at work. The 1917 Revolution heralded a revolution in industrial relations as great as, if not greater than, the overthrow of the autocracy. The whole industrial relations system was to be transferred in accordance with socialist principles. The age-old dream of liberating the worker from bondage to the machine, and from a nondemocratic system of factory management, appeared to be nearing realization. Management was to be democratic. The system was to be run by, and in the interests of, the workers. This too had been the promise of the Revolution.

But the revolution in industrial relations that started with workers' control and collective management was stillborn. There is little question that objective difficulties like economic backwardness and the civil war contributed substantially to their failure, but I also consider the Bolsheviks' messianic approach to industrial relations as the prime source of their difficulty.

As good Marxists, the Bolsheviks started out with the humanistic idea that in work men could realize themselves socially and individually and thus be free. Work was seen as the cardinal activity in life, socially necessary and the source of all value. But they then interjected repressive propositions which condoned the maxim that "he who does not work, neither shall he eat"; they revised the meaning of socially useful work to allow its use for punishing wrong and correcting evil. Men, with antisocial ways could be rehabilitated through enforced, useful work. It was not long before the idea of work as rectitude and penitence began to creep into their view of the future society. With this step they deviated far from the original idea of Marx.

But the issue is more complex. Tension existed between various commitments in their thought system. This point can be seen in their simultaneous espousal, on the one hand, of liberating the worker from the drudgery of the work process, and on the other, of rationalizing the work process to make it as efficient as possible. This in effect represented a dual commitment—to a concept of organization so all-embracing that it was quite totalitarian, and to a concept of individual freedom and autonomy that was quite humanistic. In the final analysis it was their strong belief in a highly technocratic and scientific approach to production that prevailed. Their choice was not based merely on objective need. Their devotion to the idea of efficiency and discipline was much more than a response to the chaos in industry and the economic need produced by the Revolution, though it was that too. Rationality and scientific management of the work process held great appeal to them and, once introduced, their condemnation of the idea of the worker reduced to a mere cog in the industrial process dropped on their priority scale. Indeed, the worker was to be liberated, but now by means of the rationalized work process. This was in keeping with Lenin's theories of discipline and organization. What they did not see was that the tension within their thought system and the choice they made marked the triumph of the implicit totalitarian ideas of socialist organization over the explicit humanist ideas of socialism.

If consequences are the measure, their millenarian approach and labor policies were clearly repressive. Job assignment, disenfranchisement, denial of ration books for not performing socially useful work, a labor draft, labor armies, severe labor discipline extending through N.E.P., imprisonment, and at times execution—these are just some measures which indicate the dominant character of Soviet labor policy in those early, formative years. These policies cannot be explained as men bowing to necessity alone. Some need existed, but the impetus to adopt draconian measures was reinforced, if not accelerated, by their original ideas of obligatory and socially useful work. They felt few restraints and many ample justifications for their severe labor policy.

For a Party committed to the liberalization and humanization of the work process, they have ended with strange results. Most important of all, they have offered the world little, if anything, that is either new or compatible with their original objectives. They have made a major impact with nationalization and economic planning, but regarding the humanization of the work process and worker participation in management and economic decision-making, they have had little or nothing to contribute. In the field of management, what they instituted after the abandonment of workers' control could hardly be considered a socialist innovation. Their system was little out of the ordinary, and more ruthless than some. No meaningful worker participation in management occurred. With the destruction of the trade unions, labor participation in the creation and regulation of the work process fell far below that of capitalist systems, where trade unions, primarily through the collective bargaining process, contribute to the determination of plant policy. There has been some attempt in Russia in recent years to search for new paths in worker participation in management, but they are scarcely as imaginative as the Yugoslav attempt—and the Yugoslavs have a long way to go. The rub is that their emphasis on efficiency did not produce the results they needed or wanted. If anything is true in the Soviet Union today, it is that they are learning not only that worker satisfaction is essential to efficiency but, more important, that efficiency is not everything. It is quite a lesson to learn after fifty years of rule.

In the field of bargaining and labor-management relations, the Bolsheviks ended with the destruction not only of the unions but also of a real bargaining relationship. Union power was not only checked but reduced to the point where the unions were a shadow of themselves. Labor had no way of compelling attention to its demands. Management's price for disregarding them was lower than that of yielding. Management was essentially free to do what it wanted to. The net effect was that the unions lost their ability to control the work force and the labor market. They were in fact, though not in form, close to being functionless institutions in the field of labor relations. With the decline of the unions, the need to regulate worker behavior remained as great a problem as ever. Economic backwardness, unemployment, low wages, and poor living conditions, and then the Five Year Plan with its enormous opportunity for mobility—all reinforced the need. But the unions were unable to provide the levels of labor stability and discipline needed for efficient plant operations. They could give their members some few satisfactions, but they had no means of commanding respect or loyalty or of performing their originally designed functions. The net effect was more and more direct state control. It would thus seem hard to say that the introduction of direct state control was a necessary function of socialism. It would appear to be rather a by-product of the destruction of the unions. Large industrial societies can achieve their objective of control of the labor market in more ways than one, and effective collective bargaining appears to be one of the less torturous ways of doing it, whether the system is socialist or nonsocialist. What is important is that for less draconian solutions unions possess real functions and real powers.

In the Soviet Union today there appears to be a general awareness that the Soviet system is up against a labor problem—low worker satisfaction with life in the plant and an arbitrary and inconsiderate management. It appears that some policy-makers now believe an effective method for the resolution of this problem is, among other things, a series of reforms upgrading labor, the strengthening of the unions, and the creation of a real bargaining relationship. Collective bargaining in the West has posed its problems, and in an age when strikes occur on an industry- and nationwide basis adversely affecting the national economy, many now question them as an effective and desirable mechanism for the resolution of labor problems. This may be, yet Soviet problems point up a dimension of collective bargaining that reveals its effectiveness: the introduction of a system of rules and regulations that cover all dimensions of life in the industrial process. Today the Soviets are struggling to redistribute power and eliminate inequity. One can only hope they will be successful.

However, regarding one of the most important questions of modern industrial societies, that of groping with problems of impersonalization and alienation due to organization, bigness, and the work process itself, the Russians so far have precious little to offer us in the field of industrial relations. Without a fundamental reorganization of their system, it is doubtful they will have very much to offer.

The Leninists are still millenarians, and they still repress people to remake and save them. They have lost much feeling and enthusiasm for the worker and the workers' state, but not all of it; the idea of the withering away of the state may be passing as an important factor influencing behavior, though, indeed, some still cherish the idea; and the idea of communal property and a classless society may ring hollow, though men still think and respond in these terms. This may all be the case, but one concept that is very much alive and has contributed to an operative social ethic and to policy is their Leninist idea of work. They still see work as socially utilitarian and morally necessary. It is still a cornerstone of their social ethic used to measure the moral worth of men. In their eyes, it is still the case that men have an obligation to work, not for personal reward but for the common good of society and their own moral salvation. And they still believe men can be made to work for their own rehabilitation. In the Communist ethic of work there still lives an element of ideological vitality and a millenarian commitment. In this sense the Party is more than a mere power-seeking institution concerned with preserving the status quo. Talented Russian poets like Brodsky are persecuted and sentenced to hard labor by officials who indeed may be men who see good career prospects in such a case, but they are also men who have been so asocialized by a Leninist value system and a millenarian approach that they are incapable of understanding or tolerating intellectual and social heretics, or anyone for that matter who does not conform to expected Communist norms. The poetry of the deviants may be subtle and creative, but it is seen as empty and decadent. Socially useful labor, as applied by law courts and comradely courts, by judges, neighbors and associates, is, in their opinion, the best way for correcting evil and developing a healthy moral and social climate for the society of the future. The Leninist idea of work is very much alive in the Soviet Union today. It is a living mystique, a whole way of looking at the world. It is a key to Soviet politics and behavior and to their present commitment to remake man and society.

The humanism and ideals of the 1917 Revolution are also very much evident. They are espoused by many who are critical of the present system, though paradoxically they are also sought by some who are Party millenarians. Men as unlikely as Khrushchev and Mikoyan, motivated by hard but multifold political objectives, con-tributed to destalinization. Deliberately or not they were pressing Russia back to the ideals of 1917, and to completing an unfinished revolution. Leninism and 1917 were important to Khrushchev, and so powerful are both ideals that they have provided the only legiti-mate standards which he and others employed to reject Stalin.

The neo-Stalinist revival and the invasion of Czechoslovakia cannot but leave one with a profound sense of despair. Yet the destalinization process and the vitality of the ideas of 1917 leave one feeling that there is something to be hopeful about on the Russian scene. The Soviet Union is changing. There are strong pressures at work which commit the Russians to secure the objec-tives for which the Revolution was fought and to which so many have remained committed for so long. Many inside and outside the Party are consciously committed to these goals. The tragedy is that the Bolsheviks were their own worst enemies, and it was through their acts that they diverted Russia from the very goals they so anxiously wanted to achieve and were closer to in 1917 than they have been for most of the fifty years since. Perhaps they will get close again, and one can feel the surge of hope run through one's veins for the Russian people, a hope that mitigates apprehen-sions about the repressive forces still dominant in Soviet society. But at the same time one also feels an all-pervasive sadness. Fifty years ago, when Russia was on the threshold of democracy and a great and noble revolution, a handful of men, deluded by their own sense of infallibility and by the ideological proposition that they were leading the people, took the wrong road. It was tragic, for democracy was a real option on a scale of credible possibilities. The hopes and dreams of a democratic system are still alive, and though elements of a virile and despotic millenarianism are still active, there is reason to hope that the Russians will ultimately find the right road.

Notes

Notes to Chapter 2

1. John Reed, *Ten Days That Shook the World* (New York: 1960), pp. 75–77. This event took place on the eve of the meeting of the Second Congress of Soviets as Trotsky tried to enter Smolny, the Soviet headquarters. Reed was a witness to the incident.
2. Leon Trotsky's retort to Martov at the Second Congress of Soviets, quoted from Nikolai N. Sukhanov, *The Russian Revolution, 1917,* edited and translated by Joel Carmichael (New York: 1955), pp. 639–640.
3. V. I. Lenin, *Sochineniia* (*Works*), 3rd ed. (Moscow: 1935), Vol. XXII, pp. 27–29.
4. Robert Payne, *The Life and Death of Lenin* (New York: 1964), p. 402. One recent account would have it that Lenin was not so vague. In reminiscing in 1965 about experiences in the Bolshevik Revolution 48 years earlier, Nikolai F. Izmailov, a sailor in the Baltic Fleet in 1917, stated that a month before the Revolution, when Lenin wanted to organize support within the fleet, he (Izmailov) became a member of the embryonic Central Committee of the fleet. He further stated: "The Baltic Fleet had already withdrawn its support from the Provisional Government, and on November 6 we received a telegram saying 'Send manuals.'" That, he said, "was the code meaning that the revolution was beginning."
    "On November 9 they summoned me to the telegraph office saying that Vladimir Ilyich Lenin was calling me. I did not believe it at first, but I went and Lenin himself asked me how many torpedo boats we could send to Petrograd to help fight the counterrevolutionaries. I replied we could send two torpedo boats and one battleship. They could be in Petrograd in 18 hours. Vladimir Ilyich asked if we had enough food and gave me precise instructions on where the ships should anchor in the harbor."
    This account was reported in *The New York Times* by Peter Grose on November 3, 1965. Because of the time span and Lenin's own official account, I am inclined to give less credence to Izmailov's account.

5. Lenin, *Soch.*, 2nd ed., Vol. XXX, p. 222.
6. George Lichtheim, *Marxism: A Historical and Critical Study* (New York: 1965), p. 332.
7. See Reed, *op. cit.*, p. 21, note 5.
8. *Bolshaya Sovetskaya Entsiklopediya* (1930 ed.), Vol. XI, p. 534.
9. Reed, *op. cit.*, p. 6.
10. S. An-sky's account of the negotiations to form a socialist coalition government, November 10–14, 1917. S. An-sky (Rapoport), "Posle perevorota 25-go Oktiabria 1917 g.," in *Arkhiv Russkoi Revoliutsii* (1923), Vol. VIII, pp. 45–54. See also James Bunyan and H. H. Fisher, *The Bolshevik Revolution, 1917–1918* (Stanford: 1934), pp. 167–168; henceforth referred to as Bunyan and Fisher. Although most citations were researched in the original, this work is cited for the convenience it provided the author and can provide the reader.
11. Reed, *op. cit.*, pp. 211–216.
12. *Ibid.*, p. 312.
13. *Pervyi Vserossiiskii S"ezd Professional'nykh Soiuzov, 7–14 ianvaria 1918 g., Polnyi Stenograficheskii Otchet* (Moscow: 1918), pp. 29–30, 134, 338; henceforth referred to as *Pervyi S"ezd*. Of the remaining 147 delegates, there were 67 Mensheviks, 32 Independents, 21 Left Socialist Revolutionaries, 10 Right Socialist Revolutionaries, 6 Maximalists, and 6 Anarcho-Syndicalists. A discrepancy should be noted: the figures total 142, not 147.—J.B.S.
14. *Pervyi S"ezd*, p. 134.
15. International Labor Office, *The Trade Union Movement in Soviet Russia, Studies and Reports*, Series A, No. 26 (Geneva: 1927), p. 22.
16. *Pervyi S"ezd*, pp. 29–30.
17. Yury Martov, "Nasha Programa," *Sotsialisticheskii Vestnik*, October 4, 1922, pp. 3–8; quoted in Leonard Schapiro, *The Origin of the Communist Autocracy* (Cambridge: 1955), pp. 198–199; henceforth referred to as Schapiro, *The Origin*.
18. *Pervyi S"ezd*, p. 80.
19. *Ibid.*, pp. 111, 122.
20. *Ibid.*, p. 103.
21. *Ibid.*, pp. 11, 22.
22. *Ibid.*, p. 38.
23. *Ibid.*, p. 97.
24. *Ibid.*, p. 38.
25. *Ibid.*, p. 27.
26. *Ibid.*, p. 75.
27. *Ibid.*, pp. 119–120.
28. *Ibid.*, p. 193.
29. *Ibid.*, p. 235.
30. *Ibid.*, p. 374.
31. *Ibid.*, pp. 233–234.
32. *Vtoroi Vserossiiskii, S"ezd Professional'nykh Soiuzov, 16–25 ianvaria 1919 g., Stenograficheskii Otchet, Chast' 1 Plenumy* (Moscow: 1921), pp. 31, 37; henceforth referred to as *Vtoroi S"ezd*.
33. *Ibid.*, p. 38.
34. *Ibid.*, p. 66.
35. *Ibid.*, p. 257.
36. *Ibid.*, pp. 400–402.
37. *Pervyi S"ezd*, p. 80.
38. Cf. Tomsky's Preface, *Pervyi S"ezd*.
39. N . . . sky, *Vtoroi Vserossiiskii S"ezd Professional'nykh Soiuzov* (Moscow: 1919), p. 96; henceforth referred to as N . . . sky, *Vtoroi S"ezd*. Translated in *The Trade Union Movement in Soviet Russia*, Appendix III.
40. *Loc. cit.*

Notes to Chapter 3

1. Sukhanov, *op. cit.*, p. 65.
2. Representative of the executive committee of the railwaymen's union addressing "several thousand sailors massed, bristling with rifles ready to leave for Moscow," quoted from Reed, *op. cit.*, p. 279.
3. Sukhanov, quoting the union representative at the closing session of the Second Congress of Soviets in November 1917. See Sukhanov, *op. cit.*, p. 665.
4. Conversation between John Reed and a young unnamed Socialist Revolutionary on the eve of Kerensky's march on Petrograd. Reed, *op. cit.*, p. 207.
5. Lenin in a conversation with Maxim Gorky just after Lenin had been shot. From Gorky, *Days with Lenin* (New York: 1932), p. 11ff.
6. *Pravda*, January 22, 1927.
7. P. Vompe, *Dni Oktiabr'skoi Revoliutsii i Zheleznodorozhniki* (Moscow: 1924), p. 10. Also A. Taniaev, *Ocherki Dvizheniia Zheleznodorozhnikov Revoliutsii 1917 g* (Moscow: 1925), p. 91. Also Bunyan and Fisher, p. 153.
8. A different interpretation of this affair is to be found in Edward H. Carr's *A History of Soviet Russia. The Bolshevik Revolution*, Vol. II (London: 1958), p. 395. For a personal though rather abbreviated account, see Sukhanov, *op. cit.*, pp. 664–665.
9. Sukhanov, *loc. cit.*
10. *Delo Naroda*, No. 191, November 10, 1917, p. 2.
11. *Novaia Zhizn'*, No. 167, November 12, 1917, p. 2. See also Bunyan and Fisher, pp. 155–156.
12. *Proletarskaia Revoliutsiia*, No. 10, 1922, pp. 465–470.
13. *Loc. cit.*
14. *Ibid.*
15. Leon Trotsky, *Stalinskaia Shkola Fal'sifikatsii* (Berlin: 1932), pp. 116–124.
16. *Delo Naroda*, No. 203, November 21, 1917, p. 2.
17. *Ibid.*
18. *Delo Naroda*, No. 204, November 22, 1917, p. 3.
19. *Delo Naroda*, No. 195, November 13, 1917, pp. 1–2.
20. Cf. Schapiro, *The Origin*, p. 79.
21. *Delo Naroda*, No. 228, December 22, 1917, p. 4; also Bunyan and Fisher, p. 230.
22. From Shlyapnikov's report to the Central Executive Committee, March 20, 1918. *Protokoly zasedanii Vserossiiskogo Tsentral'nogo Ispol'nitel'nogo Komiteta 4-go sozyva* (*Stenograficheskii Otchet*), pp. 44–45. See Bunyan and Fisher, pp. 654–655.
23. Report of Protnitsky, *Protokoly i-oy Vserossiiskoi Konferentsii Zheleznodorozhnikov Kommunistov* (Moscow: 1918). Also Bunyan and Fisher, pp. 653–654. Also *Sbornik Dekretov i Postanovlenii po Narodnomu Khoziaistvu* (Moscow: 1918), pp. 820–822. Cf. Carr, *The Bolshevik Revolution*, Vol. II, p. 396.
24. Sovnarkom Narodnoe Kozhiaistvo, *Sobranie Uzakonenii i Rasporiazhenii Rabochego i Krestianskogo Pravitel'stva, 1918*, pp. 86–89; henceforth referred to as SNK, SU.
25. *Proletarskaia Revoliutsiia*, No. 10, 1922. Also Leon Trotsky, *My Life* (New York: 1930), p. 293, and Bunyan and Fisher, pp. 227–228.
26. *Izvestiia*, November 13, 1917, p. 5.
27. Trotsky, *Sochineniia*, Vol. III, Book 2 (Moscow: 1924–1927), p. 120. Also Bunyan and Fisher, p. 230.
28. *Novaia Zhizn'*, No. 10, January 27, 1918, p. 4, and No. 18, February 7, 1918, p. 3. Also Bunyan and Fisher, p. 231.

29. *Pravda*, No. 25, February 14, 1918, p. 3. Also Bunyan and Fisher, *loc. cit.*
30. *Novaia Zhizn'*, No. 26, February 16, 1918, p. 3. Quoted in Bunyan and Fisher, *loc. cit.*
31. Report on the dissolution of the Moscow Printers Union in the *British Labor Delegation to Russia 1920: Report* (London: 1920), pp. 63–72, and in *Revoliutsionnaia Rossiia*, No. 5 (Tallin: 1921), pp. 23–24. For protests of oppositionists, see F. Dan, *Dva Goda Skitanii: 1919–1921* (Berlin: 1922), pp. 7–15; also Victor Chernov, *Pered burei* (New York: 1953), pp. 409–412.
32. *British Labor Delegation Report*, pp. 64–65.
33. *Vtoroi S″ezd*, p. 31.
34. Documents given to C. R. Buxton, the last member of the British labor delegation to pass through Moscow, June 23, 1920, in *British Labor Delegation Report*, pp. 64–65.
35. *Novaia Zhizn'*, No. 46, March 20, 1918, p. 3. Also Bunyan and Fisher, pp. 645–646.
36. *Nash Vek*, No. 59, March 28, 1918. Also Bunyan and Fisher, pp. 646.
37. *Novaia Zhizn'*, No. 80, April 30, 1918, p. 4.
38. Schapiro, *The Origin*, p. 201; see Chapter 10 for further evidence.
39. *Ibid.* See also *Protokoly Desiatogo S″ezda RKP(b)*, mart 1921 g. (Moscow: 1933), p. 353; henceforth referred to as *Protokoly X*.
40. Lenin, *Soch.*, 2nd ed., Vol. XXVI, p. 348. Schapiro, *The Origin*, p. 204.
41. Lenin, *Soch.*, 2nd ed., Vol. XXIV, p. 760.
42. Schapiro, *The Origin*, pp. 208–209. The Mensheviks split on the question of overthrowing the Bolsheviks. See Zaria, *Organ Sotsialdemokraticheskoi mysli*, No. 8 (Berlin: 1922), p. 239.

Notes to Chapter 4

1. Sukhanov, *op. cit.*, p. 212.
2. S. A. Lozovsky, *Trade Unions in Soviet Russia* (New York: 1920), pp. 14–15.
3. *Ibid.*, p. 15.
4. See *Verkhoven in Voprosy Istorii*, No. 10, 1948, pp. 7–8. The account above also follows closely one presented by Margaret Dewar, *Labor Policy in the U.S.S.R., 1917–1928* (London: 1956), p. 23.
5. V. A. Auerbach's Memoirs, quoted in Bunyan and Fisher, p. 625.
6. *Novaia Zhizn'*, No. 95, May 21, 1918, p. 1.
7. *Izvestiia*, No. 84, April 27, 1918, p. 1.
8. *Pervyi S″ezd*, pp. 175, 194.
9. *Oktiabrskaia Revoliutsia i Fabsavkomy: Materialy po istorii fabrichnoz-avodskikh komitetov* (Moscow: 1927), Vol. 1, p. 32.
10. *Vtoroi S″ezd*, pp. 98–99.
11. N . . . sky, *Vtoroi S″ezd*, p. 10.
12. Komissiia Po Izucheniiu Istorii Professional'nogo Dvizhenia v Rossii Pri V.Ts.S.P.S. (1st Prof.) Seriia Istoricheskikh Dokumentov, *IV Vseros-siiskaia Konferentsiia Professional'nykh Soiuzov 12–17 marta 1918*, V.Ts.S.P.S. (1st Prof., Moscow: 1923), pp. 27–28.
13. *VKP(b) Rezol.* 4th ed. (Moscow: 1941), Vol. i, pp. 290–291.
14. See *Protokoly Deviatogo S″ezda RKP(b)*, mart-aprel' 1920 g. (Moscow: 1934); henceforth referred to as *Protokoly IX*.
15. Isaac Deutscher, *Soviet Trade Unions* (London: 1950), p. 29.
16. *Ibid.*, p. 64.
17. *Ibid.*, p. 137.
18. Lenin, *Soch.*, 2nd ed., Vol. XXVI, p. 66.

Notes to Chapter 5

1. "Lenin's Speech at the Third All-Russian Trade Union Congress," *Trade Unions in Soviet Russia,* a collection of documents compiled by the International Labor Party (New York: 1920), pp. 63–64.
2. *Tretii Vserossiiskii S"ezd Professional'nykh Soiuzov,* 6–13 aprel'a 1920 g. (Moscow: 1920), p. 80; henceforth referred to as *Tretii S"ezd.*
3. *The Economic Condition of Soviet Russia* (London: 1924), p. 25, quoted in Dewar, *op. cit.,* p. 52.
4. *Trudy I Vserossiiskogo S"ezda Sovetov Narodnogo Khoziaistva,* 25 maia-4 iunia 1918 (Moscow: 1918), pp. 381–382.
5. *Novaia Zhizn',* No. 173, November 18, 1917, p. 3.
6. Sukhanov, *op. cit.,* p. 42.
7. *Pravda,* December 17, 1919.
8. Arakcheev was a former Tsarist official who set up military farming colonies. See Isaac Deutscher, *The Prophet Armed* (New York: 1965), p. 492.
9. Leon Trotsky, *Dictatorship vs. Democracy (Terrorism and Communism)* (New York: 1922), p. 175.
10. *Pravda,* March 27, 1919; *Protokoly X,* pp. 869–870.
11. For criticisms, see Zinoviev, *Sochineniia,* Vol. VI, p. 344.
12. Lenin, *Soch.,* 2nd ed., Vol. XXVI, p. 68.
13. *Protokoly IX,* p. 62.
14. *Sed'moi S"ezd Professional'nykh Soiuzov,* 6–18 dekabria 1926 g. *Plenumy i Sektsii, Polnyi Stenograficheskii Otchet* (Moscow: 1927), p. 201; henceforth referred to as *Sed'moi S"ezd.*
15. Lenin, *Soch.,* 2nd ed., Vol. XXV, p. 593.
16. *Odinnadtsatyi S"ezd RKP(b), Stenograficheskii Otchet,* mart-aprel' 1922 g. (Moscow: 1936), p. 254.
17. Trotsky, *Soch.,* Vol. XV, p. 126. See Deutscher, *The Prophet Armed,* p. 499.
18. *Protokoly IX,* pp. 81–84.
19. *Protokoly IX,* p. 254.
20. *Ibid.,* p. 257.
21. See Schapiro, *The Origin,* p. 253, for a different interpretation.

Notes to Chapter 6

1. Alexandra Kollontai, *Rabochaia Oppozitsiia* (Moscow: 1921), pp. 39, 47. Thanks to Eleanor Buist, librarian and specialist on Russian material at Columbia University, I was able to obtain Madame Kollontai's manuscript in Russian while I was doing research for my Masters Essay on the Workers' Opposition. It is amusing to note that the English version has been politically edited by its I.W.W. translators. The word "peasant" has been omitted every time reference was made to "a worker-peasant state"!
2. This speech was reportedly not preserved. My interpretation is based on Lenin's writings of a short time later. See Lenin, *Soch.,* 2nd ed., Vol. XXVI, p. 100; Schapiro, *The Origin,* p. 274.
3. Lenin, *Soch.,* 2nd ed., Vol. XX, p. 28. See Schapiro, *The Origin,* p. 275.
4. Lenin, *Soch.,* 2nd ed., Vol. XXVI, p. 624.
5. *Otchety o deiatel'nosti tsentral'nogo Komiteta RKP(b-ov) s VIII do X S"ezda.* Perepechatany iz "Izvestii Ts.RKP" (Moscow: 1921), pp. 47–48; henceforth referred to as *Otchety.* Also Lenin, *Selected Works,* Vol. IX (New York: n.d.), p. 30.

6. Leon Trotsky, *On the Tasks of the Trade Unions* (New York, n.d.), pp. 15–21.
7. Schapiro, *The Origin*, p. 279.
8. *Pravda*, December 14, 1920; *Otchety*, pp. 47–49; Lenin, *Soch.*, 2nd ed., Vol. XVIII, p. 29, Schapiro, *The Origin*, p. 280.
9. *Protokoly X*, p. 826.
10. Lenin, *Soch.*, 2nd ed., Vol. XVIII (I), p. 28; Schapiro, *The Origin*, p. 280.
11. Lenin, *Soch.*, 2nd ed., Vol. XXVI, p. 28.
12. Lenin, *Soch.*, 3rd ed., Vol. XVI, p. 71.
13. See Schapiro, *The Origin*, note 23, p. 281.
14. Lenin, *Soch.*, 2nd ed., Vol. XXVI, pp. 61–68.
15. Lenin, *Selected Works*, Vol. IX, p. 4.
16. Lenin, *Soch.*, 2nd ed., Vol. XXVI, p. 87; *Selected Works*, Vol. IX, p. 28. (Emphasis added, J.B.S.)
17. Lenin, *Selected Works*, Vol. IX, p. 28.
18. *Ibid.*, p. 30.
19. *Ibid.*, p. 36.
20. Lenin, *Soch.*, 3rd ed., Vol. XXVI, pp. 103–104.
21. *Loc. cit.*
22. Lenin, *Soch.*, 2nd ed., Vol. XXVI, p. 563.
23. *Loc. cit.*
24. Kollontai, *op. cit.*
25. *Protokoly X*, p. 103.
26. Kollontai, *op. cit.*, p. 5.
27. *Ibid.*, pp. 6, 22.
28. *Ibid.*, pp. 36–37.
29. *Ibid.*, p. 45.
30. *Ibid.*, p. 39.
31. *Ibid.*, p. 40.
32. *Ibid.*, p. 38.
33. *Ibid.*, p. 47.
34. *Ibid.*, pp. 36–37.
35. Alexander Berkman, *The Kronstadt Rebellion* (Berlin: 1922), p. 7.
36. Lenin, *Soch.*, 2nd ed., Vol. XXVI, pp. 227–228. Earlier he had said: "Of course it is permissible (especially before a congress) to organize in blocs (and canvas for votes). But it must be done within the limits of Communism (and not syndicalism)." *Ibid.*, p. 94.
37. *Loc cit.* See also Schapiro, *The Origin*, p. 316.
38. See Schapiro, *The Origin*, p. 317. For this meeting see Marx-Engels-Lenin note, *Protokoly X*, pp. 891–892.
39. Lenin, *Soch.*, 2nd ed., Vol. XXVI, pp. 262–264.
40. *Ibid.*, pp. 259–261.
41. *Protokoly X*, p. 540.
42. Lenin, *Soch.*, 2nd ed., Vol. XXVI, pp. 259–261.

Notes to Chapter 7

1. Lenin, *Soch.*, 2nd ed., Vol. XXI, pp. 128–129.
2. *SU 1917–1924*, 51–582.
3. *VTsIK, SU 1918*, 87–905.
4. Adriano Tilgher, *Homo Faber: Work Through the Ages* (Chicago: 1930), p. 3.
5. Thessalonians 3:10.
6. R. H. Tawney, *Religion and the Rise of Capitalism* (New York: 1926), p. 96.
7. *Ibid.*, p. 101.

8. Calvin, *Institutes*, bk. iv, ch. xii, par. 1.
9. *Ibid.*, p. 104.
10. *Ibid.*, p. 100.
11. *Ibid.*, p. 115.
12. *Loc. cit.*
13. John Kenneth Galbraith, *The Affluent Society* (Cambridge: 1958), pp. 26ff.
14. Quoted from John Bowle's excellent treatment of Saint-Simon in *Politics and Opinion in the Nineteenth Century* (London: 1964), p. 105.
15. Hannah Arendt, *On Revolution* (New York: 1963), p. 61.
16. Quoted from manuscript of 1857–58, in A. Leontyev, *Work Under Capitalism and Socialism* (New York: 1942), p. 21.
17. Lewis S. Feuer, ed., *Karl Marx and Friedrich Engels. Basic Writings on Politics and Philosophy* (New York: 1959), pp. 483ff.
18. Karl Marx, *The German Ideology*, quoted in *Ibid.*, p. 254.
19. Lenin, *State and Revolution*, pp. 82–84.
20. *Ibid.*, p. 80.
21. Lenin, *Selected Works*, Vol. IX, p. 447.
22. Lenin, *Selected Works*, Vol. IX, p. 418.
23. Nicolas Berdyaev, *The Origin of Russian Communism* (Ann Arbor: 1960), p. 127.
24. Lenin, *State and Revolution*, p. 75.
25. N. N. Sukhanov states: "Lenin's pamphlet *State and Revolution* was very soon to become gospel. But first of all this gospel, as always, served merely as something to swear by—God forbid that anything should be done in accordance with its visionary words!—and secondly, it had not yet been published [at the time of the Bolshevik insurrection]." Sukhanov, *op. cit.*, pp. 570–571.
26. Daniel Bell, "Two Roads From Marx," *The End of Ideology* (New York: 1962), p. 375.
27. Lenin, *Selected Works*, Vol. IX, p. 421.
28. *Ibid.*, p. 433.
29. Lenin, *State and Revolution*, pp. 84–85.
30. Lenin, *The Soviets at Work*, English translation (New York: 1919), p. 23.
31. Lenin, *Soch.*, 2nd ed., Vol. XXIV, p. 342.
32. *Protokoly II Vserossiiskogo S"ezda Kommissarov, Truda, Predstaviteli Birzh Truda i Strakhovykh Kass, 18–25 maia 1918* (Moscow: 1918), p. 251.
33. *Trudy I Vserossiiskogo S"ezda Sovetov Narodnogo Khoziaistva, 25 maia-4 iunia, 1918* (Moscow: 1918), No. 2, p. 38.
34. VTsSPS and NKTruda, *SU 1919*, 26–293. I recommend M. Dewar's *Labour Policy in the U.S.S.R. 1917–1928*, for an excellent and succinct survey of the measures traced in this chapter. I used her book extensively in preparing this chapter.
35. SNK, *SU 1920*, 36–172.
36. SNK, *SU 1920*, 35–168.
37. SNK, *SU 1919*, 56–537.
38. Lenin, *Soch.*, 2nd ed., Vol. XXIV, p. 329.
39. Lenin, "A Great Beginning," *Selected Works*, Vol. IX, pp. 438–439.
40. *Ekonomicheskaia Politika SSSR: Sbornik Dokumentov* (Moscow: 1947), pp. 32–35, 500–502.
41. *Izvestiia*, February 18, 1918.
42. *VKP(b) Rezol.* (1941), Vol. I, p. 278.
43. Y. Larin and L. Kristman, *Ocherk Khoziaistvennoi Zhizni i Organizatsii Narodnogo Khoziaistva Sovetskoi Rossii, 1 noiabria 1917 g.-1 iulia 1920 g.* (Moscow: 1920), pp. 39–40.

44. *Trudy I Vserossiiskogo S"ezda Sovetov Narodnogo Khoziaistva, 19 de-kabria-27 dekabria 1918* (Moscow: n.d.), p. 15.
45. NKTruda, *SU 1918*, 60–704; *SU 1919*, 81–855; and SNK, *SU 1920*, 65–288.
46. SNK, *SU 1918*, 73–792.
47. NKTruda, *SU 1918*, 90–979.
48. NKTruda, *SU 1918*, 67–204.
49. *Ibid.*
50. SNK, *SU 1918*, 98–999.
51. SRKO, *SU 1919*, 14–163.
52. VTsIK, *SU 1919*, 12–124; 20–235.
53. SRKO, *SU 1919*, 9–100; 28–316.
54. SNK, *SU 1919*, 18–204.
55. VTsIK, *SU 1919*, 28–315.
56. SRKO, *SU 1919*, 57–543.
57. NKTruda, *SU 1919*, 65–587.
58. NKTruda, *SU 1919*, 34–338, 48–471.
59. SRKO, *SU 1919*, 53–506.
60. SRKO, *SU 1920*, 3–15.
61. SNK, *SU 1920*, 415–426.
62. STO, *SU 1920*, 27–146.
63. *Pravda*, January 22, 1920.
64. Trotsky, *Dictatorship and Democracy*, p. 175.
65. Lenin, *Soch.*, 2nd ed., Vol. XV, pp. 52–83.
66. Trotsky, *Dictatorship and Democracy*, pp. 138–145.
67. *Tretii S"ezd*, pp. 87–96.
68. *Ibid.*, pp. 97–98.
69. *Loc. cit.*
70. *Ibid.*, pp. 97–98.
71. Trotsky, *Dictatorship and Democracy*, p. 152.
72. I. Deutscher, *The Prophet Armed*, p. 500.
73. Lenin, *State and Revolution*, p. 84.
74. Lenin, *Soch.*, 2nd ed., Vol. XXII, pp. 445–447.
75. *VKP(B) i Rezol.*, 5th ed. (Moscow: 1936), Vol. i, p. 128.
76. Dewar, *op. cit.*, p. 7.
77. Lenin, *Soch.*, 2nd ed., Vol. XX, p. 459. See also M. Dewar's *Labour Policy*. Her coverage of this question is excellent.
78. Lenin, *Soch.*, 2nd ed., Vol. XXII, pp. 50, 125.
79. *XIV S"ezd Vsesoiuznoi Kommunisticheskoi Partii (B), 18–31 dekabria 1925 g., Stenograficheskii Otchet* (Moscow: 1926), p. 730.
80. Robert Dunn, *Soviet Trade Unions* (New York: 1928), p. 140.
81. *Trud*, December 14, 1926.
82. *Vos'moi S"ezd Professional'nykh Soiuzov SSSR, 10–24 dekabria 1928 g., Plenumy i Sektsii, Polnyi Stenograficheskii Otchet* (Moscow: 1929), pp. 41–43.
83. *Trud*, August 9, 1928.
84. *Trud*, May 1, 1928.
85. Quoted in Daniel Bell, *Work and Its Discontents* (Boston: 1956), p. 7. I am indebted to Bell not merely for his section on Taylor, but for his whole treatment of the work problem in this incisive and penetrating essay.
86. Taylor, from Georges Friedmann, *The Anatomy of Work* (New York: 1961), p. 86.
87. F. Engels, "On Authority," in L. S. Feuer, ed., *Marx and Engels*, p. 483.
88. Marx, *Communist Manifesto* [authorized English translation, edited and annotated by Friedrich Engels (Chicago: 1947), p. 22.
89. V. I. Lenin, *Collected Works, Towards the Seizure of Power* (New York: 1932), Vol. II, p. 89.

90. Lenin, *Soviets At Work*, p. 25.
91. Lenin, *Selected Works*, Vol. IX, p. 435.
92. See A. Gerschenkron, "Patterns of Economic Development," in Cyril Black's *The Transformation of Western Society* (Cambridge: 1960), and Karl Polanyi, *The Great Transformation* (Boston: 1964).

Notes to Chapter 8

1. From Trotsky's defense at the Tenth Party Congress, March 14, 1921, pp. 353–360.
2. *Pravda*, March 24 and 31, 1921.
3. *Spravochnik*, I, pp. 68–69, 122. Schapiro, *The Origin*, p. 323. Schapiro's work served as an outline.
4. Zorky, *Materiali* (Moscow: 1926), pp. 146–147. Schapiro, *The Origin*, p. 326.
5. *Protokoly XI, S"ezd RKP(b)*, p. 652.
6. *Chetvertyi Vserossiiskii S"ezd Professional'nykh Soiuzov, 17–25 maia 1921 g. Pts i: Plenumy Pt; Sektsii* (Moscow: 1921), pp. 153–162, 202. E. H. Carr, *The Bolshevik Revolution*, pp. 325–326.
7. *Izvestiia*, August 6, 1921.
8. *Pravda*, July 30, 1921.
9. *Odinnadtsatyi S"ezd RKP(b)*, p. 768.
10. *Ibid.*, pp. 261–262.
11. *Ibid.*, pp. 223–224.
12. *Ibid.*, pp. 223–224.
13. *Ibid.*, p. 729.
14. *Ibid.*, pp. 188, 196.
15. *Ibid.*, p. 83.
16. Zorky, *Materiali*, pp. 51–54.
17. See Zorky, *Materiali*, pp. 48–49; Schapiro in The *Origin* presents the report in full in Note 33, p. 327.
18. Schapiro, *The Origin*, Note 33, p. 327.
19. Lenin, *Soch.*, 2nd ed., Vol. XXVII, 147–156, 515, Note 56: *Stenograficheskii Otchet Piatogo Vserossiiskogo S"ezda Professional-nykh Soiuzov, 17–22 sentiabria 1922 g.* (Moscow: 1922), pp. 71, 88–89, 99, 105.
20. *IV Sessia Vserossiiskogo Tsentral'nogo Ispolnitel'nogo Komiteta IX Soiuza R.S.F.S.R., 28–31 oktiabria 1922, Stenograficheskii Otchet, Biulleten' No. 1, 25 oktiabria 1922*, pp. 1–20.
21. *Vestnik* (Berlin), January 31, 1923, pp. 12–14.
22. See V. L. Zorin, *Rabochaia Gruppa (Miasnikovshchina)* (Moscow: 1924). *Izvestiia*, No. 9–10 (1923), pp. 13–16.

Notes to Chapter 9

1. Rykov's speech, *Tretii S"ezd*, p. 91.
2. Walter Duranty, *I Write As I Please* (New York: 1935), pp. 110–111.
3. C. E. Bechhofer, *Through Starving Russia . . . A Journey to Moscow and the Volga Provinces in August and September, 1921* (London: 1921), pp. 84–95, quoted from Stanley W. Page, ed., *Russia in Revolution* (New York: 1965), pp. 177–178. With some additions, most of the selections describing the social problem are from Page's book.
4. Duranty, *op. cit.*, p. 128, quoted by Page.
5. *Ibid.*, pp. 131–132, also quoted by Page.
6. Anna Louise Strong, *I Change Worlds* (New York: 1937), p. 123.
7. Duranty, *op. cit.*, p. 140.
8. *Ibid.*, p. 145.

266

9. *Ibid.,* pp. 138–150.
10. *Ibid.,* pp. 147–148.
11. *Ibid.,* pp. 182–183.
12. N. Popov in his *Outline History of the C.P.S.U.* (New York: 1934) states that 1922 signified the end of N.E.P., Vol. II, p. 166.
13. W. Reswick, *I Dreamt Revolution* (Chicago: 1952), pp. 166–173, quoted from Page, *Russia in Revolution,* p. 189.
14. Duranty, *op. cit.,* p. 276. However, unlike in China, the Russian "red guard" was not used to attack the Party itself.
15. *Pravda,* February 9, 1928.
16. *Trud,* March 17, 1928.
17. *Trud,* August 22, 1928.

Notes to Chapter 10

1. Melnichansky in *Trud,* December 17, 1926.
2. *Blizhe K Massam: Sbornik Statei* (Moscow: 1925), p. 37.
3. Lozovsky, *Trade Unions in Soviet Russia,* p. 12.
4. *Stenograficheskii Otchet Piatogo Vserossiiskogo S"ezda Professional'nykh Soiuzov SSSR, 17–22 sentiabra 1922 g.* (Moscow: 1922), translated in *The Trade Union Movement in Soviet Russia,* Appendix V.
5. *Loc. cit.*
6. *Statistique du Travail,* No. 3, 1926 (Geneva: 1926), quoted in *The Trade Union Movement in Soviet Russia,* p. 102.
7. N . . . sky, *Vtoroi S"ezd,* p. 128.
8. Robert Dunn, *Soviet Trade Unions* (New York: 1928), p. 8.
9. *Professional'nie Soiuzov SSSR, 1921–1922, Otchet,* VTsSPS (Petrograd: 1922), pp. 26, 91–92.
10. *Odinnadtsatyi S"ezd RKP(b),* pp. 223–224.
11. Chart adapted from *Labor Messenger,* May–July 1924, as cited in *The Trade Union Movement in Soviet Russia,* pp. 27–28.
12. *Sed'moi S"ezd,* pp. 37ff.
13. *Bol'shaia Sovetskaia Entsiklopediia* (1930 ed.), Vol. XI, p. 534, quoted in Merle Fainsod, *How Russia Is Ruled* (Cambridge: 1953), p. 213.
14. *Ibid.,* p. 212.
15. *Pravda,* September 2, 1927 and June 19, 1928.
16. See *Itogi Vsesoiuznoi Partiinoi Raboty, 1922–23 g.* (Moscow: 1923), pp. 146–147. See also TsK VKP(b) *Statisticheskii Otdel, Sotsial'nyi i Natsional'nyi Sostav VKP(b), Itogi Vsesoiuznoi Partiinoi Perepisi 1927 g.* (Moscow-Leningrad: 1928).
17. VTsIK and NKTruda, *SU 1922,* 70–903.
18. *Loc. cit.*
19. *Pravda,* October 7–9, 1921.
20. N . . . sky, *Vtoroi S"ezd,* Appendix III.
21. *Stenograficheskii Otchet Piatogo Vserossiiskogo S"ezda,* pp. 66, 93, 574.
22. *VKP(b) i Rezol.,* 5th ed., i, 588–589.
23. *Trud,* July 19, 1925.
24. *Trud,* July 19, 1925.
25. *Trud,* November 21, 1923.
26. *VKP(b) i Rezol.,* 5th ed., i, 626–629.
27. *XIV S"ezd Vsesoiuznoi Kommunisticheskoi Partii (B), 18–13 dekabria 1925 g., Stenograficheskii Otchet* (Moscow: 1926), pp. 722–748.
28. *Shestoi S"ezd Professional'nykh S.S.S.R., 11–18 noiabria 1924 g., Plenumy i Sektsii, Polnyi Stenograficheskii Otchet* (Moscow: 1925), p. 87; henceforth referred to as *Shestoi S"ezd.*
29. *Sed'moi S"ezd,* pp. 47–48.

30. *Trud*, December 17, 1926.
31. *Sed'moi S"ezd*, p. 151.
32. *Vos'moi S"ezd Professional'nykh Soiuzov, S.S.S.R., 10–14 dekabria 1928 g., Plenumy i Sektsii, Polnyi Stenograficheskii Otchet* (Moscow: 1929), p. 33.
33. *Shestoi S"ezd*, p. 87.
34. *Vos'moi S"ezd*, p. 157.
35. *Ibid.*, p. 180.
36. *Trud*, September 30, 1928.
37. *Trud*, August 18, 1928.
38. *Trud*, July 25, 1928.
39. *Trud*, September 28, 1928.
40. *Trud*, August 17, 1928.

Notes to Chapter 11

1. Peter Wiles, "The Importance of Being Djugashvili," *Problems of Communism*, Vol. XII, No. 2 (March–April 1963), p. 78.
2. *Sed'moi S"ezd*, pp. 36–75.
3. Simon A. Zagorsky, *Wages and Regulation of Conditions of Labor in the U.S.S.R.* (Geneva: 1930), p. 182.
4. *XIV S"ezd Vsesoiuznoi Kommunisticheskoi Partii (B)*, 1925, pp. 780–781.
5. *Sed'moi S"ezd*, pp. 51, 54–55.
6. Abram Bergson, *The Structure of Soviet Wages* (Cambridge: 1944), p. 70.
7. *Sed'moi S"ezd*, pp. 51–52.
8. Zagorsky, *op. cit.*, p. 153.
9. *Ibid.*, pp. 152–158.
10. *Statistica Truda*, 1929, No. 1, and *Ekonomicheskaia Obozreniia*, 1929, No. 10. Quoted from Zagorsky, *op. cit.*, pp. 15–16.
11. *Stenograficheskii Otchet Piatogo, Vserossiiskogo S"ezda Professional'nykh Soiuzov, 17–22 sentiabria 1922 g.* (Moscow: 1922), p. 51.
12. *Shestoi S"ezd*, pp. 90, 103.
13. *Vos'moi S"ezd*, p. 65.
14. *Sed'moi S"ezd*, pp. 333–334.
15. *Ibid.*, p. 344; *Vos'moi S"ezd*, p. 333.
16. *Sed'moi S"ezd*, p. 333.
17. Zagorsky, *op. cit.*, p. 53.
18. *Shestoi S"ezd*, pp. 62, 83.
19. *Ibid.*, pp. 55–56.
20. *Trud*, June 16, 1921.
21. *Bolshevik*, No. 8, 1928.
22. *Sed'moi S"ezd*, p. 193.
23. *XIV S"ezd, VKP(B), Stenograficheskii Otchet*, pp. 730–731.
24. *Shestoi S"ezd*, pp. 103, 121–122, 458–464; also *Sed'moi S"ezd*, p. 687.
25. *Trud*, January 13, 1924.
26. *Ekonomicheskaia Zhizn'*, January 13, 1929.
27. *Trud*, July 27, 1928.
28. *Trud*, April 1, 1928.
29. *XIV S"ezd, Vsesoiuznoi Kommunisticheskoi Partii (B), Stenograficheskii Otchet*, p. 781. Cf. *Sed'moi S"ezd*, pp. 161, 371, 373, 382; *Vos'moi S"ezd*, pp. 328–331; *Trud*, June 14, 17, 22, 1928; July 15, 27, 1928; August 14, 1928.
30. *Shestoi S"ezd*, p. 184.
31. *Trud*, June 7, 1928.
32. STO, *SU 1923*, 68–655.
33. *Professional'nye Soiuzy S.S.S.R., 1926–1928; Otchet VTsSPS K VIII S"ezdy*

Professional'nykh Soiuzov (Moscow: 1928), p. 394. Soviet statistics are also ambiguous on total union membership. There is reason to believe the official figures are inflated. Figures on the size of the industrial labor force for the same years also vary depending upon the source used.

34. TsIK and SNK, *Sobranie Zakonov i Rasporiazhenii Rabochego i Krestianskogo Pravitel'stva 1925, Soiuz Sovetskikh Sotsialisticheskikh Respublik, 1924–1928*, pp. 2–15.
35. *Trud*, March 10, 1928.
36. *Trud*, March 16, 1928.
37. *Trud*, July 21, 1928.
38. *Trud*, July 21, 1928.
39. *Trud*, April 28, 1928.
40. *Trud*, July 1, 1925, quoted in E. H. Carr, *Socialism in One Country, 1924–26*, Part I (London: 1958), Vol. V, p. 367.
41. Cf. Leon Trotsky, *The Real Situation in Russia* (London: 1928), p. 44.
42. *Sed'moi S"ezd*, p. 348.

Notes to Chapter 12

1. "On the Results of the Controversy and on the Petty-Bourgeois Deviation in the Party," *VKP(b) i Rezol.*, I, 780–782.
2. "On Intra Party Affairs," February 9, 1929, *VKP(b) i Rezol.*, II, 558–562.
3. Leon Trotsky, *The Revolution Betrayed*, translated by Max Eastman (New York: 1945), pp. 87–104.
4. Quoted from R. V. Daniels, *A Documentary History of Communism* (New York: 1960), pp. 235–237.
5. Stalin, *Soch.*, Vol. VII, p. 376.
6. Quoted from John S. Reshetar, *A Concise History of The Communist Party of the Soviet Union* (New York: 1960), p. 205.
7. *XIV S"ezd, Steno. . .* , pp. 273–275.
8. *Loc. cit.*
9. *Ibid.*, pp. 289–292.
10. *Loc. cit.*
11. *Ibid.*, p. 288.
12. *The Case of Leon Trotsky*, pp. 322–323, quoted in I. Deutscher, *The Prophet Unarmed*, pp. 248–249.
13. *Loc. cit.*
14. M. Zorky, *Materialy*, pp. 188–189.
15. W. Reswick, *I Dreamt Revolution* (Chicago: 1952), pp. 175–183, quoted in S. Page, *Russia in Revolution* (New York: 1965), p. 192.
16. For Radek's remarks, see I. Deutscher, *The Prophet Unarmed*, p. 286.
17. *Loc. cit.*
18. Stalin, *Soch.*, VIII, pp. 262ff.
19. *K.P.S.S. v rez.*, II, pp. 511–517. See Schapiro, *The Origin*, p. 365.
20. Stalin, *Soch.*, Vol. XI, pp. 144–187.
21. Leonard Schapiro, *The Communist Party of the Soviet Union* (New York: 1960), p. 366, and *Sotsialisticheskii Vestnik*, Nos. 6 and 9, March 22 and May 4, 1929.
22. See Bertram D. Wolfe, *Khrushchev and Stalin's Ghost* (New York: 1957), pp. 295–315. This is a slightly abridged version, but, astonishingly, it is the first English translation of the article. L. Schapiro has an excellent digest of Bukharin's "Notes" in *The Communist Party*, pp. 368–369.
23. Cf. *Vos'moi S"ezd, Stenograficheskii Otchet*, pp. 373 *passim*.
24. *Ibid.*, p. 24 *passim*.
25. *Pravda*, December 29, 1928.
26. *Trud*, June 7, 1929.

27. *VKP(b) i Rezol.*, 5th ed., i, 389.
28. *Ibid.*
29. *Piatiletnii Plan Narodno-Khosiaistvennogo Stroitel'stva*, SSSR, Vol. I, II, p. 20, quoted in Maurice Dobb, *Soviet Economic Development Since 1917* (New York: 1967), p. 236.
30. Alexander Erlich, *The Soviet Industrialization Debate, 1924–1928* (Cambridge: 1960), Chap. IX.

Bibliography

OFFICIAL REPORTS OF TRADE UNION CONGRESSES

First: Pervyi Vserossiiskii S″ezd Professional'nykh Soiuzov, 7–14 ianvaria 1918 g. Polnyi Stenograficheskii Otchet. Moscow: 1918.
Second: N . . . sky. Vtoroi Vserossiiskii S″ezd Professional'nykh Soiuzov. Moscow: 1918.
Vtoroi Vserossiiskii S″ezd Professional'nykh Soiuzov 16–25 ianvaria 1919 g. Stenograficheskii Otchet. Chast '1 Plenumy. Moscow: 1921.
Third: Tretii Vserossiiskii S″ezd Professional'nykh Soiuzov, 6–13 aprelia 1920 g. Moscow: 1920.
Fourth: Chetvertyi Vserossiiskii S″ezd Professional'nykh Soiuzov, 17–25 maia 1921 g. Pt i: Plenumy; Pt ii: Sektsii. Moscow: 1921.
Fifth: Stenograficheskii Otchet Piatogo Vserossiiskogo S″ezda Professional'nykh Soiuzov, 17–22 sentabria 1922 g. Moscow: 1922.
Sixth: Shestoi S″ezd Professional'nykh Soiuzov S.S.S.R., 11–18 noiabria 1924 g., Plenumy i Sektsii, Polnyi Stenograficheskii Otchet. Moscow: 1925.
Seventh: Sed'moi S″ezd Professional'nykh Soiuzov, 6–18 dekabria 1926 g. Plenumy i Sektsii, Polnyi Stenograficheskii Otchet. Moscow: 1927.
Eighth: Vos'moi S″ezd Professional'nykh Soiuzov S.S.S.R., 10–14 dekabria 1928 g., Plenumy i Sektsii, Polnyi Stenograficheskii Otchet. Moscow: 1929.
Professional'nye Soiuzy S.S.S.R., 1921–1922, Otchet, VTsSPS. Petrograd: 1922.
Professional'nye Soiuzy S.S.S.R., 1926–1928, Otchet, VTsSPS K VIII S″ezdu Professional'nykh Soiuzov. Moscow: 1928.

REPORTS OF PARTY CONGRESSES AND CONFERENCES

Ninth: Protokoly Devyatogo S″ezda RKP(B), mart-aprel' 1920 g. Moscow: 1934.
Tenth: Protokoly Desiatogo S″ezda RKP(B), mart 1921 g. Moscow: 1933.
Eleventh: Odinnadtsatyi S″ezd RKP (Bol'shevikov), Stenograficheskii Otchet, mart-aprel' 1922 g. Moscow: 1936.

Twelfth: Dvenadtsatyi S"ezd Rossiiskoi Kommunisticheskoi Partii (Bol'she-vikov), Stenograficheskii Otchet, 17–25 aprelia 1923 g. Moscow: 1923.
Thirteenth: Trinadtsatyi S"ezd Rossiiskoi Kommunisticheskoi Partii (Bol'she-vikov), Stenograficheskii Otchet, 23–31 maia 1924 g. Moscow: 1924.
Fourteenth: XIV S"ezd Vsesoiuznoi Kommunisticheskoi Partii (B), 18–31 dekabria 1925 g., Stenograficheskii Otchet. Moscow: 1926.
Thirteenth Conference: Trinadtsataia Konferentsiia RKP(B), 16–18 ianvaria 1924 g. Moscow: 1924.
Vsesoiuznaia Kommunisticheskaia Partiia (B) v Rezoliutsiiakh i Resheniiakh S"ezdov, Konferentsii i Plenumov TsK, 1888–1932. Pt i: 1898–1924; pt ii: 1924–1932. 4th ed., Moscow, 1932; 5th ed., Moscow, 1936; 7th ed., Moscow: 1954.
Statisticheskii Otdel, Sotsial'nyi i Natsional'nyi Sostav VKP(b), Itogi Vsesoi-uznoi Partiinoi Raboty, 1922–1923 g. Moscow, 1923; Itogi Vsesoiuznoi Partiinoi Perepisi 1927 g. Moscow-Leningrad: 1928.

COLLECTIONS OF LAWS AND DECREES

Sobranie Uzakonenii i Rasporiazhenii Rabochego i Krestianskogo Pravitel'stva, 1917–1924.
Sobranie Zakonov i Rasporiazhenii Rabochego i Krestianskogo Pravitel'stva. Soiuz Sovetskikh Sotsialisticheskikh Respublik, 1924–1928.
Ekonomicheskaia Politika SSR: Sbornik Dokumentov. Moscow: 1947.

SELECTED CONGRESSES, CONFERENCES, AND REPORTS

Trudy I Vserossiiskogo S"ezda Sovetov Narodnogo Khoziaistva, 25 maia-4 iiunia 1918. Moscow: 1918.
Trudy II Vserossiiskogo S"ezda Sovetov Narodnogo Khoziaistva, 19 dekabria-27 dekabria 1918. Moscow: n.d.
Protokoly II Vserossiiskogo S"ezda Kommissarov Truda, Predstavitelei Birzh Truda i Strakhovykh Kass, 18–25 maia 1918. Moscow: 1918.
IV Sessia Vserossiiskogo Tsentral'nogo Ispolnitel'nogo Komiteta IX Sozyva RSFSR, 23–31 oktiabria 1922, Stenograficheskii Otchet, Biulleten No. 1, 25 October 1922. Moscow: 1922.

NEWSPAPERS AND PERIODICALS

Bol'shevik. Moscow, 1924–
Ekonomicheskaia Politika SSSR: Sbornik Dokumentov. Moscow: 1947.
Ekonomicheskaia Zhizn', 1921–
International Press Correspondence. Moscow.
Izvestiia, Petrograd, Moscow, 1917–
Novaia Zhizn', Petrograd, 1917, and Moscow, 1918.
Pravda. Petrograd, Moscow, 1917–
Revolyutsionnaia Rossiia. Tallin, December 20, 1920–
Sotsialisticheskii Vestnik, Organ zagranichnoi delegatsii R.S.-D.R.P., Berlin: February 1, 1921.
Trud. Moscow, 1921–
Vestnik Truda, Ezhemesiachnyi organ vserossiiskogo tsentralnogo soveta pro-fessional'nykh soiuzov. Moscow: 1920.
Voprosy Truda.

SELECTED BOOKS

Arendt, Hannah. *The Origins of Totalitarianism.* New York: Harcourt, Brace, 1951.
———. *On Revolution.* New York: Viking Press, 1963.
Arkhiv Russkoi Revoliutsii. Berlin: 1921–1934, 21 vols.
Bauer, Raymond A., Alex Inkeles, and Clyde Kluckhohn. *How The Soviet System Works.* Cambridge: Harvard University Press, 1956.
Baykov, Alexander. *The Development of the Soviet Economic System.* London: The University Press, 1946.
Bechhofer, Walter. *Through Starving Russia.* London: Methuen, 1921.
Bell, Daniel. *Work and Its Discontents.* Boston: Beacon Press, 1956.
———. *The End of Ideology.* New York: The Free Press, 1962.
Berdyaev, Nicolas. *The Origin of Russian Communism.* Ann Arbor: University of Michigan Press, 1960.
Bergson, Abram. *The Structure of Soviet Wages.* Cambridge: Harvard University Press, 1944.
Berkman, Alexander. *The Kronstadt Rebellion.* Berlin: Der Syndikalist, 1922.
Blizhe K Massam: Sbornik Statei (Closer to the Masses: Collection of Articles). Moscow: 1925.
Bol'shaia Sovetskaia Entsiklopediia. Moscow: 1926–1939, 65 vols.
Bowden, Will, Michael Karpovich, and Abott Payton Usher. *An Economic History of Europe Since 1750.* New York: American Book Company, 1937.
Bowle, John. *Politics and Opinion in the Nineteenth Century.* New York: Oxford University Press, 1964.
British Labour Delegation to Russia, 1920: Report. London: Trade Union Congress General Council, 1920.
Bukharin, N. I. *Put'k Sotsializmu i Raboche-Krest'ianskii Soiuz (The Road to Socialism and the Worker-Peasant Movement).* 4th ed. Moscow: Gos. izd-vo, 1927.
———. "Zametki Ekonomista" ("Notes of an Economist"). Published first in *Pravda,* September 30, 1928.
Bunyan, James, and H. H. Fisher. *Bolshevik Revolution, 1917–1918.* Stanford: Stanford University Press, 1934.
Calvin, John. *Institutes of the Christian Religion,* trans. J. Allen, n.d.
Carr, E. H. *A History of Soviet Russia.* 6 vols. London: Macmillan, 1958.
Chamberlain, Neil. *The Union Challenge to Management Control.* New York: Harper & Row, 1948.
Chamberlin, William H. *The Russian Revolution, 1917–1921.* New York: Macmillan, 1935.
Chernov, Victor. *Pered burei (Before the Storm).* New York: Chekova, 1953.
Dan, Theodore. *Dva Goda Skitanii (Two Years Wandering).* Berlin: N. S. Hermann & Co., 1922.
———. *The Origins of Bolshevism.* New York: Harper & Row, 1964.
Daniels, R. V. *The Conscience of a Revolution.* Cambridge: Harvard University Press, 1960.
———. *The Left Opposition: 1917–1921.* Harvard University, unpublished Ph.D. dissertation.
Deutscher, Isaac. *Soviet Trade Unions.* London: Royal Institute of International Affairs, 1950.
———. *The Prophet Armed. Trotsky: 1879–1921.* New York: Vintage Press, 1965.
———. *The Prophet Unarmed. Trotsky: 1921–1929.* New York: Vintage Press, 1965.

————. *Stalin, A Political Biography.* New York: Oxford University Press, 1949.

Dewar, Margaret. *Labour Policy in the U.S.S.R., 1917–1928.* London: Royal Institute of International Affairs, 1956.

Dobb, Maurice. *Soviet Economic Development Since 1917,* rev. ed. New York: International Publishers, 1967.

Dunn, Robert. *Soviet Trade Unions.* New York: Vanguard Press, 1928.

Duranty, Walter. *I Write As I Please.* New York: Simon & Schuster, 1935.

Erlich, Alexander. *The Soviet Industrial Debate, 1924–1928.* Cambridge: Harvard University Press, 1960.

Fainsod, Merle. *How Russia Is Ruled.* Cambridge: Harvard University Press, 1953.

————. *Smolensk Under Soviet Rule.* Cambridge: Harvard University Press, 1958.

Feuer, L. S. (ed.). *Karl Marx and Friedrich Engels. Basic Writings on Politics and Philosophy.* New York: Doubleday, 1959.

Fischer, Louis. *The Life of Lenin.* New York: Harper & Row, 1964.

Fromm, Erich. *Escape from Freedom.* New York: Holt, Rinehart & Winston, 1941.

Galbraith, John Kenneth. *The Affluent Society.* Boston: Houghton Mifflin, 1958.

Gerschenkron, Alexander. "Patterns of Economic Development," *The Transformation of Russian Society,* ed. C. Black. Cambridge: Harvard University Press, 1960.

Golden, Clinton S., and Harold J. Ruttenberg. *The Dynamics of Industrial Democracy.* New York: Harper & Row, 1942.

Gordon, Manya. *Workers Before and After Lenin.* New York: E. P. Dutton & Company, 1941.

Gorky, Maxim. *Days With Lenin.* New York: International Publishers, 1932.

Grinevitch, Vladimir. *Professional'noye dvizhenie rabochikh v Rossii (Trade Unionism in Russia),* 1908.

Haimson, Leopold H. *The Russian Marxists.* Cambridge: Harvard University Press, 1955.

————. "The Problem of Social Stability in Urban Russia, 1905–1917," Parts One and Two, *Slavic Review,* Vol. XXIII, No. 4, December 1964, and Vol. XXIV, No. 1, March 1965.

Hazard, John N. *Law and Social Change in the U.S.S.R.* London: London Institute of World Affairs by Stevens, 1953.

International Labor Office. *The Trade Union Movement in Soviet Russia.* Studies and Reports, Series A, No. 26. Geneva: G. Thone, 1927.

Jakobson, M. *Die Russischen Gewerkschaften.* Berlin: 1932.

Kateb, George. *Utopia and Its Enemies.* New York: The Free Press, 1963.

Kollontai, Alexandra. *Rabochaia Oppozitsiia (The Workers' Opposition).* Moscow: 1921.

Kornhauser, William. *The Politics of Mass Society.* New York: The Free Press, 1959.

Krasnii Arkhiv Tsentroarkhiv RSFSR, Moscow: 1922.

Larin, Y., and L. Kristman. *Ocherk Khoziaistvennoi Zhizni i Organizatsii Narodnogo Khoziaistva Sovetskoi Rossii, 1 noiabria 1917 g.-1 iiulia 1920 g. (Outline of the Economic Life and the Organization of the National Economy of Soviet Russia, November 1, 1917–July 1, 1920).* Moscow: 1920.

Leontyev, A. *Work Under Capitalism and Socialism.* New York: International Publishers, 1942.

Lenin, V. I. *Collected Works,* 7 vols. *Towards the Seizure of Power.* Book II. New York: International Publishers, 1932.

————. *Selected Works.* 12 vols. New York: International Publishers, n.d.

————. *Sobranie Sochinenii (Collected Works).* 30 vols., 2nd ed. Edited by N. I. Bukharin, V. Molotov, and I. Skvortsova-Stepanov. Moscow: 1927.

——. Sochineniia (Works). 30 vols., 3rd ed. Moscow: Partizdat TsK VKP(b), 1935.
——. The Soviets at Work. English translation. New York: The Rand School of Social Science, 1919.
Liashchenko, Peter I. History of the National Economy of Russia to the 1917 Revolution. Trans. L. M. Herman. New York: Macmillan, 1949.
Lichtheim, George. Marxism: A Historical and Critical Study. 2nd ed. New York: Praeger, 1965.
Lindblom, Charles E. Unions and Capitalism. New Haven: Yale University Press, 1949.
Lipset, Seymour Martin. "Working Class Authoritarianism," Political Man. New York: Doubleday, 1960.
Lozovsky, Solomon Abromovich. Trade Unions in Soviet Russia. New York: The Rand School of Social Science, 1920.
——. Rabochii Kontrol (Workers' Control). Moscow: 1918.
Marx, Karl. Communist Manifesto. Authorized English translation, edited and annotated by Friedrich Engels. Chicago: C. H. Kerr and Company, 1947.
——. The German Ideology. Edited by R. Pascal. Parts 1 and 2. New York: International Publishers, 1939.
Michels, Robert. Political Parties. New York: The Free Press, 1949 and 1958.
Moore, Barrington, Jr. Soviet Politics: The Dilemma of Power. Cambridge: Harvard University Press, 1950.
——. Terror and Progress U.S.S.R. Cambridge: Harvard University Press, 1954.
Nicholaevsky, Boris. Power and the Soviet Elite. New York: Praeger, 1965.
Oktiabrskaia Revoliutsia i Fabzavkomy: Materialy po istorii fabrichnozarodskikh Komitetov. 2 volumes. Moscow: 1927.
Page, Stanley W. ed. Russia In Revolution. New York: Van Nostrand, 1965.
Parsons, Talcott. "Some Sociological Aspects of Fascist Movements," Social Forces. Vol. XXI. December 1942.
Payne, Robert. The Life and Death of Lenin. New York: Simon and Schuster, 1964.
Perlman, Selig. A Theory of the Labor Movement. New York: Macmillan, 1949.
Pipes, Richard. Social Democracy and the St. Petersburg Labor Movement, 1885–1897. Cambridge: Harvard University Press, 1963.
Polanyi, Karl. The Great Transformation. Boston: Beacon Press, 1957.
Popov, N. Outline History of the Communist Party of the Soviet Union. 2 vols. New York: International Publishers, 1934.
Prokopovich, S. N. Russlands Volkswirtschaft. Zurich: 1944.
——. Narodnoe Khoziaistvo SSSR (The National Economy of the U.S.S.R.). Vol. I, New York: 1952.
Radkey, Oliver Henry. The Elections to the Russian Constituent Assembly of 1917. Cambridge: Harvard University Press, 1950.
Reed, John. Ten Days That Shook the World. Ed. Bertram D. Wolfe. New York: Random House, 1960.
Reshetar, John S. A Concise History of the Communist Party of the Soviet Union. New York: Praeger, 1960.
Reswick, William. I Dreamt Revolution. Chicago: Regnery, 1952.
Rostow, Walter W. The Stages of Economic Growth. Cambridge: Cambridge University Press, 1960.
Rozenfeld, Y. S. Promyshlennaia Politika SSSR. (Industrial Policy of the U.S.S.R.). Moscow: 1926.
Schapiro, Leonard. The Communist Party of the Soviet Union. New York: Random House, 1959.
——. The Origin of the Communist Autocracy. Cambridge: Harvard University Press, 1955.

Schwartz, Solomon. *Labor in the Soviet Union.* New York: Praeger, 1951.

Stalin, J. *Collected Works.* Moscow: Foreign Languages Publishing House, 1952–1955.

Steinberg, I. N. *In the Workshop of Revolution.* London: Victor Gollancz Ltd., and New York: Holt, Rinehart & Winston, 1953.

Strong, Anna Louise. *I Change Worlds.* New York: Holt, 1937.

Sturmthal, Adolf. *Unity and Diversity in European Labor.* New York: The Free Press, 1953.

Sukhanov, N. N. *The Russian Revolution, 1917.* Ed. and trans. by Joel Carmichael. New York: Oxford University Press, 1955.

Sviatlovsky, Vladimir. *Istoriia Professional'nogo Dvizheniia (The History of Trade Unionism in Russia).* 2nd ed. Leningrad: 1925.

Tawney, R. H. *Religion and the Rise of Capitalism.* New York: Harcourt, Brace, 1926.

Taylor, George W., and Frank C. Pierson. *New Concepts in Wage Determination.* New York: McGraw-Hill, 1957.

Tilgher, Adriano. *Work: What It Has Meant to Men Through the Ages.* Trans. by Dorothy Canfield Fisher. New York: Harcourt, Brace, 1930.

Trotsky, Leon. *Dictatorship vs. Democracy (Terrorism and Communism).* New York: Worker's Party of America, 1922.

———. *My Life.* New York: Scribner's, 1930.

———. *Novy Kurs. (The New Course).* Moscow: 1924.

———. *On the Tasks of the Trade Unions.* New York: Pioneer Publishers, n.d.

———. *The Real Situation in Russia.* London: Harcourt, Brace, 1928.

———. *The Revolution Betrayed.* Trans. Max Eastman. New York: Pioneer, 1945.

———. *Sochinenii (Works).* 21 vols. Moscow: Gos. izd-vo, 1924–1927.

Turin, Serge. *From Peter the Great to Lenin.* London: P. S. King & Son, Ltd., 1935.

Veblen, Thorstein. *The Instinct of Workmanship.* New York: Macmillan, 1922.

Webb, Sidney and Beatrice. *The History of Trade Unionism.* London: Longmans, 1919.

Wiles, Peter. "The Importance of Being Djugashvili," *Problems of Communism,* Vol. XII, No. 2, March–April 1963, p. 78.

Wolfe, Bertram D. *Three Who Made a Revolution.* New York: Dial Press, 1948.

———. *Khrushchev and Stalin's Ghost.* New York: Praeger, 1957.

Zagorsky, Simon A. *Wages and Regulation of Conditions of Labor in the U.S.S.R.* Geneva: World Peace Foundation, 1930.

Zinoviev, Grigorii. *Sochineniia.* Vol. VI. Moscow: Gos. izd-vo, 1926.

Zorky, Mark S. *Rabochaia Oppozitsia, Materiali i Dokumenty, 1920–1926.* Moscow: Gos. izd-vo, 1926.

Index

For Product Safety Concerns and Information please contact our EU
representative GPSR@taylorandfrancis.com
Taylor & Francis Verlag GmbH, Kaufingerstraße 24, 80331 München, Germany

* 9 7 8 0 2 0 2 3 6 3 5 0 9 *